'With *Lest*, Mark Dapin transforms his trademark humour into serious history: a beguiling blend of erudition, insight and wit. *Lest* forces us to look again at stories we think we all know – or should know – and reframe them with intellectual rectitude and rigour. Never a piss-take (the lazy writer's way to make history fun), *Lest* offers new perspectives on the past from one of Australia's most interesting and provocative thinkers. This is one for the savvy book club *and* for the classroom. I loved it.'

CLARE WRIGHT

'In *Lest*, Mark Dapin trains a wry eye and an acute historical bullshit detector onto the "sacred" shibboleths of Australia's highly contestable but largely unchallenged birthing story – Anzac. He lifts the veil on its myths, its bizarre cosplay, and the cheap political jingoism that has long inoculated Anzac from the scrutiny good history demands while allowing commemoration to transmogrify into celebration. It's a fabulous book – intelligent, witty, but most importantly, earthed in fact. It should be fast-tracked onto the national curriculum.'

PAUL DALEY, AUTHOR AND JOURNALIST

LEST

ALSO BY MARK DAPIN

Carnage
Prison Break
Public Enemies
Jewish Anzacs
The Nashos' War
Australia's Vietnam

MARK DAPIN

LEST

AUSTRALIAN WAR MYTHS

SCRIBNER

SCRIBNER

First published in Australia in 2024 by Scribner, an imprint of
Simon & Schuster (Australia) Pty Limited
Suite 19A, Level 1, Building C, 450 Miller Street, Cammeray, NSW 2062

Simon & Schuster: Celebrating 100 Years of Publishing in 2024.
Sydney New York London Toronto New Delhi
Visit our website at www.simonandschuster.com.au

SCRIBNER and design are registered trademarks of The Gale Group, Inc.,
used under licence by Simon & Schuster LLC.

10 9 8 7 6 5 4 3 2 1

© Mark Dapin 2024

All rights reserved. No part of this publication may be reproduced, stored in a
retrieval system, or transmitted in any form or by any means, electronic, mechanical,
photocopying, recording or otherwise, without prior permission of the publisher.

A catalogue record for this book is available from the National Library of Australia

9781761108068 (paperback)
9781761108075 (ebook)

Cover design by Luke Causby
Cover image: Alamy
Typeset by Midland Typesetters in Adobe Caslon Pro 11.5/17
Printed and bound in Australia by Griffin Press

The paper this book is printed on is certified against the Forest Stewardship Council® Standards. Griffin Press holds chain of custody certification SCS-COC-001185. FSC® promotes environmentally responsible, socially beneficial and economically viable management of the world's forests.

FOR BEN AND SARA

Contents

Before We Start . . .   xi

The Myths of Anzac Day   1
The Myths of White Feather Women   23
The Myths of the Gallipoli Landing   43
The Myths of the Dardanelles Campaign   65
The Myths of Monash and the Western Front   89
The Myths of the Emu War   119
The Myths of the POWs   147
The Myth of No Poofters   167
The Myths of Victimised Veterans   185
The Myths of Vietnam Veterans, Anzac Day and the RSL   209
The Myths of Movements   227
The Shape of Myths to Come   245

Notes   *269*

Before We Start . . .

This is a book about separating truth from myth in Australian war history. It's salted with jokes – because I can't seem to help myself – but it has a serious purpose. It's about questioning received truths and realising that the most widely accepted are often the most woefully misguided. It's about accepting that historians (especially this one) have flawed personalities and eccentric agendas and that our opinions and interests are coloured by our own experiences. The scope of the book is shaped by my own knowledge. I know little of significance, for instance, about the Second World War and much of insignificance about the Emu War.

By training, I am a journalist as well as a historian. Small sections of this book formed part of my Radio National show, *Myths of War*, in which I interviewed historians who knew more than me about – well, everything, really. I realise that it is unusual in a history book to quote conversations with historians rather than their writing, but this is an unusual book. It's driven by the conviction that a document can be found to support any proposition that is accurate, and that anything unprovable is likely to be untrue. Most of all, it's about loving history and having fun with it, and using the past to understand the present – which you can only do if you've got your facts straight.

The Myths of Anzac Day

That Anzac Day has always been commemorated rather than celebrated. That Anzac Day developed unchallenged. That only a tiny activist fringe questions Anzac Day.

It's always dangerous to make a claim for historical singularity, but I'm willing to take a risk and say that this is the only book ever to have been inspired by a statement by Alan Tudge, who was Minister for Education and Youth in Scott Morrison's Coalition government between December 2020 and May 2022.

While it's difficult to pinpoint any of Tudge's achievements in the field of education, he was able to attract a fusillade of publicity when he criticised what he claimed to be planned changes to the national curriculum. He was particularly troubled by the proposal that Year 9 history students might study 'contested debates about the nature and significance of the Anzac legend' and perhaps consider 'the difference between commemoration and celebration of war'.

In fact, this was not a change to the curriculum. The only significant alteration to the existing wording was the insertion of 'contested' before 'debates' (which is offensive, true, as it's tautological) but the thought of it nonetheless made Tudge angry.

If these revisions were to be made, Tudge declared, children would be taught to doubt the sanctity of Anzac Day, 'the most sacred of all days in Australia'. In an interview with the ABC's youth radio station, Triple J, he said that Anzac Day was 'not a contested idea, apart from an absolute fringe element in our society'. He believed that the new national curriculum was advocating that 'instead of just accepting these for the things which they are, such as Anzac Day', students should 'really challenge them'.[1]

But Anzac Day, like so many other 'sacred' days, has always been a contested idea. As has Christmas Day: there is little intellectual or theological support for the proposition that Jesus Christ was born on December 25. Good Friday is another contested idea: certain Christian denominations believe Christ to have been crucified on a Wednesday. Australia Day is publicly and vigorously challenged by First Nations people and others, some of whom nurse the ambitious goal that it will one day be commemorated as Invasion Day.

Anzac Day has a history. It is marked today differently from the way it was in 1916. War is thought of differently. The Anzacs are remembered differently. The ways that events are remembered have histories themselves – even histories have histories – and, as any high-school history teacher knows, the history of Anzac Day is a story of the tension between celebration and commemoration.

Tudge's comments were unworthy of an education minister. But in his confected exasperation, he was acting as a man of the people – or, more accurately, a man with an MBA from Harvard University mimicking the way that he imagined 'the people' might be: incurious, uninformed and reflexively belligerent. The celebration of pugnacious obtuseness has been the fashion among populist politicians for a while, and one unmistakable characteristic of militant ignorance emerges when privately educated Australians such as Tudge adopt the common tongue. This anti-Anzac malarky had really got his goat. 'I can tell you, I'm not putting up with it,' he told presenter Chris Kenny on Sky News. 'I won't have a bar of it.'

He may have been a Haileybury old boy with an Ivy League education, but bonza bloke Tudge was ridgy-didge.

Kenny was ropeable too. He described the wording of the curriculum as 'the demolition of Anzac Day' and demanded of Tudge, 'Can you explain to me why I should be ashamed or guilty about Anzac Day? ... And who are these people who think that we should?'

'Chris, I cannot explain that to you,' said Tudge.

Fair dinkum.

By then, Tudge had refined his critique and invented a statistic. He said that the draft curriculum pandered to a possible '0.1 per cent of fringe activists' who believed Anzac Day was 'about warmongering'.[2]

This is a myth, so we may as well start here.

The Anzacs are still with us, in effigy. More than a century after the Armistice, there are Anzacs in our cities, young men with shoulders squared and jaws set tight – tough, unaffected and 25 per cent larger than life. At the western end of Sydney's Anzac Bridge, a bronze statue of a digger (unveiled on Anzac Day in 2000) stands with head bowed, sightless eyes following the barrel of a Lee-Enfield rifle to the handful of sand from Gallipoli that is buried beneath his boots. On the other side of the bridge is a newer Anzac, the digger's Kiwi comrade in arms (unveiled on Anzac Sunday in 2008), similar in build and bearing but about five centimetres taller because he's wearing a bigger hat. The statues are often described as 'standing guard', although they're not: they're both frozen in the 'rest on arms reversed' position. In the event of a surprise attack, they would be as slow to respond as the security guards who listlessly patrol the walkway below.

Every morning, columns of tradespeople and hot-deskers drive haltingly to work beneath the statues' unseeing gaze. At the turn of the millennium, I lived in a unit overlooking the bridge and passed under the Australian digger each day. I found him quietly comforting, and it was his statue that sparked my interest in Anzac. Until then, I had not thought much about the Anzacs outside of Anzac Day, when the city I loved turned abruptly into the town where I grew up – Aldershot, the home of the British army – and drunken soldiers dressed in civvies spilled out of crowded pubs to claim the pavements by right of conquest and force of numbers. I did not fully grasp the point of what appeared to me to be one massive regimental reunion: I did not learn much about the First World War (or anything else, really) at school, and I had only heard of Gallipoli through Eric Bogle's ballad 'And the Band Played Waltzing Matilda' (and although the song mentions a parade of veterans 'every April' and famously predicts that 'someday no-one will march', I had no idea it was about Anzac Day).

There are other motionless Anzacs forever at their posts in Melbourne, Sydney and Canberra (and Beersheba, Bullecourt and Fromelles), all cast – sometimes literally – from the same rugged mould. The Centenary of Anzac and the years that followed saw a new generation of statuary born, more than a decade after the last Anzac had died. As I grew older and more boring, I found that I wished I knew more about them, and I began to investigate their histories through journalism.

I became interested in unknown soldiers, an idea I was familiar with from England, where the grave of the Unknown Warrior lies in Westminster Abbey. On Remembrance Day 1993, to mark the seventy-fifth anniversary of the end of the First World War, the remains of an Australian unknown soldier exhumed from Adelaide Cemetery near Villers-Bretonneux in France were reinterred in the Hall of Memory at the Australian War Memorial. In his eulogy over the body, Prime Minister Paul Keating – aided immeasurably by his speechwriter, Don Watson – described the Anzac story as 'a legend of free and independent spirits whose discipline derived less from military formalities and customs than from the bonds of mateship and the demands of necessity ... a democratic tradition'.[3]

Like all traditions, Anzac was invented over time and has to be reinvigorated regularly. 'I sometimes wish we could withdraw the unknown soldier speech,' Don Watson told me, 'because it seems to have triggered the rebirth of Anzac, in a way. I think it's grown into 60 per cent bullshit these days. It's awful what's happened to it.'

Alec Campbell, the last remaining Australian to serve at Gallipoli, passed away in 2002 at the age of 103. At Campbell's funeral, Prime Minister John Howard made a 'silent promise' (out loud, somehow) to protect the values by which Campbell had lived – even though Campbell's lived values were those of a trade unionist, republican and socialist. When Howard later endowed Campbell and his comrades with 'courage, valour, mateship, decency ... a willingness as a nation to do the right thing, whatever the cost', Watson wrote that he 'may as well have emptied his old sock drawer on the cenotaph'.[4]

Curiously, as the First World War has become more prominent in our daily lives, the modern military has virtually disappeared from public view. In the early twentieth century, militia units could have been seen drilling in every country town. During the world wars, hundreds of thousands of uniformed men swamped the cities. In the 1950s, a national service scheme saw almost every young male in the country engaged in military training. Selective conscription was introduced to quickly expand the army in the 1960s and early 1970s. About one-third of 'nashos' from the later national service scheme were sent to fight in Vietnam, and the public was acutely aware of their plight. Despite bizarre claims to the contrary, huge welcome-home parades greeted the return of battalions from Vietnam to Sydney, Brisbane, Adelaide and Townsville. But today, most Australians outside of Seymour/Puckapunyal, Wagga Wagga/ Kapooka, Townsville, Darwin and Canberra barely see a soldier and seem to have only a hazy idea of what the armed forces do.

As the Australian Defence Force increasingly lost its connections with civilian society, we came to remember past wars with a greater urgency, and in a strange cultural shift, everyone who'd ever served in any branch of the military, at home or overseas, with or without New Zealanders, became an Anzac.

James Brown, a veteran of Australia's wars in Afghanistan and Iraq, wrote about a Sydney Anzac Day parade where he had asked a woman marching behind him whereabouts she had served: 'She hadn't, it turned out, but was marching to support her husband, who had spent a brief moment in the Army Reserve.' After the marching bands, cadets, boy and girl scouts, widows' guilds and Legacy clubs came what Brown felt was 'the strangest sight of all: military enthusiasts in period costumes, some standing alongside their jeeps or trucks from bygone wars.

'I couldn't help but wonder,' wrote Brown, 'on a day dedicated to respecting military service, what made these men and women dress up in uniform despite never having served a day themselves. They may as well put their arm in a sling, or wear an eye patch to simulate war wounds. Some people will do anything to be a part of the Anzac legend.'[5]

There isn't room in the military for everyone – as diehard advocates of a return to national service might do well to bear in mind – but if you cannot be an Anzac, you can at least find an Anzac in your lineage. Towards the beginning of the late twentieth-century family-history boom, many Australians were animated by the idea that they might be heirs to a 'convict past' – often in riotous contrast to their law-abiding present – and went in search of forebears in the desolate transports of the Georgian and Victorian eras.[6] In the years leading up to the Centenary of Anzac, it became more fashionable for IT specialists and HR managers to seek out an Anzac to stiffen their family tree.

Australians are fantastically lucky that every military service record from the First World War has been digitised and is available from the National Archives of Australia website, instantly and at no cost. The digitisation of Second World War records is an ongoing process, and any not-yet-digitised files can be ordered through the Archives for use in its reading rooms. Vietnam War records were once available too, until they were withdrawn from public access to protect the privacy of surviving veterans, in a setback for historians that was probably my fault.[7] Other documents have been exhaustively collected and catalogued by the Australian War Memorial, whose website promises: 'Our collection contains a wealth of material to help you research and find your connection with the wartime experiences of the brave men and women who served in Australia's military forces.'[8]

Once Malcolm from Marketing has tracked down his uniformed forebear, he will ideally discover that his ancestor was a hero – and, happily, this has recently become a more attainable goal. An idea has sprung up that once would have been risible: anybody who has ever worn their nation's uniform is a hero. Anzac creep has been accompanied by medal creep. Australian National University professor David Horner, a Vietnam veteran and official historian, told me, 'People want more recognition for what they have done than was ever the case in the past. Guys who serve in the ADF now, and who've been overseas, have got more medals than guys who served in World War II. We'll have a medal for volunteering, a medal for national service, a medal for being in the army for four years. I've got more medals for serving in Vietnam in the past four years than I ever got when I was there. Every time there's an election, the government comes up with the bright idea of a new medal: they'll get more votes. And why do they get more votes? Because everybody wants to be an Anzac.'

By the 1930s, Anzac Day on April 25 had become a funeral mass for the 60,000 who died in the First World War. Solemn marchers walked through silent cities, with thoughts of the butcher, the postman and the railwayman whose names were engraved on the memorial plinths in every country town. After the Second World War, a new generation of former servicemen marched as the Sons of Anzacs, the inheritors of the mantel. But what must it mean to actual war heroes when they hear that reluctant, conscripted, stay-at-home base troops were heroes too?

In 1995, the Keating government launched the Australia Remembers campaign to mark the fiftieth anniversary of the end of the Second World War. From the late twentieth century until recently, the heroes of that war were considered broadly unimpeachable, as they were held (quite reasonably) to have helped save democracy from fascism, Nazism and Japanese imperialism. But the people behind Australia Remembers did not necessarily support every other military adventure – including their own.

Vietnam veteran Noel Turnbull was a principal of Turnbull Fox Phillips, a PR agency that worked on Australia Remembers. Turnbull, who once marched in a Vietnam moratorium demonstration, told me that he 'wouldn't march [on Anzac Day] in a fit' (although he has done since) and that he regretted 'the notion that Anzac Day and Gallipoli shaped Australian society'. He said, 'I feel sick in the stomach when I see some young guy wearing an Australian flag and saying, "The people at Gallipoli died for our freedom." No, they didn't. They were invading another country in one of the great military stuff-ups of all time. We're ending up a bit like America, where we wear our patriotism on our arse.'

More visibly, we wear it in public spaces, in the form of those ubiquitous sculptures in marble and bronze. Modern Anzac statues often have a 'certain look that First World War volunteer soldiers had', Victorian sculptor Peter Corlett told me. 'It was probably due to the fact they were posing in front of a camera that had a long time exposure, so they had to sit very still. There was a strange, jovial formality about all the images.'

Corlett's bronzed soldiers can be found at memorials and museums all over Australia, as well as at Beersheba in Israel and Bullecourt in France. His Anzacs are all tall, fit, handsome and physically complete. 'You're trying to capture national characteristics,' he told me, 'and it's probably quite inaccurate.' They are statues of an idea, an Anglo-Celtic ideal, rather than men as they were.

Corlett also created the statue of John Simpson Kirkpatrick and his donkey at the Australian War Memorial, the statues of Ernest Edward 'Weary' Dunlop that stand at the AWM and in Melbourne's Kings Domain gardens, and the statue of John Monash at Monash University. Corlett told me that he was proud of his work and the acknowledgement it offers to the sacrifices of a lost generation, but remained troubled by a statue he cast of 'Mad' Harry Murray, who won a Victoria Cross for leading fearless and bloody raids against German trenches on the Western Front in 1917. 'I didn't get to design this sculpture,' he said. 'It's not the concept I had.'

Corlett wanted to sculpt Murray the farmer, sitting on his porch after the war. He saw Australia's most decorated soldier as a 'reluctant hero' back on the land, but the commission stipulated he be shown in the act for which he was cited for his medal: throwing a grenade and rushing forward, pistol in hand, to take an enemy trench.

Corlett said, 'I thought, Bugger this, I don't want to do someone with weapons. I was going to walk.' But he felt bound to the job by his respect for a retired officer who had spent years lobbying for the statue. 'I ended up sick, with really high blood pressure, and the only issue was me making a sculpture I really didn't want to make. I made it, but didn't sign it. But they've put my name on it since. And I didn't stop them. I'm not proud of it at all,' said Corlett. 'I won't get into that situation again.'

But in fact Murray was not a reluctant soldier. He landed at Gallipoli at the age of thirty-four, a trained fighting man with six years' service in the militia. He wrote, 'I am cursed with a vivid imagination, and before going into battle I went through it all, had blood, brains, "innards", limbs etc., spattered all over me, and I fought my fight with self then, fixed my code, and it only remained to prove it. The real thing being less terrible than pictured, and an intense curiosity as to how I would react, got me through. The dominating factor was curiosity.' He added, 'My one wish before I landed was that I would not have to kill a man. This went at the sight of our dead and wounded.'[9]

Harry Murray was decorated for fighting – for killing human beings – not for farming, and fighting he stands outside the Memorial Hall in the town of Evandale in northern Tasmania, in death as in life, hurling destruction at Germans.

But most military statues are about remembering soldiers as men, not what they did in battle. Otherwise the Anzacs on the bridge would be limbless, blind and screaming. And nobody wants to look at that driving to work. It would put us off our breakfast. It might even put us off our wars.

James Brown believed that Anzac Day began as 'a well-deserved day of rest for returned servicemen' but is now 'a holiday for all but the serving military'.[10] He was glad to see Anzac Day respected – insofar as respect played a part in the festivities – but felt that its current form might help to extend 'a cycle of jingoistic commemoration that does little to help the way we think about war or to stitch veterans back into the fabric of the society from which they came'.[11]

In 2016, Tom Frame, a former naval officer and Anglican bishop to the defence force, edited an anthology of essays in which he 'confessed' to 'being uncomfortable with many aspects of contemporary commemoration and to feeling less than free to share my anxieties about the Anzac Day "experience".' He argued that 'the identification of historical fallacies and the questioning of historical interpretations ... are, at times, painful necessities if Anzac Day is to avoid descending into empty sentimentality or being hijacked for nationalist propaganda'.[12]

So, the '0.1 per cent' of 'fringe activists' rounded on by Tudge for questioning the spirit of Anzac Day included the former speechwriter for a prime minister; a Vietnam veteran who helped promote the commemoration of the Second World War; a former bishop to the Australian Defence Force; and, fringiest of them all, James Brown, a former army officer, the former son-in-law of former Liberal prime minister Malcolm Turnbull (in whose government Tudge served), former president of the New South Wales branch of the RSL, and president of the Paddington branch of the Liberal Party.

*

The prime-ministership of Scott Morrison – like the tenure of Alan Tudge as Minister for Education and Youth – was somewhat overshadowed by the COVID-19 pandemic. This left Morrison with comparatively few opportunities to coopt the Anzacs into whatever his peculiarly opaque value system may have been. However, a few weeks into the pandemic, at the Anzac Day service at the Australian War Memorial in 2020, Morrison used the occasion to promote national unity through social distancing. He cast his mind back to 1919 and the first Anzac Day after the First World War when, he said, 'There were no city marches or parades for the returning veterans, because Australians were battling the Spanish flu pandemic. Though our streets were empty, the returning veterans were not forgotten.' He spoke of a small group of men who had held a service for their mates on the beach at Gallipoli, with 'no dignitaries, no bands, just the sound of lapping water on a lonely shore.

'And so our remembrances – small, quiet and homely – will be today,' said Morrison.

However, Morrison's characterisation of Anzac Day 1919 was not entirely accurate. While there were no big marches in Sydney or Melbourne, many smaller cities and towns staged days of solemn commemoration and unashamed celebration. In Byron Bay in New South Wales, for example, most of the population assembled at the railway gates to express 'pride for the glorious deeds of the living and sorrow for the splendid dead'.

Although the extent of the casualties of the war had become clear – the 60,000 Australians killed and 156,000 wounded, gassed or taken prisoner – and the memories of the dead were still fresh in the minds of their families and friends, the townsfolk of Byron Bay saw no reason to put on a glum face. Their Anzac Day procession was led by schoolchildren and trailed by adults in fancy dress: Charlie

The Myths of Anzac Day

Chaplin marched with the comic character 'Ard Luck and the fictitious bush patriarch Dad Wayback (the mainstay of a 1918 Dad and Dave-style movie farce) on a painted horse. Their costumes were judged and ranked. Prizes were awarded for guessing the correct height of a pole and the length of a ribbon. A soldiers-versus-civilians tug of war was won by the military team.[13]

Gatherings like this were always reported in meticulous detail by the relevant local newspaper. A similar spectacle took place in Euroa in Victoria, where a procession from the Post Office was led by two flag-bearing soldiers, followed by returned men, the emergency services and a 'miscellaneous collection of Indians, stockmen, swagmen, gollywogs, Waybacks, boot-grapplers [and] hair-raisers ... the best fancy-dress procession yet witnessed in the town'. At the showground, the slow-horse race and the tilting-of-a-bucket-from-a-wheelbarrow event offered uncommon amusement.[14] The Waybacks won the prize for most original turnout, but lost the tug of war.

Bearing in mind the facts of 1919, it would have been just as appropriate historically if Morrison had announced that he planned to celebrate a pandemic Anzac Day by rolling around in a Bluey onesie and dyeing his pet schnoodle green.

Nor did the unlikely association between the hugely popular Waybacks and the Anzacs end with the passing of the pandemic. People dressed as the Waybacks won the best humorous turnout at Lawloit in northwestern Victoria on Anzac Day in 1920, while at Waikerie in South Australia the Waybacks were joined by an associated group of 'aboriginal' people on a truck.[15] At Tamworth in New South Wales, 'a queer combination on a horse lorry' styled as 'Dad Wayback's Chocolate Wheel Company' sadly failed to capture best individual turnout.[16] Finally, in Mullumbimby, the diggers themselves dressed as 'The Waybacks in Town'.[17]

Customs do not appear fully formed and continue untransformed through the generations. There was no template for the observance of the first Anzac Days after the Armistice, and communities did what they felt was best to raise money for servicepeople's charities such as the Wounded Soldiers Fund. Just as early Christmas Day celebrations absorbed the Roman Saturnalia and the December 25 festival for the sun god Sol Invictus, the first Anzac Day in South Australia was incorporated into the October 13 public holiday for Eight Hours Day (Labour Day).

In Adelaide, Eight Hours Day was traditionally marked with a trade-unions pageant. In 1915, the principal organiser resolved to hold a patriotic parade instead, and involve the government and prominent (that is, wealthy) local people in the planning. The parade organising committee originally conceived of a 'Monster Procession, Pageant, and Carnival', but appealed to the public for a more appropriate name. As always, there was a prize for the winning suggestion and, when 'Anzac Day' was 'sent in by a number of competitors', lots were drawn to choose the winner.[18]

Adelaide's Anzac Day Committee was supported by a motley collection of stakeholders, notably theatre managers, commercial travellers, and the Shopkeepers Defence League.[19] The South Australian League of Wheelmen took charge of the bicycle races to be held at Adelaide Oval.[20]

On this first Anzac Day many Anzacs were still dug in and pinned down on the beaches at Gallipoli, but there remained hope that the Dardanelles stalemate might end in a victory for the Allies. The march in Adelaide was led by the Naval Brigade, followed by wounded men from Gallipoli, 2,281 soldiers from the nearby camps, the traditional trade-union procession, more than forty young ladies on horses, and then seasoned entertainers such as 'Mr. Freeman's Nigger Minstrels'.

Less than a minute of fitful film survives of the watching crowd, all frocked up and behatted for a fine day out – councillors in bowlers, men in trilbies, women in bonnets, cadets in slouch hats, John Bull in his top hat – and a bareheaded performer in blackface, kneeling in front of what appears to be a Joan of Arc, tipping back his head to best show off his prosthetic nose. The young ladies trot in formation on their mounts and the war seems as distant as the Dardanelles.[21]

Several of the trade-union floats illustrated Gallipoli themes, and all the unions would have had members in the Australian Imperial Force. The Builders' Labourers Union apologised: 'Our numbers are small. Two hundred fighting at the front.' The Federated Theatrical Employees made Australia's largest-ever papiermâché sculpture: a model of the rugged heights of Gaba Tepe, as stormed by the Anzacs on April 25, defended by Turkish soldiers whose 'spiteful-looking machine gun . . . cracked out death and defiance' while 'the gleaming bayonets of the Australians in a declivity below spoke of the glorious charge that was to come'. The tableau was co-designed by the union's branch president, J. Till, who had lost his eldest son in that same charge.

Servicemen, tradesmen and minstrels aside, the Adelaide *Advertiser* judged the highlight of the procession to be the 'curious tribe' that came dressed as cavemen and prehistoric animals, and included 'a chief and his followers, attired in skins, wielding stone and wooden weapons, carrying shields of hide, and looking the very picture of ferocity'.

When the march reached the oval, the cycle races were overshadowed by the diversion offered by 'The Great Tramway Crash', 'a real American novelty' in which two obsolete, formerly horse-driven tramcars were set against each other 'at something approaching top speed on a single line of track' which was elevated at both ends. According to the *Advertiser*, 'The effect of the collision was startling.

Explosions of detonators placed on the rails added to the din', causing the cars to burst into flames and thereupon melt into 'a shapeless mass of twisted iron and splintered wood'. The movie rights to the smash were sold for £25, which was put towards the total of £3,157 raised throughout the day (equivalent to about $380,000 today).[22]

Patriotic committees throughout the state organised similar Anzac Day diversions. At Kapunda in the Barossa Valley, the centrepiece of the afternoon tea stall was a 'Gallipoli cake' designed and baked by Mrs B. Standen, who 'with the aid of chocolates and other confections built an admirable representation of the cliffs of Gallipoli augmented by pictures of soldiers among the rocks'.[23] At Onkaparinga, south of Adelaide, a fleet of vehicles from miles around took part in a pageant, where the prize for most humorous turnout was awarded to a tableau representing ... the Waybacks. Members of the Adelaide Gollywog Company 'amused young and old'.[24] Meanwhile in Renmark on the Murray River, 'a projected nigger minstrel group was arrested by influenza and had to go to bed'.[25]

Nor was the extreme oddness of wartime Anzac Days confined to South Australia. In Ballarat in Victoria, Anzac Day was declared on 14 January 1916, and the procession was led by a wrestling champion dressed as a Norse war god, followed by a woman in costume as the goddess of peace. After the returned wounded came groups of citizens dressed as 'Red Indians' and, of course, the Melbourne Gollywog Club – this time on motorcycles.

By the time the first anniversary of the Anzac landing dawned at Gallipoli, the AIF was back in Egypt, enjoying an Anzac Day of its own making. After a memorial ceremony, wrote the Commander of the 4th Brigade, Brigadier General John Monash, 'We spent the morning in cricket matches and other amusement, and in the afternoon the whole Division went down to the Canal to swim and take part in a great Aquatic Carnival ... [B]oth sloping banks of the

Suez Canal for fully a mile north was one teeming mass of naked humanity – at times there were over 15,000 men in the water.

'Of course, we had many comic items not on the program, including a skit on the memorable landing by a freak destroyer manned by a lot of corked blackfellows hauling ashore a number of tiny tin boats full of tiny tin soldiers. It was screamingly funny.'[26]

In 1916, April 25 was officially recognised as Anzac Day, but arguments continued over whether it should be marked with sombreness, frivolity or an AIF-style mixture of the two. The day was used to promote recruitment during the war years and was not observed as a national holiday in all states until 1927, by which time the ritual silence, the old soldiers marching, and the beery reunions with former comrades had become established features. But the strangeness lived on in South Australia as late as 1929, when Port Lincoln's local newspaper insisted that, while some people called for solemnity on Anzac Day, 'most were for rejoicing'. In Port Lincoln, Anzac Sunday had been kept as the day of the remembrance. Since April 25 marked the anniversary of the birth of Australia as a nation, suggested the *West Coast Recorder*, 'let Anzac Day be a genuine birthday and rejoice'. In Port Lincoln the nation's birthday was celebrated with a carnival. A local man ran second in the 75-yard Somme Handicap but was not officially placed as he was 'in his negro minstrel costume and the judges evidently thought he was having a run for fun'. Competitions were held to guess the weight of sheep and the quantity of wheat in a bottle. A Queen of the Carnival was crowned to great applause, and dancing went on to 'the wee small hours'.[27]

The truth about the early Anzac Days has been genuinely forgotten – except by certain painstaking historians – and replaced by the mythological idea that things have always been the way they are, and therefore that is the way they always should be. There are all sorts of problems with remembering Anzac Day as a sacred day when people dressed up as gollywogs – but that is how it was.

In this book, I frequently use the word 'myth' to describe a story based around a misunderstanding of an event, or an alleged occurrence that did not actually happen, and then used as a cautionary tale to promote a fallacy.

It has been suggested to me in private correspondence that I have called veterans 'liars' when I have pointed out that they have misrepresented their experience, but I contend that a myth can represent an honest attempt to give flesh to a feeling. When some Vietnam veterans claim to have been physically spat upon, what they mean is that they felt their service, their values and their sacrifice were metaphorically spat upon by the society that sent them to war. They attach this feeling to an allegory to make it easily understood. Whether or not the feeling was based on fact – and even whether they felt this way at the time, rather than in retrospect – is another matter. But I do not believe that veterans who claim to have been spat upon are lying – even when they were not spat upon.

Nor do I think that disregard for facts is necessarily nefariously motivated. When the authorities in Australia and Turkey continue to promote the idea that Kemal Atatürk decreed that there was 'no difference between the Johnnies and the Mehmets to us, where they lie, side by side' – even in the face of overwhelming evidence that Atatürk said no such thing – they are expressing a feeling, sometimes a hope, that Australia and Turkey are friends and allies who have put the enmities of the past behind them. However, while there must be few Turks who begrudge the Anzacs their lonely graves on the Gallipoli Peninsula, that does not mean that there are many who hold that there is 'no difference' between the invaders and defenders of their nation.

A myth may thus be created and nurtured out of a simple desire for something to be true. The impossible story that John Simpson Kirkpatrick rescued hundreds of seriously wounded men on the back of a donkey gives Australians a war hero who did not kill anybody, permitting even pacifists and anti-militarists (that phantom '0.1 per cent') to remember his life and memorialise his death with pride.

'Weary' Dunlop was another Australian hero who saved lives – but perhaps not in the way most people imagine. The inaccurate portrayal of Dunlop as the surgeon-rescuer, rather than the administrator-protector, of POWs on the Burma Railway attributes his success to his medical prowess instead of his astounding strength of character. But it's easier to understand a doctor helping sick men than a leader shielding them from their captors' savagery.

Most of the myths examined and debunked in this book have been propagated by journalists, or journalist-historians, not academics. While I wear my PhD from the Australian Defence Force Academy like body armour, I am a journalist too, and as guilty as any other of sensationalising and oversimplifying complex and nuanced stories. When I criticise a journalist, it is not because they misname a military unit, or mis-rank an officer, or misspell a surname. This can happen to anyone. Certain idiots might even have called the distinguished military historian Professor David Horner by the name 'Derek Horner' in a newspaper feature, only to have David Horner examine (and fail) their doctoral thesis seven years later (spoiler: he passed me in the end).

When I take a writer to task, it is because they do not check their sources. People often remember events incorrectly; this is not the interviewee's problem – anybody is entitled to say whatever they like about their own lives – but it is a historian's responsibility to verify their testimony. I learned this the hard way from a number of academics, including David (aka Derek) Horner: a writer who fails to check the facts is not a historian, but a storyteller.

I used to think that exposing myths was an important, amusing but futile exercise. I did not imagine that I could really alter what people thought, but another impetus for this book was a rare and unexpected success. In an earlier work, *Australia's Vietnam: Myth vs History*, I had prosecuted a wearying and wearisome campaign against the ideas that Vietnam veterans were routinely rejected and insulted upon their return to Australia, and that they did not receive a welcome-home parade until 1987.

I was surprised to discover that the rejected-veteran folklore was taught to students. For example, in the absence of a suitable textbook in Victoria, use was made of *Australia and the Vietnam War*, a lively primer and workbook published by the Department of Veterans' Affairs and distributed free to every school. Depressingly, the first edition included an anecdote about a schoolteacher from the anti-war group Save Our Sons who spat on a soldier who was once her pupil, and a story from a soldier 'who remembered' being met at Sydney Airport by 'people waving placards and someone [holding] up a page out of a newspaper about women and children being killed'. The book also made the argument that the 'first significant act of commemoration' of Australia's Vietnam War was the famous Australian Vietnam Forces National Reunion and Welcome Home Parade in Sydney in 1987, which was for many veterans 'the admission that they should not have been shunned or abused on their return from Vietnam'.[28]

However, in 2022, I was mailed a copy of Cambridge University Press's *Analysing Australian History: War and Upheaval 1909–1992*, in which a section headed 'Perception versus evidence' includes eight quotes from my own book describing how returned men were enthusiastically welcomed home by cheering crowds at least sixteen times before the 1987 parade – and no mention of the previously ubiquitous spitting stories.

It is exciting for me to be quoted anywhere, but *Analysing Australian History* is the textbook series for the new Victorian Certificate of Education Australian History syllabus, and I was told that my work was pivotal in the reframing of the Vietnam War homecoming section. Amazingly, I seemed to have succeeded in getting changes made to a history curriculum.

Which, I believe, is more than Alan Tudge ever managed to do.

The Myths of White Feather Women

That white feather women did not exist. That women are more peace-loving than men. That white feather women handed out feathers to disabled war veterans. That white feather women were always serious. That only women distributed white feathers.

The white feather women of the First World War were a phenomenon that some historians believe to have been a myth, but which certainly did exist in Australia – even though many of the anecdotes told about white feather women are probably mythical.

White feather giving seems to have been born in the imagination of Alfred Edward Woodley Mason, a popular English author at the turn of the twentieth century. Mason's 1902 novel *The Four Feathers* tells the story of British army officer Harry Faversham, who resigns his commission during the Mahdi rebellion in the Sudan and is accused of cowardice by three fellow officers, who each send him a white feather. When Harry's fiancée learns of his spinelessness, she is revolted by the very thought of him (and particularly the idea that 'their lips had touched'). She returns her engagement ring and plucks Harry a fourth feather from her fan. Harry then secretly travels to North Africa to wage a private war against the Mahdi.

When his friends find out what he has done they take back their feathers, and his fiancée marries him.

The family-history boom that saw many Australians embrace a rediscovered Anzac ancestor came almost a century after the publication of *The Four Feathers*, and the fact that every man in the 1st AIF was a volunteer was a source of pride for many descendants. But few arborists of the family tree would have enjoyed the thought that their great-grandmother might have cried 'shirker' at young men reluctant to enlist in the war that eventually killed 60,000 Australians. This is probably part of the reason that so little is known about the Australian women who used white feathers to shame men into going to the front.

Nicoletta Gullace, a historian of the white feather movement internationally, told me, 'Even today I get feminist scholars who'll come up to me and say, "Oh, you're that woman who writes about white feathers. It didn't happen. Don't you know it was a myth?" In fact, all my research suggests it wasn't a myth,' said Gullace. 'And I think one of the reasons feminist scholars have shied away from it is that they wish to claim more laudable aspects of the feminist movement; there's been a lot of scholarship on feminist pacifism, and women who opposed the war.' Genealogically, the white feather women have no living descendants who want them; ideologically, they have no living descendants at all.

The myths around white feather women are contradictory, often framed as cautionary tales, but their origins seem clear. Myths often start out as fiction and become accepted as history. And in the case of the white feather, Mason's literary creation appears to have inspired later events – but with a particularly gendered outcome.

*

The Myths of White Feather Women

In the years before the vote was granted to women in Australia in 1902, some politicians feared that the extension of the franchise might lead to the end of state-sponsored slaughter (not to mention popular sports). 'Woman suffrage would abolish soldiers and war,' warned Victorian MP Frank Madden, 'also racing, hunting, football, cricket and all such manly games.'[1]

Many early feminists also held the view that women were innately peace-loving and that warfare was 'the ultimate destruction of femininity'.[2] In 1914, on the outbreak of the First World War, the Women's Political Association of Victoria expressed the hope that 'women everywhere, the life-givers of the world' would work together to 'destroy the perverted sense of national honour' that led to wars between nations, and demand instead that international disputes be 'adjusted by arbitration'.[3] Campaigners believed that women were 'created to care, nurture and harness the fruits of peace, pacifism, tolerance and co-existence in the world', an idea that continued to hold strong appeal for later generations of feminist activists.[4]

But it is a myth.

The findings of a major 2021 empirical analysis of cross-sectional national public-opinion surveys in twenty-one countries confirmed previous studies that could pinpoint virtually 'no difference between men and women with respect to war and peace perceptions and behaviors' anywhere in the world.[5]

There is no reason to believe that the balance was much different in the past. When Britain declared war on Germany on 4 August 1914, Australian forces were automatically included in the British order of battle. Men literally fought to be among the first recruits to the 1st AIF. Newspapers reported Victoria Barracks in Melbourne 'besieged' by insistent volunteers. The population of Australia was only about 4.9 million, but more than 52,000 men enlisted in 1914 alone.

Hostilities began well: the closest enemy territory, lightly defended German New Guinea, fell to Australian troops after not much more than a scuffle on 21 September. The troops of the 1st AIF were sent to train in Egypt, whence they embarked for Gallipoli, often via the Greek island of Lemnos, in April 1915. Partially fraudulent newspaper dispatches about the heroic deeds of the Anzacs in the Dardanelles fuelled a fresh recruiting frenzy, which reached an all-time high when more than 16,000 men enlisted in the single month of June.

Very few Australian women went to war. Three hundred volunteer nurses helped care for the sick and wounded on Lemnos, but women mainly contributed to the war effort through the patriotic-funds movement, involving organisations ranging from the Lady Mayoress's Patriotic League in Victoria to the League of Loyal Women in South Australia, which ultimately raised an incredible £14 million of Australia's total wartime defence expenditure of £188.5 million.[6] By such means as running market stalls and patriotic parades, and knitting 1.35 million pairs of socks, more women worked voluntarily to raise money for the patriotic funds than ever joined the paid workforce.

Historian Joan Beaumont writes that it was 'troubling to later generations of feminists' that the war 'did not transform prevailing ideas about femininity in Australia'. Instead, 'traditional gender stereotypes were, if anything, reinforced by the war – that is, Australian men were expected to fight while women remained at home, "waiting and weeping" and "keeping the home fires burning". Whereas in Britain the war offered women new employment opportunities, in Australia women generally did not replace men in factories, transport and public administration ... By one estimate, the percentage of women in paid employment in Australia actually declined between 1911 and 1921.'

The Myths of White Feather Women

Feminists, writes Beaumont, tend to see the First World War as a 'lost opportunity' to challenge patriarchy, and therefore the labour of the patriotic women has been neglected. 'Even more significantly, the values that these middle-class women espoused were not those of later generations. Rather, they spoke the language of imperial loyalty and militarism, and supported with a growing passion official efforts to persuade more men to enlist.'[7]

As a consequence, their efforts are generally not even derided but neglected, as if the patriots were in the minority and historically favoured figures such Vida Goldstein, founder of the Women's Peace Army, were somehow more influential.

The Order of the White Feather was founded in England in August 1914 by Admiral Charles Cooper Penrose Fitzgerald, who organised a group of women to hand out feathers to eligible-looking men in the channel ports. The event was widely reported in the press and imitated elsewhere in Britain. Word reached Australia of the young men of Deal in Kent accepting feathers from smiling women and girls in the belief that they were 'favours', or tokens of affection. According to the consistently mendacious London *Daily Mail*, the town's bachelors proudly wore the feathers in their buttonholes and hatbands until, at noon, the town crier announced: 'Oyez! Oyez! Oyez!' (Of course.) 'The White Feather Brigade Ladies wanted to present, to the young men of Deal and Walmer who have no one dependent on them, the order of the white feather for shirking their duty in not coming forward and offering their services to uphold the Union Jack of old England. God Save the King.' At which point, the men supposedly removed the gifts.[8]

The first calls for white feathers to be handed out in Australia seem to have been published in the *Brisbane Courier* in November 1914, in support of a letter writer calling herself 'Town Girl', who said young Australian men were unwilling to bear their fair share of the burden of the war. 'I should love to see "Town Girl" and her girlfriends make a raid in a Queensland street some Friday night,' wrote a correspondent, 'Jelly'. 'There are such a lot of pretty lads there doing nothing but enjoying themselves [while] British heroes lie weltering the trenches ... Each man who hasn't come forward to help might be induced to, if he had a present of a feather.'[9] Another pro-white-feather writer suggested that young women should 'refuse to have anything to do with' young men who did not join up.[10]

White feather giving was not widely supported, even by those newspapers that delighted in reporting on the process. A typically intemperate editorial in the Brisbane *Truth* rained hell upon 'the feminine furies [i]diotically insulting the young men of the community, by indiscriminately imputing cowardice to those who do not enlist for the war to please them'. According to *Truth*, white feather women were 'merely seeking to gratify the primitive sexual desire, which is innate in every woman, to see the men slay each other for the sake of a smile from their foolish and false lips'.[11]

The feminist historian Clare Wright admitted to me that the editorial was correct. 'The only reason women ever do anything is that they're driven by their animal desires,' she confessed. 'It's the same reason that women wanted the vote, apparently: they wanted to see more handsome men in parliament.'[12]

Back at the *Truth*, the call was made for the likes of the white feather women to be 'smacked or bastinadoed' and it was argued that they would be happy to share the fate of the Sabine women (that is, rape) if it meant they would become the property of the victors. Furthermore, they were probably *no good at housework*: 'We have an idea of the way these "tarts" take on at home,' thundered the *Truth*. 'No doubt a peep under their bed would disclose months of unswept fluff.'[13]

The Myths of White Feather Women

Wright told me, 'These are the kind of standard, archetypal arguments pulled out any time that women show a degree of power or influence, either for or against the cause that you want them to show it for: they are either oversexed and therefore under-rational or the sky is going to fall in – in that women will no longer want to marry or have babies or have sex with their husbands if they are allowed to do things like vote or work or give out white feathers.'

When army recruitment numbers dropped off during the bloody stalemate on the Western Front, Prime Minister William 'Billy' Hughes called a referendum on his intensely held view that men (although not politicians) should be conscripted to fight overseas. He knew that a parliamentary vote would split his party, so in October 1916 he appealed directly to the people, who rejected compulsory military service by a narrow margin. Hughes and his fellow travellers left the Labor Party but continued to govern in coalition. The coalition itself later became the Nationalist Party of Australia.

The white feather women were one expression of female patriotism and martial zeal, but more formal and respected bodies, such as the National Council of Women, the Women's National League, and the Women's Christian Temperance Union, played far more significant roles in pro-conscription campaigns, although some of their arguments seem a little eccentric today. Women's National League President Eva Hughes appeared to take curiously semantic issue with those who objected to compulsion. 'Why has the word become so objectionable?' she asked. 'Only because implied in connection with the word military. Every action of our daily lives is more or less compulsory from the day we are born.'[14]

She was echoing comments made by Labor MP Frederick Bamford (essentially that citizens were already compelled to register the birth of a child, go to school, vote and so on) who also fielded objections to sending troops to a distant war with an argument more familiar to modern Australian ears (as it has been employed by every wartime prime minister since): 'Where else will they fight in the defence of this country except on foreign battlefields? Where is Australia now being defended, if not on foreign soil?'[15]

But the sterner case for compulsion was best summarised by the Church leader who declared the principle of voluntarism to be 'wrong in conception, unfair in its incidence and inadequate in its results', as 'it treats the supreme question of the preservation of the nation as if it were purely a matter of private inclination instead of being the inalienable duty of each individual'.[16]

No literature has been left by the white feather movement in Australia. There are only a few vague press reports of anonymous white feather women meeting formally at unspecified locations, the most detailed of which come from Tasmania.

In 1915, women were reportedly seen at a corner of Melbourne Town Hall 'insulting men' by passing white feathers in envelopes, but this seems to have been an infrequent occurrence.[17] However, many Australian newspaper reports of the time recounted men of military age receiving white feathers in the mail.

While documentary evidence is scant, apocryphal stories abound: 'A man in Gisborne (M.L.) who got a white feather through the post the other day with a note making violent remarks at him decided that it was about time he got into the argument. Going to the recruiting office he put his services at the disposal of his King and country. He would have squeezed through, too, if his age hadn't settled him. He was 98.'[18]

Blame for the feathers often fell – with no deliberate linguistic irony – upon 'flappers'. One newspaper story had it that 'a band of flappers who have been carrying on the white feather foolishness in a seaside suburb saw a sturdy-looking young man sunning himself in a deck chair on a front verandah. He had a rug wrapped round his knees, a cigarette in his mouth and a magazine in his hands. The damsel strode on to the verandah and thrust a white feather into the youth's hand, with the brief salutation, "Cold feet!" The sun-bather grinned. "Well, one of them is, I guess – it's buried in Gallipoli," he observed, and from beneath the rug thrust the stump of a leg.'[19]

Feather-giving lent itself generously to fables of this kind, where the set-up preceded the punchline with uncanny prescience.

A woman on Princes Bridge in Melbourne was reported to have handed a white feather to a lad wearing an eye shield, who returned it with the words, 'Better take this yourself, madam . . . I've done my bit, and lost an eye in doing it.'[20] An Anzac fighting in the Dardanelles turned out to have enlisted – against the wishes of his terminally ill widowed mother – after his sweetheart had sent him a white feather with the message that she planned only to marry 'a man'. Within a fortnight of his leaving, a newspaper reported, his mother died. He subsequently fell in Gallipoli 'but before dying asked a comrade to return the white feather to the girl, who had written him by every mail. This the comrade did, and the boy's sweetheart received the white feather dyed red with her lover's blood.'[21]

While the anonymous and dramatic white feather stories were almost certainly invented, less spectacular episodes involving known and named individuals were clearly factual. For example, it was widely reported in February 1915 that the Minister for Defence, George Pearce, had been moved to issue a statement defending two permanent officers of the Commonwealth Military Forces, 'both of whom occupy high positions in the Defence Department', who had received white feathers in the mail. Pearce said that both officers had made applications to go overseas with the AIF, but he had refused them because their services were needed in Australia. While most newspaper reports described the names and addresses on the envelopes as 'printed in rude, uneven lettering in order to ensure the perfect disguise of the sender's handwriting', the *Geelong Advertiser* had them 'addressed in what appears to be a woman's handwriting'.[22]

A dispatch from Wangaratta in Victoria suggested that local men had received their feathers in envelopes on which 'the handwriting is that of a female', but other stories show that many recipients believed their tormentors to be men.[23] A prominent member of the Moree Recruiting Association in New South Wales apparently received a white feather with the urging that he should 'get into khaki and not hide behind recruiting schemes any longer', signed by 'An Admirer of a Man not a Shirker'. His local newspaper responded with a message for the sender: 'If he has in his odious construction reasonable comprehension – even though he may have the soul of a gnat – we might inform him that his idea is not original. In sending his message through the post, enshrouded in cowardly anonymity, he has plagiarized the method adopted by other scurrilous skunks of his ilk.' The *Moree Champion* does not seem to have even entertained the idea that the sender might have been a woman.[24]

The South Australian Labor MP Thomas Hyland Smeaton was enraged to receive a piece of white feather with no note attached. 'It had no message for me excepting that the sender is a low coward, who if he will do me the favour of giving me five minutes with him, will have my answer written on his hide,' stormed Smeaton. 'I am too old to be sent away with our gallant boys, but I believe I am still a good enough man to write my reply physically on the cur.'[25] When federal Labor members began to receive white feathers, one minister commented, 'The Ladies Political League is moulting.'[26] But the South Australian Labor MP Alfred William Styles had earlier received a white feather and the message, 'You would do more good at the front,' and since the note was written on House of Assembly letterhead, he guessed it had come from one of his colleagues, all of whom were male.[27]

White feather recipients outside the realm of politics were rarely named. An exception was made in the *Murray Pioneer*, which told the standard story of a feather that came to an unnamed 'young man on whom a sick mother and seven children relied for their main support', along with another that had reached a Mr Arthur Prince who was 'hurt considerably' but not driven to enlist as he had already tried to join up and been rejected. The newspaper suggested that the nice young lady responsible ('and we are sure from her handwriting that she's a *very* nice young lady') should send a note of apology to Prince. One week later, however, the *Murray Pioneer* was forced to issue its own mea culpa, which was refreshingly forthright: 'We regret that through the editor's stupidity Mr. Arthur Prince, instead of Mr. Arthur Lucas, was mentioned in connection with the white feather incident... Like Mr. Lucas, Mr. Prince has tried to enlist and has been thwarted by an unsympathetic doctor, but no young lady has so far favoured him with a white feather token.'[28]

The idea of the white feather continued to excite writers of prosaic fiction. In December 1915, the magazine *The Lone Hand* published a short story centred around Ted, an eighteen-year-old Sydney boy who is eager to join the AIF in the face of opposition from his mother, a Boer War widow who believes that he should wait until he is twenty-one. But Ted is worried that the war will be over by then. He opens a thin letter at the breakfast table to find it contains a white feather and a typewritten note that reads 'For a shirker'.

'A shirker, yes, and a coward, they might have put that,' says Ted. 'It's only the shirkers and cowards that don't go. God knows it makes a fellow feel pretty cheap.'

It turns out that Ted sent the feather to himself, but his distress prompts his mother to finally realise her mistake and allow him to enlist.[29]

Other mundane authors expanded upon the theme. It is a commonly held idea that early twentieth-century female novelists have been unjustly ignored and forgotten. But Ray Ellis Phillips, who wrote as Mrs M.M. Phillips, may well have been deservedly overlooked. Mrs Phillips published her only novel in 1917 and I found a copy on the shelves of the library of the Australian Defence Force Association.

As had become the convention, the book concerned a young man who was sufficiently fit, skilled and courageous to go to war but who nonetheless was forced to stay behind for hidden reasons of his own. Phillips' hero is Dick Harper, an outcast even in his gentlemen's club, where he feels 'the covert sneers that his presence elicited from some of the younger men', although 'the pitying coldness of the elders cut him more deeply still'. Dick regards his club as his address and so calls in occasionally for mail. He picks up a letter from his sweetheart, Neville. 'In his present isolation,' writes Phillips, 'it counted for more than ever to get a message from her. He pulled out the paper, unfolded it and the little white feather fell through his fingers to the floor.'

This twist has a limited impact on the reader, as it occurs on page 187 of a book called *The White Feather*, but it is a dagger in the heart for Dick. 'Unheeding he let it lie there,' writes Phillips, 'as he stood with grey face and unseeing eyes. The revulsion of feeling made him swallow nervously, as if he had difficulty in breathing. If Neville had felt that she wanted to strike him, she had but to see him as he stood now. She had struck him hard.'

He was knocked down with a feather.

Dick, of course, goes off to war (it is surprising how often the feathers do the trick) and comes back to find that Neville has waited for him. He kisses her for the first time – 'I've been waiting for that for years,' he says – and tells her he has always kept a talisman to conjure her before his eyes.

He draws his wallet from his coat and takes out 'a shabby object', which he lays in her hand.

It is, of course, a cigarette case.

Just kidding. It is a 'little piece of white feather'.[30]

Smaller groups of patriotic women in Australia included the League of Honour, whose parent organisation was founded in London at the beginning of the war. 'Women were supposed to swear never to be seen with a man out of uniform,' said Nicoletta Gullace. 'And the idea was that if these young men on the home front couldn't get women to go out with them, they would eventually join up because that was the only way they were going to get any sex. So this kind of raising of recruits by shaming men who didn't serve became a kind of military service for women.'

The Australasian branch of the League of Honour was formed in Sydney in May 1916, but its activities – a 'week of humiliation and prayer' and a 'thrift week' – may not have excited many serving men. As the war came to an end, a meeting in Melbourne was addressed by a military chaplain who 'appealed to all not to run to excess in welcoming returning men'.

'Let the head rule the heart,' he urged. 'The soldiers [do] not want it.'[31]

This may have been one of the most profound misreadings of the military mindset in modern Australian history.

While earlier anti-suffrage arguments may have found echoes in the livelier corners of debate about white feather women, the association of women's suffrage with men's recruitment was far weaker in Australia than in England. At the outbreak of the First World War, British women still lacked the vote, despite a controversial campaign of civil disobedience that had led to the imprisonment of suffragette leaders, such as Emmeline Pankhurst and her daughters Christabel, Sylvia and Adela.

The suffragettes are heroines of popular memory in the UK. Their battle for enfranchisement is widely commemorated and celebrated, especially the role of Emmeline and Christabel's Women's Social and Political Union (WSPU), but, said Gullace, there has been 'very little emphasis on their extreme pro-war position'.

'Christabel and Emmeline *embraced the war* and thought that a woman's pro-war attitude would exemplify female patriotism and their worthiness of the vote', said Gullace, whereas Sylvia and her younger sister Adela (who emigrated to Australia in 1914 and joined the Women's Peace Army) were both expelled from the WSPU and opposed the war. It has even been said that Christabel and Emmeline handed out white feathers themselves. 'The only person who said that, that I can actually find, is Sylvia Pankhurst,' said Gullace. 'The Pankhurst family was a very acrimonious family.'

Sylvia wrote that in September 1914 'Christabel re-appeared at the London Opera House, after her long exile, to utter a declaration, not on women's enfranchisement, but on "The German Peril." Mrs. Pankhurst toured the country, making recruiting speeches. Her supporters handed the white feather to every young man they encountered wearing civilian dress, and bobbed up at Hyde Park meetings with placards: "Intern Them All."'[32]

Gullace enjoyed the idea of Pankhursts as shame-sayers, but admitted, 'I don't have any evidence (and, believe me, I've looked for it) that they themselves handed out white feathers.' In fact, Gullace's research has led her to conclude that white feather giving was often not the aggressive act it appeared to be, in the UK at least. She said, 'My sense is that usually it was just a couple of girls who would cut open a pillowcase and say, "Let's go and have a bit of fun." And they'd take a handful of these goose feathers or duck feathers and they'd go around and they'd stick them on young men in civilian clothes. And there was also, in a lot of these cases, a bit of flirtation and hijinks … They'd go into the West End. They'd hang around theatres, they'd pin a feather into some guy's buttonhole.' And there are accounts from soldiers, who were handsome young officers at the time, talking about how they'd specifically go to the West End, in their mufti or their civilian clothes, in the hope of getting a white feather, because when they told the white feather girls that they were actually in the military, they could often get off with them. And they were often – quote – 'quite young and pretty'. And there was one officer who claimed he had a whole fan's worth of white feathers that he liked to show off to his pals in the trenches. Now, this may be a bit of an exaggeration, but there's clearly some flirtatious give and take in some of these situations that we've now forgotten, because we look back on it all with such horror.

'Feminist historians who still claim this is a myth do so because very few women have stepped forward and owned up, "I gave out a white feather,"' said Gullace. 'Very few people would want to claim, "I went to the Shaftesbury Theatre and stuck a white feather in a man and ran away. And later, he got his legs blown off."'

Considering the horrifically high 64.8 per cent casualty rate among Australian forces, that outcome was more likely than not for an Anzac. But as Joan Beaumont told me 'We don't have any numbers on how many women handed white feathers out. We have a lot of anecdotal evidence, including my great-uncle who, according to family memory, was handed a white feather and off he went ... and he was back within fifteen months *without his leg*, which he lost in the Battle of Polygon Wood.'

Even true history is irony exercised. Adela Pankhurst, who arrived in Australia as a fearless and unrepentant feminist, socialist and pacifist, was fated to become what she most despised. She was a founder of the Communist Party of Australia in 1920 and then a founder of the anti-communist Australian Women's Guild of Empire in 1928. She turned her back on feminists, who, she came to believe, drained the dynamism of men who had 'spilled their blood over the whole surface of the earth, and strewn their bones thick beneath every sea in the interests of future generations'.[33] In the 1930s she became an anti-Semite, and in 1941 a founder of the fascist Australia First Movement, and she was interned as an enemy sympathiser in 1942. And yet today, when the dead are forgiven nothing, her name and picture decorate the plinth of a recently erected London statue of suffragist leader Millicent Fawcett, along with those of Christabel and Emmeline.

The white feather movement left behind its monuments too. From 1916, Rejected Volunteer Associations formed across Australia, in part because 'ladies were not kind to shirkers'.[34] Members were issued with badges to distinguish them as rebuffed patriots. Meanwhile, the government also pressed an array of badges identifying discharged and demobilised soldiers and sailors, home-service volunteers, medically unfit volunteers, munitions workers and war workers, among others.[35] Some failed volunteers, desperate not to be remembered as cowards, asked that their names be included with the successful recruits on their local war memorial's roll of honour. Their appeals were mostly ignored, but the sandstone pillars on the memorial gates in Montville in southern Queensland record among

The Myths of White Feather Women

the local volunteers six 'Fallen', thirty-three 'Enlistments' and a further six 'Rejects'.[36] In time, of course, even the bathetic Rejected Volunteer Associations came to march on Anzac Day.[37]

The white feather recurred in Australian story and song long after the last plume was plucked from a pusillanimous goose. Just as I had first heard of Gallipoli in Eric Bogle's ballad, the first I learned of white feather giving in Australia was through the Melbourne folk-punk band Weddings Parties Anything's mournful 'Scorn of the Women'. The lyrics deliberately echo 'And the Band Played Waltzing Matilda', and capture the forgotten truth that white feather giving enjoyed a brief renaissance during the Second World War.

Although they had a certain cultural and political impact, the white feather women in Australia were more of a phenomenon than an organisation, and they were outliers even among patriotic women. Rather than being accepted as allies in the cause of conscription, they were ridiculed as women by patriotic men who believed that undeveloped female brains could not conceive of the logistics of modern warfare, which required able-bodied males to remain at home to supply the troops.

Again and again in this book, I will be drawn back to Australia's fascinatingly shifting mischaracterisation of the 'home front' during the Vietnam War. In the perverse but pervasive mythology of some Vietnam veterans and journalist-historians, women feature only as spitters on soldiers, or demonstrators for the Save Our Sons movement (or even, ridiculously, both at once). The mythical spitters of the Vietnam years are the equal but opposite of the white feather women. They were as vigorously opposed to one war as the white feather women were militantly supportive of another, and yet they had in common the fact that they were women and therefore (a) ignorant of military reality, and (b) in need of being spanked or raped to set them right.

During the First World War, both women and men were credited with sending white feathers in the mail, but for the subsequent stories to have the necessary impact, and for their meaning to be clear, the feathers had to be seen to be handed personally by an unthinking woman to an undeserving man. The man then must show her an injury – to his body, not his pride – or a war medal, and thereby teach her a lesson: it is not for a woman to judge.

At a visceral level, the white feather myths served as revenge fantasies for men who perhaps resented the social pressure put upon them to enlist. The feather may well have been feared more as a feeling than a thing, and perhaps came to represent all the relentless arguments made to reluctant soldiers to join their fellows at the front. There is no reason to believe that the white feather would have become a gendered weapon were it not for Admiral Penrose Fitzgerald's mobilisation of the 'flappers' of Kent in 1914. After all, the idea that women might hand out feathers came from the minds of two men – an author and an admiral – and the first three feathers received by the fictitious Harry Faversham were all given to him by his fellow officers.

The potency of the symbol endured even once the cause was lost. When a second conscription referendum failed in December 1917, *Women's Realm* magazine despaired: 'The great Yes-No question appears to have ended in a white feathery mist ... The "No" victory proclaims to the world the fact that Australia, the land of the free – free because the Mother Country and our Allies protect her shores from invasion – has shown the white feather.'[38]

In August 1918 the *Geelong Advertiser* ran a piece claiming that recruiters detested 'the sort of person who hands out white feathers' since they 'shoot very often at the wrong target'. The case in point was a young Stanley William Gurr, who had 'suffered much for the past four years from the white feather fanatic' although he had attempted to enlist 'no less than eight times'. But still he would not give up. After his ninth ignominious knockback, he returned to the recruiting office and joined the Citizen Military Forces for home service in the reserve.[39]

Thus the white feather myths carried the gentler lesson that people should not be judged on appearances. They were agile, pliable and rich in meaning, but among all the Australian white feather stories of the First World War, I could find none where a man is presented with a plume by a woman, goes off to war, becomes a hero and returns home to marry her. It could be that the infinite ranks of marble tombstones on the Western Front put paid forever to the myth of the happy ending.

The Myths of the Gallipoli Landing

That Albert Facey was at the Gallipoli landing. That reportage of the Gallipoli landing is reportage of the Gallipoli landing. That film of the Gallipoli landing is film of the Gallipoli landing. That the Australian nation was born at Gallipoli.

Every year on 25 April, thousands of young Australian and New Zealand expats decamp from their sharehouses and hostels in Clapham and Balham to gather at the beaches of Gallipoli in Turkey, there to commemorate Anzac Day on the sands where it all began. Exactly why travellers might choose to do this, more than a century after the disastrous military campaign and the Anzac evacuation, is a source of much faux-bemused debate among scholars.

But it is not only backpackers who flock to Turkey on Anzac Day: Australian prime ministers do it, too. The first PM to arrive was Labor's Bob Hawke in 1990, accompanying a group of dangerously elderly Gallipoli veterans on the seventy-fifth anniversary of the landings. At a dinner given by the Turkish prime minister, Hawke explained that 'many of the qualities we still value most in the Australian character' were forged in the fires of Gallipoli, although he also allowed that the campaign marked 'an important step in the emergence of modern Turkey'. He quoted Mustafa Kemal Atatürk's recently popularised – if highly unlikely – assurance that the Turks saw no difference between the remains of 'the Johnnies and the Mehmets' lying buried beneath their soil, before rather alarmingly introducing the veterans as 'surviving representatives of the invasion'.[1] At Anzac Cove itself, Hawke even seemed to imply that the invasion had been a success. 'This place is in one sense a part of Australia,' he said, although it is not.[2] Similar sentiments were apparently shared by Hawke's mate Alan Bond, who in 1983 compared his own America's Cup win with the Australian 'victory' at Gallipoli.[3]

In 2005, two years after he had spoken at the funeral of Alec Campbell, John Howard popped up at Anzac Cove on the ninetieth anniversary of the Gallipoli landings to expand once more on the achievements and imagined values of Campbell and his generation. Howard said that the men of Gallipoli had 'bequeathed Australia a lasting sense of national identity' and 'sharpened our democratic temper and our questioning eye towards authority' – although Howard's own questioning eye to authority (whatever that might be) was about as evident as his taste for public-bar mateship.

The 2005 Anzac Day service had the air of a carnival, and was therefore dismissed as disrespectful and non-traditional by commentators who had no idea of the dress-ups and gollywog clubs of the war years. The planning for the day was beset with unhelpful debate when the suggestion that John Farnham should sing at a concert before the service was vetoed by both Howard and the New Zealand prime minister, Helen Clark, who deemed it 'totally inappropriate to have loud entertainment on a place which was a killing field'. Clark's reservations were apparently misconstrued by Australian Democrats leader Lyn Allison, who said, 'If New Zealand can put up a better singer than our Johnny Farnham then I would be surprised.'

Clark retaliated with the claim that she had never even heard of Farnham. Alec Campbell's daughter Mary Burke chipped in with support for the 57-year-old recording artist, saying that most veterans had wanted to enjoy their peace and freedom and it was 'a strange freedom that bans talented, energetic young men singers'.[4]

Even without Farnham, the director of the Office of Australian War Graves promised the ceremony would be 'a world-class event, although it will only last about ten minutes. That's all we can afford.'[5]

Proceedings began before dawn. The story of Anzac was enunciated in the professionally plausible tones of radio announcer John Laws. His measured words and significant pauses rode the subdued melodies of Albinoni's 'Adagio in G Minor', the theme tune of the 1981 Peter Weir movie *Gallipoli*, presented as if it were the soundtrack to the actual war. Later in the program, First Nations musician William Barton played the folk song 'Çanakkale İçinde' on the yidaki. But not everyone appreciated the entertainment. Particularly criticised were giant video screens playing soft rock, disco music and Bee Gees hits, including – disastrously – 'Stayin' Alive'.

'I wouldn't've had that,' said Victorian RSL official Keith Rossi, when bothered for comment by *The Age*.[6] Howard's only remark was that he was no great fan of the Bee Gees, and history does not record whether the New Zealand prime minister had ever heard of them.

In the aftermath of the event, parts of Anzac Cove were left littered with drink bottles, bin bags, shopping bags, rotting food, Pringles tubes and biscuit wrappers. Queensland RSL president Bill Mason, who watched the ceremony on TV, described the rubbish as 'disgusting'.[7] Other voices contributed descriptions of the careless travellers as 'scumbags', a 'blight on society' and 'the slobbering, filthy, unkempt Yobbo/Bogan Aussie backpacker', although the real problem was probably the inadequate number of onsite litter bins.[8]

The backpackers have their own reasons for including the dawn service at Gallipoli on their trail to the Hofbrau tent at Oktoberfest. The politicians hope to remake the Anzacs in their own image, or remake their own image with the help of the Anzacs. But the beaches of Gallipoli also hold a longstanding attraction for writers and historians, who visit in the hope that standing on the sands and gazing up at the cliffs might offer some understanding of the experience of the Anzacs – or at least help them choose the most incisive adjective to describe it. And wherever there is a lost cause, you will find me there, tirelessly failing where others have failed before me.

So it was that I travelled to Turkey in 2023.

Unbeknown to me, 2023 happened to be the centenary of the foundation of the Republic of Turkey. Throughout the country, images of Mustafa Kemal Atatürk enjoyed even more prominence than usual, which is no small achievement for a nation always awash with Atatürkia. Huge street posters advertised the freshly released TV series *Atatürk 1881–1919*, showing the great man looking brooding and purposeful – which, judging by the trailer, is the way the actor plays him throughout.

I could not make it to Gallipoli in time for Anzac Day and, in any case, the decimal anniversaries are the big ones, and this was the unglamorous and clumsy 108th. Luckily, expeditions to the battlefields run every day of the year, largely servicing the same demographic as the Anzac Day crowd. I booked a seat on a minibus tour run by a company named Crowded House, after the Australian/New Zealand rock band that played songs about the weather. Although several different tours were available, most of them seemed to be repackagings of the same offering.

The Myths of the Gallipoli Landing

The excursion originated in Istanbul but I met the minibus in Çanakkale, a lovely city on the 60-kilometre-long Dardanelles strait that connects the Aegean Sea with the Sea of Marmara and divides Asian Turkey from the Gallipoli peninsula on the European side.

The cafes that tiara Çanakkale's waterfront are scattered with impassive old men with skin like freshly ploughed fields, who look as though they've been sitting over the same cup of sticky coffee since the fall of the Ottoman Empire, watching merchant ships ply the straits with the resolute ease of swans.

Just outside the ferry port squats Sons of Gallipoli, a single-storey multimedia centre whose audiovisual displays tell the Gallipoli story from the point of view of ordinary Turkish soldiers. Presentations include interviews with elderly veterans, two iterations of Atatürk's 'Johnnies and Mehmets' speech, and the interactive documentary around which the centre is based. Displays highlight the hubris and overconfidence of the Allies, like the fact that some troops carried travel guides to Istanbul, and that the British soldier-poet Rupert Brooke looked forward to celebrating the first Holy Mass in the Hagia Sophia since the capture of Constantinople by the Ottoman Empire in 1453. There is much acknowledgement of the pain of motherhood and the grief and sacrifice of women.

A little further along the esplanade stands the Trojan Horse used in the 2004 epic movie *Troy*. The giant prop dominates this unlikely location because Çanakkale is also a starting point for trips to the Troy archaeological site where, apparently, there is little to photograph except for a bigger and even more improbable model of a horse (with a barracks on its back – which might have been a bit of a giveaway to the legendary defenders of the city). The Crowded House Gallipoli tour makes a selfie stop at the Çanakkale horse, mixing myth with history, and film with fact. But this is not as anomalous as it might seem: several historians have conflated the mythology of the Trojan War with the mythology of Gallipoli and argued convincingly that the framework – and even the vocabulary – for viewing the Dardanelles campaign as a glorious, heroic (albeit failed) military endeavour was drawn from Classical antiquity. British historian Jenny Macleod wrote that the 'romantic understanding' of Gallipoli was rooted in the British education system, particularly the public schools, with their emphasis on Homeric literature, sports and chivalry.[9] Classically educated British and Australian soldiers knew the Dardanelles by its ancient name, Hellespont, and filled the skies and seas with the spectres of the warriors, gods and kings of *The Iliad*.

Sir Ian Hamilton, the British Commander in Chief of the Mediterranean Expeditionary Force, which comprised all the Allied forces that came together on the Greek island of Lemnos to prepare for the invasion of Turkey, wrote upon passing the mouth of the strait: 'There, Hero trimmed her little lamp; yonder the amorous breath of Leander changed to soft sea form. Far away to the Eastwards, painted in dim and lovely hues, lies Mount Ida. Just so, on the far horizon line she lay fair and still, when Hector fell and smoke from burning Troy blackened the midday sun.'[10]

More prosaically, Thomas 'Rusty' Richards of the 1st AIF wrote, 'The great warrior of the siege of Troy – Achilles – is buried here, or at any rate there is a place described as the "Tomb of Achilles". Lemnos island is also known to mythology, as it was here that Vulcan landed when he was thrown out of Mount Olympos by Juno.'[11]

On the Ottoman side, at least one German officer drew similar parallels. Major General Hans Kannengiesser, who commanded the Ottoman 9th Division, noted that 'The high hill south of Akbash [east of Çanakkale, on the European side of the straits] was the site of the old Sestos to which Leander is supposed to have swum to Hero from Abydos (Nagara).'[12]

The Myths of the Gallipoli Landing

Hamilton, unusually certain of his place in history, later wrote that the siege of Troy was 'almost the duplicate' of the Dardanelles campaign, except that 'instead of a wooden horse, we made use of a steel ship'. Confidently, he added, 'That's about the extent of the difference.'[13]

At Çanakkale in 2023, the Crowded House guide, Ibrahim – whom I will identify only by his first name, as is traditional in sloppy travelogues – helped our party onto the car ferry across the strait. It is a glorious 25-minute voyage from Asia to Europe, cruising towards the town of Eceabat. The heart-shaped fortifications of the fifteenth-century Kilitbahir Castle watch over the strait, and a towering hill bears the Dur Yolcu Memorial, a huge rock carved with a dramatic image of a Turkish soldier in front of a burning brazier and words that translate as 'Traveller, halt! The soil you tread once witnessed the end of an era.'

The ferry pulled in at Eceabat near Memorial Park, the site of a complicated sculpture that seems ambitiously determined to tell the entire Turkish story of Gallipoli in a single installation. Curiously, our tour ignored it altogether, in favour of a flavourless lunch in a nearby tourist cafe.

We drove on towards Anzac Cove, and parked in a clearing where Ibrahim unfurled a large map and gave us a military-style briefing, the gravity of which was undermined only when the chart kept threatening to fall over. Ibrahim, who spoke English unfeasibly quickly, cantered through the story of the Dardanelles campaign. As a historian, I was prepared – even hoping – to be unimpressed, but Ibrahim knew his history better than I had imagined and he gave a largely accurate, nuanced and neutral picture of the Gallipoli campaign, although a couple of his notions were fanciful at best. For example, he insisted that the British executed the commander of the Royal Navy's minesweepers for his failure in the Dardanelles, whereas in real life he died in 1945, a peer of the realm.

Nor had I ever come across the idea that the Anzacs were warned to evade capture out of a fear that the Turks would eat them, but it was worth listening to the story to hear Ibrahim's lip-licking punchline: 'Australian soup . . . I like Australian soup.'[14]

Obviously, Ibrahim was not a historian – he wasn't even known by his surname! – but the stories he told highlighted the same events as the reconstructions in the various local museums and dioramas. He focused on what had been memorialised, Turksplaining statues to tourists, and these were the episodes central to the Turkish mythology of Gallipoli. While popular Australian accounts of the campaign have tended to find explanations for the Anzac defeat in the weaknesses of the Triple Entente (Britain, France and Russia) and poor (British) leadership, Ibrahim's tales painted the Turkish victory as a product of Turkish strength and planning. He propagated the official line that the triumph at Gallipoli was the most important battle in the history of the First World War, which is only true if you happen to be Turkish – which, of course, he was.

Early in 1915, the British hoped to break the stalemate on the Western Front by defeating the Kaiser's ally in the Ottoman Empire and steaming through the Dardanelles to capture the Ottoman capital of Constantinople. This would push Turkey out of the war, and recruit – in some unlikely and unspecified way – the motley and mutually hostile armies of the Balkan states to the Entente cause; and Austria-Hungary would then be attacked from the southeast. The Ottomans – for the sake of consistency rather than accuracy, I will call them the Turks – had closed the Dardanelles to shipping in September 1914, cutting Britain off from cheap wheat supplies from Russia and Romania.

Although Ibrahim did not touch on the subject – perhaps because it was unlikely to arouse the sympathy of his audience – Mehmed V, the sultan of the Ottoman Empire and holder of the caliphate, had declared a military jihad against the Entente in November 1914. The historian Ulrich Trumpener notes that the declaration of jihad had been promised to the Germans several times before the Ottomans entered the war, and 'most of Germany's political and military leaders were eagerly looking forward to that event'. The German government reminded its ambassador to the Ottomans that the *'fetva'* by the *'sheik-ul-Islam'* concerning 'the need for a holy war' must be 'forwarded immediately to Berlin so that it could be translated into "Arabic and Indian" [*sic*] for leaflet propaganda among the "enemy Moslem soldiers in France"'. When the formal proclamation was made in Constantinople, it was greeted by 'well-organised demonstrations in the streets', and a large group of marchers, accompanied by a band, paraded around the German and Austro-Hungarian embassies.[15] In February 1915, Muslims in the British Indian Army's 5th Light Infantry in Singapore mutinied in the face of rumours that they would be sent to fight the Turks, and forty-seven so-called sepoys were later publicly executed by firing squad.

The British had a better navy than they had an army and the Turks had few significant naval assets. First Lord of the Admiralty Winston Churchill favoured a naval offensive, and Secretary of State for War Earl Kitchener did not want to commit ground troops. Both men underestimated the Turks, who had recently lost the Balkan Wars but whose forces had since been bolstered with German weapons and German commanders.

In February 1915, the Entente navies tried to force a passage through the Dardanelles. After about a month of fighting, they were driven back by Turkish artillery and shrewdly laid minefields, and the anniversary of the routing of the fleet on 18 March 1915 is celebrated in Turkey as the Martyrs Day public holiday.

Hamilton witnessed the Entente defeat from the deck of a cruiser. He had been 'frightfully keen to see the fight', since a naval battle was, he wrote, the dream of his life.

'Nor,' he wrote in his diary, 'did the reality pan out short of my hopes.'

Hamilton was particularly impressed by the moments after the British battleship HMS *Inflexible* hit a mine. 'We gazed spellbound,' he wrote. 'No one knew what moment the great ship might not dive into the depths. The pumps were going hard. We fixed our eyes on marks about the water line to see if the sea was gaining upon them or not. She was very much down on the bows ... Crew and stokers were in a mass standing strictly at attention on the main deck ... In the sight of all those men standing still, silent, orderly in their ranks, facing the imminence of death, I got my answer to the hasty moralizings about war, drawn from me (really) by a regret that I would very soon be drowned. On the deck of that battleship staggering along at a stone's throw was a vindication of war in itself; of war, the state of being, quite apart from war motives or gains. Ten thousand years of peace would fail to produce a spectacle of so great virtue.'

In a very particular way, Hamilton loved war.

'Once in a generation a mysterious wish for war passes through the people,' he wrote. 'Their instinct tells them that there is no other way of progress and of escape from habits that no longer fit them. Whole generations of statesmen will fumble over reforms for a lifetime which are put into full-blooded execution within a week of a declaration of war. There is no other way. Only by intense sufferings can the nations grow, just as the snake once a year must with anguish slough off the once beautiful coat which has now become a strait jacket.'[16]

The Turkish hero of the naval battle was artilleryman Corporal Seyit, who apparently managed three times to haul 276-kilogram

The Myths of the Gallipoli Landing

shells on his back after his gun was damaged while firing at the enemy ships. When Seyit tried to re-enact his feat for a photographer, far from the adrenaline-charged air of battle, he could not even move a shell. A famous Turkish photograph of Seyit actually shows him carrying a hollow wooden shell. 'If war breaks out, I'll lift it again,' he promised.

While the Entente ships were turned around or sunk in the Dardanelles, the 1st Division AIF was training in Egypt. Hamilton took overall command of the Australians and all the motley Allied forces and returned to the Dardanelles with an army. The Anzacs landed first, at the beach now known as Anzac Cove on the northern end of the Gallipoli peninsula. The earliest landing craft put to shore about 1.6 kilometres south of their intended drop-off point. Ibrahim cited this as a factor in the Anzacs' early difficulties, as did my doctoral supervisor and author of *A Military History of Australia*, the late Professor Jeffrey Grey. Grey blamed navigational error but Ibrahim preferred the story that the current drew them off course, as if the seas themselves were fighting for the Turkish cause.

However, the historian Robin Prior writes, 'The force did not miss the parameters which were all that they were given to delineate the landing area, and the confusion caused by the bunching of the tows only affected the first wave of 1,500 men. The others landed more or less in their designated positions and if there was confusion it was no more than might be expected after a night landing on a hostile coast.'[17]

The most commonplace observation about Anzac Cove is that the beach is smaller than most visitors expect. I knew it was going to be small, but I was still surprised it was *that* small. It has grown bigger in the Australian imagination in part because of the enormous role it is held to have played in our history, but also because the stranded troops gave a name to every rock, peak, trench and gully.

The second truism is that the cliffs that rise above the beach are taller and steeper than travellers imagine. I seemed to have internalised this to the point that I was disappointed that they were not even taller. But I would not have liked to try to climb them.

The Anzacs landed at dawn and immediately commenced to storm the heights. And it was not only Hamilton and British officers who loved war. Our ideas of the emotional life of First World War soldiers remain informed by the great British war poets, and even their feelings about battle itself are sometimes misunderstood. The words of men of baser appetites are usually less beautiful and generally less heard.

Some Australian troops at the Gallipoli landing revelled in the carnage. 'Up the hill . . . we swarm,' wrote Private B.A. Kellaher. 'The lust to kill is on us, we see red. Into the trench, out of it, and into another. Oh! the bloody gorgeousness of feeling your bayonet go into soft yielding flesh – they run, we after them, no thrust and parry, in goes the bayonet the handiest way.'[18]

The Anzacs needed to take the high ground, but they advanced harried by bombardments of artillery and were soon opposed by Turkish reinforcements under the command of Lieutenant Colonel Mustafa Kemal. Tradition – and Ibrahim – has it that Kemal was appalled to see a group of Turkish soldiers retreating towards him. He later told a journalist, 'I shouted, "You cannot run away from the enemy!" They said they had no bullets left and I replied, "If you have not ammunition you have your bayonets" and ordered them to fix bayonets and face the enemy. Upon this action, the enemy soldiers also lied down.'[19]

Mustafa Kemal became Kemal Atatürk, and Atatürk's early biographer, Lord Kinross, writes, 'It was this moment of hesitation by the Anzacs which may well have decided the fate of the peninsula.' But it may equally well not have, and it possibly did not even happen. It has the feeling of a metaphorical conception of the origins of the stalemate that lay ahead, and there does not seem to be any corroborating evidence.

However, in a written order to his troops, Atatürk declared, 'I don't order you to attack. I order you to die. By the time we are dead, other units and commanders will have come up to take our place.'

'I order you to die': these were the real Atatürk Words.

And they worked. A very large number of his men did die, to be replaced by an Arab regiment which took up the challenge to drive the Anzacs back into the sea.[20] And that almost worked too, to the extent that on the evening of the landing, the Australian commanders wanted Hamilton to withdraw his forces from the peninsula.

Instead, the diggers were ordered to dig in.

Atatürk had marked himself for death along with his men, and he was lucky to survive. The bravery of the man who lived to father modern, secular, democratic Turkey is widely acknowledged by Australian commentators – his consolations, less so. To his consort, Corrine Lütfü, Atatürk wrote that the easy comradeship of the troops 'greatly facilitates the execution of my orders, which often demand death … This leads only to two celestial results: to become a victorious Gazi or a Chehad [and] go straight away to Paradise, where the *houris*, God's most beautiful women, will come to receive them and remain permanently at their disposal. Supreme happiness!'[21]

The first dispatch to cross the world about the Gallipoli landings was the work of the British journalist Ellis Ashmead-Bartlett, whose report for the London *Daily Telegraph* was widely syndicated in Australian newspapers on 8 May 1915.

Ashmead-Bartlett wrote that the Australian troops 'waited neither for orders nor for the boats to reach the beach, but, springing out into the sea, they waded ashore, and, forming some sort of a rough line, rushed straight on the flashes of the enemy's rifles. Their magazines were not even charged. So they just went in with cold steel, and I believe I am right in saying that the first Ottoman Turk since the last Crusade received an Anglo-Saxon bayonet in him at five minutes after 5 a.m. on 25 April. It was over in a minute. The Turks in their first trench were bayoneted or ran away, and a maxim gun was captured.'

Faced with an 'almost perpendicular' sandstone cliff, and under 'terrible fire' from the enemy, the Australians, 'practical, above all else', stopped for a few moments 'to pull themselves together and to get rid of their packs, which no troops should carry in an attack, and then charged their magazines. Then this race of athletes proceeded to scale the cliffs without responding to the enemy's fire. They lost some men, but did not worry, and in less than a quarter of an hour the Turks were out of their second position, either bayoneted or in full flight.'

At sunrise, the Australians were established at the top of the ridge but their 'blood was up' and 'instead of entrenching themselves and waiting developments, pushed northward and eastward inland in search of fresh enemies to attack with the bayonet . . . It was then the turn of the Turks to counter attack and this they continued to do throughout the afternoon, but the Australians never yielded a foot of ground on the main ridge.'

When the evacuation of casualties began, and the wounded were towed among the ships, 'although many were shot to bits and without hope of recovery, their cheers resounded through the night, and you could just see, amidst a mass of suffering humanity, arms being waved in greeting to the crews of the warships'. The men may have been dying from hideous wounds but 'they were happy because they knew that they had been tried for the first time and had not been found wanting'.

This gave the troops that followed the first waves an awful lot to live up to, and it would have been an impressive piece of reportage if Ashmead-Bartlett had actually been on the ground for the landings that morning. But he had not. He did not disembark the HMS *London* and set foot on the beach until 9.30 in the evening. Ashmead-Bartlett witnessed no Ottoman receiving an Anglo-Saxon bayonet.

The report of the official Australian war correspondent Charles Edwin Woodrow Bean was not published until May 17, by which time the myth of the race of athletes laughing in the face of death had presumably already found favour among large sections of a proud and relieved public.

'I can't write about bayonet charges like some of the correspondents do,' Bean later wrote in his diary. 'Ashmead-Bartlett makes it a little difficult for one by his exaggerations, and yet he's a lover of the truth. He gives the spirit of the thing, but if he were asked: "Did a shout really go up from a thousand throats that the hill was ours?" he'd have to say "No, it didn't". Or if they said "Did the New Zealanders really club their rifles and kill three men at once?" or "Did the first battle of Anzac really end with the flash of bayonets all along the line, a charge, and the rolling back of the Turkish attack", he'd have to say: "Well, – no, as a matter of fact that didn't occur". Well, I can't write that it occurred if I know it did not.'[22]

As the godfather of the Anzac legend, Bean has himself acquired the stuff of legend. The meticulous war correspondent who went on to write the classic *Official History of Australia in the War of 1914–18*, and who was instrumental in the founding of the Australian War Memorial in Canberra, has become a familiar part of our national story. In memory, he stoops through the battlefields, bespectacled and brave, methodically counting the bullets as they pop past his quizzically inclined head.

Almost a century after the publication of the first volume of his history, Bean remains the only official historian most Australians could name. We even know his middle initials. He was a remarkable man, with courage and a commitment to the truth. But as Australia's 'official war correspondent', a role that is barely imaginable today, he was caught between his responsibilities as a journalist to report accurately on the carnage and his duty as a patriot – and army captain – to do everything he could to support the Australian war effort. The two aims may have ultimately been incompatible. The journalist Ross Coulthart opens his biography of Bean with a quote from British Prime Minister David Lloyd George in 1917: 'If people really knew, the war would be stopped tomorrow. But of course they don't – and can't know.'[23]

If Bean rarely wrote about things that he knew did not happen, he perhaps more often neglected to report things that did happen, and which might not reflect well on the Australians. For example, on the night of the landings, Bean recorded in his diary, many men began to return from the lines carrying the wounded ('an offence in war, but few realised it at this early stage'). He saw six men come down with one wounded officer, and noted wryly, 'It is very easy to persuade yourself that you are really doing a charitable soldierly action in helping a wounded soldier to the rear.' Bean made his own way up the gully and, while stretcher bearers seemed unconcerned by the falling shrapnel, 'the parties resting under some of the lower reaches of the creek were so numerous as to be of the nature of stragglers – men who had collected there as a comfortable position of having nowhere else to go – and no one to see that they went there – that is the stragglers' frame of mind'.

The Myths of the Gallipoli Landing

Acts of 'straggling' loom large in Bean's journals on 26 April, but not at all in his journalism. He later notes that some men returned quickly from the lines, while others advanced through them, 'going straight by them as you might pass a man in the street, taking not the slightest notice of them, one going up and the other coming back... Generally a man who meets another coming back will come back with him.'[24]

Ashmead-Bartlett's sometimes fanciful account of the landing was even (unofficially) adapted for the popular 1915 movie, *The Hero of the Dardanelles*. Daniel Eisenberg, Curator of Photographs, Film and Sound at the Australian War Memorial, chose the movie to represent the work of First World War cinematographers in the AWM's travelling exhibition, *ACTION! Film & War*. In flickering, faltering, blurry black and white, hordes of diggers pour from landing craft under enemy fire, rushing for the hills, while all around their comrades fall wounded and dead in the sand.

'It's the best bit of imagery we've got of men in uniform running up a beach,' said Eisenberg.

But the beach is not at Gallipoli, it is in Tamarama in eastern Sydney. And the sequence is not documentary footage, it is excerpted from *The Hero of the Dardanelles*. 'That went into archives,' says Eisenberg, 'and, because there's no footage of the landing, that became representative of the landing. But when it becomes replicated and replicated enough, it ends up entering the popular lexicon as the real thing.'

But *The Hero of the Dardanelles* was filmed only weeks after the events in Gallipoli, using AIF recruits from the army training camp at Liverpool (and footage of their training is genuine). Nor was it an unalloyed theatrical entertainment: it was used as a recruitment tool by the Australian army, which toured the film around the country to encourage young men to sign up for the fighting.

And even 'genuine' First World War footage tended to be staged anyway, as it was logistically difficult to film from the trenches. 'You can't set up a big wooden tripod camera "over the top",' said Eisenberg. 'For a start, a large object on a tripod, that has a lens that reflects the light, from a distance looks like a weapon.'

Silent movie dramas can be the best surviving representations. 'Sometimes the action is faked but all the elements are true,' said Eisenberg. 'In some cases, it's as close as we get to a truthful record.'

Much early-twentieth-century silent film has been lost, but the entire twenty-one minutes of *The Hero of the Dardanelles* has survived, and even the original screenplay has been preserved in the archives, including a note from the writers instructing 'all scenes at Dardanelles to be produced according to Ashmead-Bartlett's report'. So, as per Ashmead-Bartlett, we see the Anzacs discover that their magazines are empty and fix bayonets with 'a grim determination'. During the fighting, the hero meets a Turk on the edge of a cliff, and dispatches him 'as described in [Ashmead-Bartlett's] cable'.[25]

Perhaps the least moving account of the Gallipoli landings is a diary entry written by Sergeant Percy Smythe (later Lieutenant Percy Smythe MC) in 1915. Smythe had been training at Liverpool when the order came to pull out. His troop train was delayed outside Redfern, where a few local people waved to the soldiers. 'Another train somewhere near by was whistling its inside out with a variety of spasmodic blasts,' wrote Smythe, 'and I wondered what was wrong with it. Then we moved on, and soon another engine somewhere seemed to suddenly go mad and started demonstrating its whistling powers. Then I tumbled to what was the matter. They were cheering us.'

Smythe recounts more trains coming by and more whistling, answered with more cheers and shouts. The situation escalated until

The Myths of the Gallipoli Landing

it 'was a regular pandemonium of shrieks, wails, yells, shouts and cheers ... As we rumbled through Redfern, men quickly gathered on the platform to cheer and wave to us, sharing in the general delusion that we were leaving Australia.'

It was July 7, and Smythe's company was heading to Middle Head, to re-enact the Gallipoli landing for a movie company. They were taken by motor launch from Rushcutters Bay to Obelisk Beach in Mosman, where another group of men, dressed in Turkish uniforms, awaited their arrival.

The hills above the rusty sandstone cliffs are thickly covered with shrubs and trees, and offered some challenge to the fitness of the recruits. After an initial charge, they 'had a bit of a rest and then formed up on the beach again,' wrote Smythe, 'while a couple of chaps acted the struggle on the cliff between the Australian and the Turk. The Turk was behind a bush sniping and the Australian crept up to bayonet him, but altered his mind, and laid his rifle down and struck the Turk with his fist and then came to grips with him. A brief struggle followed and then the Turk lay helpless. He got up, and a stuffed dummy was put in his place. The brave Australian then picked up the dummy and shot him over the cliff with truly wonderful ease.

'That ended the play,' wrote Smythe. 'It didn't appear to me to be too well done, but might look all right on the pictures.'

Smythe did go to the actual Dardanelles, on 28 August 1915, where his dress rehearsal at Mosman proved to have been of limited military utility. 'The hill rising up from the beach is very steep,' he wrote, 'and a fair height, and I can't imagine how our chaps could ever have charged up it and rooted the Turks out.'

The 'World War I Diary of Percy Smythe' has been transcribed by his family and uploaded to the internet. The movie in which Smythe played a bit part was called *Within Our Gates* (also known, rather misleadingly, as *Deeds that Won Gallipoli*) and is now lost. The family website uses footage of the landing at Tamarama from *The Hero of the Dardanelles* to illustrate Smythe's story. [26]

Within Our Gates was partly based on the popular play by J.E. Harold Terry and Lechmere Worrall, *The Man Who Stayed at Home*, which was staged in the US and Canada as *The White Feather*. The play's lead character is a British secret agent intent on breaking up a German spy ring in England, and who is given a white feather by a young woman who assumes he is a shirker – thus proving women to be wrong yet again.

The Man Who Stayed at Home was a huge success in Britain and played well in Australia, where it premiered just as the news of the Gallipoli landing reached home. It was performed on the radio by the ABC Players in April 1931, but does not seem to have been revived since.

It is rare for a play or a movie or a novel to outlast the generation that spawned it, and journalism dates faster than any other literary form. More read in modern times than either Bean or Ashmead-Bartlett is Albert Facey's humble memoir, *A Fortunate Life*. First published in 1981, *A Fortunate Life* has sold more than two million copies and, as is customary, inspired a Channel Nine TV miniseries featuring Bill Hunter. A highlight of the book and a set-piece of the show is Facey's landing at Gallipoli with the 11th Battalion on 25 April 1915.

I used Facey's simple words to represent the tragedy at Gallipoli when I served as editor of *The Penguin Book of Australian War Writing* (2011). Facey remembered climbing into a landing craft with his comrades and heading for the shore at Anzac Cove, where they quickly came under attack: 'Bullets were thumping into us in the rowing-boat,' he wrote. 'The Turks had machine-guns sweeping the strip of beach where we landed – there were many dead already when we got there. Bodies of men who had reached the beach ahead of us were lying all along the beach and wounded men were screaming for help. We couldn't stop for them – the Turkish fire was terrible and mowing into us. The order to line up on the beach was forgotten. We all ran for our lives over the strip of beach and got into the scrub and bush. Men were falling all around me. We were stumbling over bodies – running blind.'[27]

Facey's account of the landing is moving, engaging and all too real.

'It's very dramatic,' First World War historian Peter Stanley told me, 'but it's completely invented. Because we know for a fact that Albert Facey landed on Gallipoli about ten days after the [first] landing. And we also now know that there were no machine guns striking the water on the landing. So, Albert Facey's supposed memoir – his recollection of the Gallipoli campaign – at least begins with something which is completely fictitious.'

Later in his life, Charles Bean wrote that 'it was on the 25th of April, 1915, that the consciousness of Australian nationhood was born'.[28]

It was not. The Australian nation was born peacefully and democratically (unless you happened to have been Indigenous) on 1 January 1901 when New South Wales, Victoria, Queensland, South Australia, Western Australia and Tasmania united to form the Commonwealth of Australia.

What was born on 25 April 1915 was a myth.

The Myths of the Dardanelles Campaign

That Gallipoli was a confrontation between Turks and Australians. That Australians are natural soldiers. That Simpson and his donkey saved lives. That British officers callously dispatched Anzacs to their deaths. That Kemal Atatürk spoke the Atatürk words.

There is an idea in Australia and New Zealand that Gallipoli was essentially a battle between Anzacs and Turks, with the British top brass guiding and ruining the show for the colonials. It is expressed to its highest degree in the earnest, excitable commentary of historian Jonathan King's documentary *Gallipoli: The Last Anzacs Tell All*, in which King has the narrator claim, 'Because the British were fighting Germany in Western Europe they ordered the Anzacs to invade Germany's ally, the Ottoman Empire, so these Anzacs (with other Allied armies) could then attack Germany from behind.'

In fact, even at the April 25 landings, there were far more British troops (27,500) than Anzacs (18,100) and almost as many French (16,800). During the course of the campaign, there were more French than Australians in the fighting, and the French suffered more deaths (8000 as against 7800) than the Australians. Contingents from the British Empire included men from British India and

Newfoundland, as well as Jews, largely Middle Eastern, operating as a British army transport unit, the Zion Mule Corps. The French Empire also contributed troops from North Africa and Senegal.

According to one study, many post-Second World War Turkish migrants to Australia only discovered in Australia that Australians had fought at Çanakkale, as 'although the battles were taught at schools in Turkey, generally, Australia was not mentioned'. While they might have heard of the Anzacs, 'even the better educated often did not associate the word Anzac with either Australia or New Zealand'.[1]

The 'Turks' in the opposing army were also more diverse than is often recognised. Fighting alongside Turkish soldiers and German officers were peoples from the breadth of the Ottoman Empire, including Greeks, Arabs, Armenians and, again, Jews. A German officer remembered the Turks doing all the heavy fighting while 'the Christians and the Jews were recruited into work battalions or were used in other ways behind the front'.[2] But even Çanakkale itself was once home to a comparatively large Sephardic Jewish community which fought to defend its homeland and which was celebrated in 2020 as part of a travelling exhibition, 'The Gallipoli War – the First World War and the Ottoman Jews' at Çanakkale's ruined and abandoned synagogue.[3] Seventy-eight Ottoman Jews died while serving in the military in the First World War and Moshe Sharrett, the second prime minister of Israel and a settler in Ottoman Palestine, was an officer and an interpreter at Gallipoli.

Although the Dardanelles campaign was a defeat for the Anzacs, it gave rise to the myth of the (white, male) Australian as a natural soldier, whose military prowess developed from a rough-and-tumble boyhood in the bush, confronting and taming the forces of nature. Charles Bean felt that 'the wild, pastoral independent life of Australia, if it makes rather wild men, makes superb soldiers'.

He wrote that some observers felt the 1st Division was one of the best prepared ever.

However, 'There is little evidence for this contention,' wrote Jeffrey Grey, 'and it seems more likely that, for all the courage of its soldiers, the 1st Division was probably the worst-trained formation ever sent from Australia's shores.'[4]

Grey explained that 'Bean believed that the best soldiers came from the "outer" states, because there the values of the bush were closest to everyday life and the inhabitants were inured to hardship. But he also held that the values of the bush permeated the towns and cities, thus getting around the problems posed for his thesis by the simple fact that Australia was one of the most highly urbanised countries on Earth in 1914.'[5]

At least 21 per cent of the 1st AIF were born overseas, anyway, mainly in the UK. As historian John Connor points out, 'Bean says that Australians at Gallipoli showed leadership, bravery, initiative and mateship. But the men Bean gives as examples of those supposedly Australian traits were often British migrants.'[6]

Among the 79 per cent of the AIF that was Australia-born, the 'outer states' were not over-represented: 55 per cent came from New South Wales or Victoria. Nor were bushmen dominant: only 21 per cent of the 1st AIF had worked in farms and fields, and almost twice as many had jobs in industry, transport and trade.

The lasting myth that Australians – or, at least, Australian bushmen – are natural soldiers much exercised the academics at ADFA, where Grey and Connor both lectured. Their interest had an intensely practical base: if the young men and women who join the modern Australian Defence Force as officers are, in fact, born warriors, they could be forgiven for thinking that they would not need to pay much attention to training at ADFA. But the myth has its purposes. It might allay the fears of people at home if they believe their family and friends at war possess an innate advantage over the enemy. It might also make the public more receptive to the idea of fresh and exciting foreign wars (although the majority do not generally need much prodding). But it also endangers the very people it lionises.

Of course, many quintessential Australians are actually British. I have only to think of myself, and the man buried in the first grave we encountered on the Crowded House tour of Gallipoli. Back on the minibus that transported us between the battlefields, our guide Ibrahim asked the tour party, 'You know John Simpson Kirkpatrick?'

Nobody did.

'The man with the donkey,' Ibrahim prompted.

'The man with the what?' somebody called out.

I was surprised at the general ignorance. The story of the man who came to be known as Simpson, and the donkey who came to be known as Murphy, is taught in Australian schools and is much loved, probably because it involves a donkey.

John Simpson Kirkpatrick was a merchant seaman born in South Shields in England, who jumped ship in Australia in 1910; he enlisted in the AIF in 1914, apparently in the hope of getting back home. Simpson, as he called himself (possibly to avoid being identified as a deserter from the Merchant Navy), became a stretcher bearer with the 3rd Australian Field Ambulance and arrived at Gallipoli on the day of the first landings. He seems to have unilaterally decided to abandon the idea of carrying men himself when he found a beast of burden that could do the job for him.

A version of the story of the man and his donkey was told in E.C. Buley's *Glorious Deeds of Australasians in the Great War* in 1916. 'Their partnership began on the second day of occupation of the Anzac zone of Gallipoli,' wrote Buley. 'The man had carried two heavy men in succession down the awful slopes of Shrapnel Gully and through the Valley of Death. His eye lit on the donkey. "I'll take this chap with me next trip," he said, and from that time the pair were inseparable.

'At times they held trenches of hundreds of men spellbound, just to see them at their work,' he wrote. Simpson would leave the donkey under cover then crawl through the scrub, make 'a lightning dash' for a wounded man, hoist him onto his back and retreat. 'In those fierce seconds he always seemed to bear a charmed life ... Then the limp form was balanced across the back of the patient animal, and, with a slap on its back and the Arab donkey-boy's cry of "Gee," the man started off for the beach, the donkey trotting unruffled by his side.'[7]

The National Library of Australia preserves a single copy of a pamphlet published in 1917, 'Simpson and his Donkey "Murphy"'. Glued to the front cover is a watercolour by sapper Horace Millichamp Moore-Jones, reproduced on a lithographic-print postcard, with the assurance that the painting is 'acknowledged a perfect portrait of the Gallipoli hero, Private "Simpson" D.C.M. and his donkey "Murphy"', since the artist had 'a personal knowledge' of Simpson and was also guided by photographs.

The photograph used as reference by Moore-Jones is well known today (and has since served as the model for the statue *Man with the Donkey*, aka *Private Simpson and His Little Donkey*, at Melbourne's Shrine of Remembrance) although Moore-Jones moved the figures of man and beast to the edge of a ridge, for dramatic effect.

The text of the pamphlet is a story reprinted from the Anzac service magazine *Coo-ee*, along with a couple of letters readers had written in response. At the time, few details of Simpson's story were certain, and when writers don't know what happened they often collate the unknowns. So we learn from the pamphlet that nobody seemed to know who Simpson had been before the war and when he met 'his friend the donkey', there was 'no formal introduction'. There was 'no special reason why Simpson should take to the donkey, or the donkey to him'. However, 'The fact remained . . . that the attachment was mutual.'

Apparently, the donkey was a 'queer sort of beast' with unusually long ears which were generally 'carried at half-cock'. This was taken to be a type of asinine early-warning system, as 'when his ears went to full-cock, the boys knew it was time to look for cover, for it was a sure sign that a big shell was on its way'.

A donkey with these skills could probably have been put to some more sophisticated tactical purpose, particularly after the abrupt end to his brief period of service with the 3rd Australian Field Ambulance. According to the pamphlet, 'Late one afternoon, he came down the gully with the wounded man on his back, but Simpson was not there. As soon as he delivered his charge he trotted up the gully again. Somebody followed, and saw the creature stoop and sniff at a form lying still on the ground. It was Simpson with a hole through his big heart.'[8]

Simpson was shot dead by a Turkish sniper on 19 May 1915. He and his donkey were remembered with enormous affection by the men of Anzac, and are mentioned in the writings of both John Monash and Albert Facey. Simpson is buried at the Beach Cemetery, along with 390 other Commonwealth servicemen, at Hells Spit at the southern point of Anzac Cove. At his tombstone, Ibrahim asked our tour party if anyone knew the name of Simpson's donkey (which seemed improbable, as they had not even heard of Simpson).

Ibrahim pointed to the gravestone behind Simpson's, which commemorates Cornelius Joseph Murphy of the 4th Australian Field Ambulance, who was killed in Gallipoli on 9 May 1915, and speculated that Simpson may have named his donkey after his mate. But Simpson used more than one donkey, and while two of them were called Murphy, other accounts name the animals as 'Duffy',

'Abdul' or 'Queen Elizabeth', so Simpson may have had an eclectic bunch of mates.

Times change, but it seems unlikely that the donkey will be known as Abdul again in a hurry.

As for the particular characteristics of Simpson's donkey, the donkey with the unusually long ears was a different donkey altogether. And the muleteer in Moore-Jones's watercolour was not John Simpson Kirkpatrick, it was Richard Alexander Henderson. And Henderson was not an Australian, he was a New Zealander. And the painting was copied from a photograph taken by Sergeant James Gardiner Jackson of the New Zealand Medical Corps. And the painter himself, Moore-Jones, was a New Zealander. Even the pamphlet 'Simpson and his Donkey "Murphy"' was published in Auckland.

Moore-Jones had been invalided out of the army after Gallipoli. In Dunedin in 1917, he was touring his Gallipoli paintings in support of the war effort, when Jackson's brother showed him a photograph of a stretcher bearer using a donkey. Moore-Jones, who claimed to have seen Simpson at Gallipoli, used the picture as the model for a series of watercolours of 'the man with his donkey', and dedicated one to 'our hero comrade Murphy', by which he meant Simpson. However, when Jackson returned from the war, he confirmed that the man in the photograph was Jackson's friend Henderson. A comparison of the faces of the men leaves no doubt that Jackson was right.

The *New Zealand Herald* claimed that Henderson had been inspired by Simpson – 'even using one of his donkeys, Murphy' – but Simpson might not have been the first stretcher-bearer to employ donkeys. The journalist drew on our rich and shared cultural history for his metaphor: 'Much like the pavlova debate, which country's soldiers were the first to use donkeys to pluck wounded troops from battle may never be settled – and arguably doesn't matter,' he wrote. However, 'The Waiouru Army Museum website says the original "man with the donkey" may have been another member of the NZ Medical Corps, Private William Henry. Soon after arriving at Anzac Cove, Henry organised two donkeys into "an independent unit for evacuating wounded". Subsequently other members of the unit used donkeys but "Henry remained the leading figure [and used donkeys] very early in the campaign" after landing at Anzac Cove on April 25.'[9]

The plot thickened, much like pavlova might thicken if it did thicken – which it does not. Henderson, an Auckland schoolteacher, apparently gave his donkey the name 'Murphy', too. Simpson himself was also known as Murphy. In fact, it is possible that most donkeys were known as 'Murphy', as an unkindness towards Irish people, since some Australian troops in Gallipoli believed Simpson to be Irish.[10]

Simpson was so closely identified with the name Murphy that a lost 1916 silent movie about his exploits (which features the hero receiving a white feather) was called *Murphy of Anzac*.

Prominent myths often attract mythbusters with motivations and methods even more eccentric than my own. In his 2012 book, *Dust, Donkeys and Delusions*, former army intelligence officer Graham Wilson undertakes a fascinatingly thorough – not to say obsessive – quest to fact-check the story of Simpson, who, he writes, is supposed to have saved 300 lives by picking up wounded men, often while under fire, and transporting them to medical facilities on the back of his donkey. Wilson demonstrates that the soldier who became known simply as 'Simpson' could not possibly have saved 300 casualties in the twenty-three working days between his landing at Gallipoli on 25 April 1915 and his death on the morning of 19 May. If this figure were correct, Simpson and his donkey would have had to save 13.4 men per hour. Wilson takes literally the contention that Simpson did not sleep, and must therefore have been attributed with saving one man every one hour and fifty minutes. In an extraordinary passage, Wilson cites the actual distance (expressed in miles, yards and kilometres) that Simpson would have had to travel with his donkey to make a round trip with a wounded man; the average walking speed of a human being; the average walking speed of a donkey, both laden and unladen; the temperament of donkeys; and the time it would have taken to load and unload a wounded man – all to prove Simpson could not have completed the task in one hour and fifty minutes: it would have had to take at least two hours.

Wilson had already examined the question of whether a donkey could transport more than one man at a time, citing hauling and tillage studies that recommended individual donkeys carry no more than one-third of their body weight ('that is, 40 to 60 kilograms depending on the size of the donkey', and warning that donkeys are too small to carry large human beings.[11] He went on to estimate the maximum number of hours that a human being might superhumanly have been expected to work (20 hours from 6 am to 2 am), and thereby reduced to 230 the maximum possible number of wounded soldiers saved. If he had worked a more average, realistic day, wrote Wilson, Simpson could have saved perhaps 180.

Wilson continued to introduce further factors and variables, such as the phases of the moon, the difficulty of the terrain, and the accumulated fatigue of man and donkey, to suggest that 138 might be a more realistic figure. Even that, however, would only have been possible given an unbroken flow of wounded men, so Wilson then examined the recorded flow of wounded during the relevant period and discovered that, on certain days, there were very few men requiring treatment by medical units. If the Simpson myth were true, wrote Wilson, Simpson would have been responsible for 70 per cent of all wounded handled by his unit, which had a strength of more than a hundred men. Wilson ploughed on unrelentingly before arriving at his next question: what kind of casualties could have been transported by donkey? His answer was, in brief, none with life-threatening wounds and probably none who could not have walked. Simpson, according to Wilson, saved nobody's life at all.[12]

Virtually nobody wants to hear this – and I suspect virtually nobody bought Wilson's extraordinary book. Brendan Nelson, a former minister in John Howard's government and later director of the Australian War Memorial, declared in 2005 that Simpson 'represents everything at the heart of what it means to be Australian' and 'everything that we should strive to be as a nation'.[13]

Curiously, what Simpson represented when he was alive was the opposite of everything Nelson represented. In a letter home dated 1912, Simpson wrote to his mother: 'I often wonder when the working men of England will wake up and see things as other people see them. What they want in England is a good revolution and that will clear some of these Millionaires and lords and Dukes out of it and then with a Labour Government they will almost be able to make their own conditions.' Simpson called England a 'Louse bound country' – unlike Australia where 'the working man out here votes for a labour Government out here but the man at home has not got the sense for that he must go and vote for the first big Liberal Capitalist that puts up for the seat'.[14]

Even conservative commentator Gerard Henderson, who generally maintains an admirable insistence on the primacy of fact over folklore, seems to feel differently about the story of the man with the donkey. He wrote, 'Whatever his background and whatever his views, the values which Simpson demonstrated in Gallipoli are much admired – from the bottom up. Indeed, the debate on

Simpson demonstrates the strength of deeply held opinion in the face of intellectualised cynicism.'[15]

So even Simpson the socialist works for the right, as well as for the left. Part of the reason rests in circumstances peculiar to army life, where the approach to warfare – at least in the ranks – reflects values closer to communism than capitalism: everyone gives their lives to a common cause, from each according to their ability, to each according to their needs.

From Simpson the larrikin Aussie hero to Simpson the Pommie socialist naval deserter, the myths of the man and the donkey change as we reconsider history, in a way that donkeys do not and cannot – since donkeys are unaware of the existence of past donkeys or, indeed, of the past itself. The original inscription on the statue at the Shrine of Remembrance in Melbourne reads 'in Commemoration of the valour and compassion of the Australian soldier'. Today, however, the statue is styled by the Shrine as a 'tribute to all stretcher bearers and their donkeys', although it is unclear how it might be possible to pay tribute to donkeys. While it is sad and terrible that people lead animals into wars, it could be argued that the heroism of human beings who selflessly act with conscious agency is diminished by an implied equivalence with the axiomatically unreflective actions of donkeys.

Australians generally love Simpson's donkey as much as they value the man himself. At least three books have been written from the point of view of the donkey, one of them by Peter Stanley. And in 2004, New Zealand military historian Glyn Harper published *The Donkey Man*, which tells the Gallipoli story through the eyes of *Henderson's* donkey.

As the stalemate at Gallipoli solidified, with the Anzacs established at Anzac Cove and other beaches, and the Turks entrenched sometimes only metres from their enemy, further parallels with *The Iliad* came to mind for Sir Ian Hamilton, who now commanded the troops on the ground: 'Here is our shelling from Asia,' he wrote, before quoting Homer: '"and the iron roaring went up to the vault of heaven through the unharvested sky." ... Take our ordinary existence: Day in and night out the clatter of weapons "resounds like an armourer's forge."'[16]

On May 30, Hamilton visited Anzac Cove, where once again he revelled in the proximity of death – for himself and for the Anzacs. 'There are poets and writers who see naught in war but carrion, filth, savagery and horror,' he wrote. 'They refuse war the credit of being the only exercise in devotion on the large scale existing in this world. The superb moral victory over death leaves them cold. Each one to his taste. To me this is no valley of death – it is a valley brim full of life at its highest power. Men live through more in five minutes on that crest than they do in five years of Bendigo or Ballarat.'[17]

Hamilton tends to attract little sympathy from Australian journalists and historians, and British officers in general usually get short shrift in Australian popular memory. This is in part due to Peter Weir's 1981 movie *Gallipoli*. If there is one single work that can be said to have captured, encapsulated, and even constructed the image of the Gallipoli campaign in Australia at the time of the family-history boom, it is *Gallipoli*. Weir's masterpiece was the most expensive Australian film made up until that time, with a cast of almost 4000 extras and a script by playwright David Williamson.

In *Gallipoli*, two bonza Aussies, a naive country bloke played by Mark Lee and a more slippery and sophisticated city slicker played by Mel Gibson, go off to war. Although they are supposed to be different character types, they are both natural athletes (as well as all the usual white, Christian, straight stuff). Both men end up in the Australian Light Horse, but are sent to Gallipoli without their horses as reinforcements for the infantry. In a masterful early scene, we see a recruitment exercise for the Light Horse carried out under the shadow of a looming wooden horse.

Weir and Williamson drew heavily on Bill Gammage's grass-roots history *The Broken Years: Australian Soldiers in the Great War* and the work of Charles Bean. Weir said that he had put his boys in the Light Horse because the Light Horse had fought at the Battle of the Nek, and 'you only had to read the official account of the battle by Bean to gain a respect and admiration for the type of man in the 10th Light Horse, a type of Australian largely vanished from the country'.[18]

On 6 August 1915, fresh troops arrived north of Anzac Cove at Suvla Bay. On August 7, in an attempt to break the longstanding deadlock, entrenched Australian troops, including elements of the Light Horse, were sent over the top as a feint, to cover for a New Zealand attack on the commanding peak of Chunuk Bair. The push was a disaster for Australians, as wave after wave of men were mown down by Turkish machine guns and rifles. Hundreds died in minutes when (Australian) brigade staff catastrophically misjudged the situation at the front and ordered the men to charge and charge again, even when it should have been clear that the offensive was doomed.

The distorted version of the Battle of the Nek that featured in *Gallipoli* – in which the officer who orders the helpless Australian heroes to their deaths is cold, ruthless and, most importantly, British – greatly coloured the memories of cinema audiences, including those who had actually fought at Gallipoli. Historian Alistair Thomson, author of the classic 1994 study *Anzac Memories*, told me, 'Soldiers and war veterans are constantly trying to make sense of their past experience. They're not usually inventing. They're not usually lying. But they are struggling to make sense, drawing upon whatever resources are available. And what happens later in their life – becoming a conscientious objector; becoming a pacifist; becoming a member of the RSL; reading a battalion history; watching Peter Weir's film *Gallipoli* – all those things are feeding into how we make sense of our past.'

As well as absorbing the movie's message that they were exploited and betrayed by the Brits, some veterans came to believe that certain events in the film had happened in real life – to them.

'There's that wonderful scene where Mel Gibson and Mark Lee are in Cairo and they see these English officers with donkeys and with monocles,' said Thomson, 'and they put these monocles in their own eyes and take them off and take the mickey out of these autocratic English officers. And I remember, in a couple of interviews [conducted as research for the book], almost exactly the same scene got replayed. Now, probably these older men, in their younger lives, had seen autocratic, snobbish English officers. But in a way, Peter Weir's film confirmed or reaffirmed that experience, rekindled it in their memory, reminded them to tell the story, and helped them to make sense of their experience.'

Gallipoli was a movie of its time – and 1981 was a very different time to 1915. 'In a way,' said Thomson, 'the British become the baddies, not the Turks. We've been at war with the Turks in Korea on the same side, so the Turks are now allowed to march on Anzac Day. Atatürk has told us that he's looking after our buried soldiers in Turkey ...'

Supposedly.

'Supposedly,' agreed Thomson. 'So that Imperial relationship – which is fracturing after Britain joins the European Community and we feel like we've been deserted – shifts in Australia. And a classic moment in Peter Weir's *Gallipoli* is the moment when the men of the Light Horse are being sent off to a suicidal death at the Nek, and the officer in the trenches is trying to get a message back to HQ. And back at HQ a man with a very posh English accent is saying, "Go over, you've got to go over the top," etc. He's ignoring all the advice. And it's quite clear to an Australian audience that this is an English officer sending the Australians to their deaths. But actually, we knew – Peter Weir knew, to be honest – it was a Western Australian farmer. But, for the purposes of the film in the 1980s, we want to see the Australians sacrificed by someone or something. And it's the British upper class and their incompetence.'

On Chunuk Bair today stands a massive bronze statue, the Atatürk victory monument, erected in 1993 to commemorate a pivotal moment in the Turkish mythology of Gallipoli. This is the spot where Atatürk ordered his troops to attack the enemy, just before dawn on 10 August 1915. Atatürk personally led the assault, raising his whip to signal his men to advance.

British guns shelled the Turkish army from the sea, tearing them to pieces, but Atatürk stood in the line of fire, commanding the surviving soldiers to fight on. As iron rained from the sky, a piece of shrapnel struck him in the chest. It shattered the watch he carried in his breast pocket, which, of course, saved the great leader's life.

Ibrahim told the Crowded House tour party that Atatürk took a direct hit and lived to tell the tale.

He paused, then added, 'It just wasn't his time.'

It was at Chunuk Bair that our tour began to intersect with much larger tour groups of Turkish people. We later merged with dense crowds of locals at the Turkish 57th Infantry Battalion Cemetery, where there is a bronze statue of the last surviving Turkish Gallipoli veteran, Huseyin Kacmaz, who died at the age of 110.

I was illogically surprised that Turkey should have its own oldest veterans, that there were exact parallels between the Turkish and

Australian stories. The two mythologies fed and formed each other. The Australian memorialising at Gallipoli influenced the Turkish government to raise its own monuments. The postwar Australian admiration for Atatürk as a leader gave international credence to his domestic reputation as a great man.

August 1915 was a fertile month for mythmaking. In *A Fortunate Life*, Albert Facey describes the enemy attack that led to the wound that had him sent him back to Egypt on August 19: 'A shell lobbed into the parapet of our trench and exploded, killing my mate. Several bags filled with sand were blown on top of me [which] hurt me badly inside and crushed my right leg ... [T]hen, while moving to the tunnel to get through to the doctor, a bullet hit me in the shoulder.'[19] However, his service record attests he was invalided out of Gallipoli with 'heart trouble' on August 21, and makes no mention of any physical injury throughout his service. In addition, the 11th Battalion does not appear to have come under shellfire either on or around August 19.

Elsewhere on the peninsula, Hamilton noticed more parallels with *The Iliad* in 'the sudden and mysterious veil of mist which was drawn over the Turkish trenches at Suvla on August 21, blinding our gunners while the weather remained bright and sunny elsewhere'. This was, he wrote, 'The very identical same phenomenon that prevented Ajax from hurling his thirty-foot pike and made him pray. "Our Father, save us from darkness, give sight to our eyes."'[20]

Ibrahim the guide told Turkish stories of acts of kindness to the enemy. The Respect to Mehmetçik Memorial near Anzac Cove is a statue of a Turkish soldier carrying a wounded Australian officer to safety, although there does not seem to be a historical account that names the man on either side. The sculpture is emblematic of the idea that the opposing troops respected and even helped each other, that they recognised in the enemy a common humanity. Ibrahim spoke of gifts of food passed between the two armies. Bean wrote of these exchanges in his diary. On November 11, the Anzacs sent some bully beef behind Turkish lines, to be rebuffed with a curt note – 'Bully beef *non*.' Biscuits and jam had a better reception – '*fini*'. The next morning, an Australian interpreter spoke to the Turks, and they were allowed to pick up a pocket knife that had been thrown over to them. On the third morning, the Australians were ordered to desist.[21]

Little tends to be said about the attitude of commanders to these friendly overtures to the enemy, but in May 1915 Colonel John Monash of the Australian 4th Brigade at Gallipoli was appalled by an incident in which medical officers from both sides had exchanged greetings and cigarettes while discussing the possibility of a truce to bury the dead. He wrote that this event 'and such interchange of good feelings at Xmas time, as the English and Germans in France, destroys the will to kill. And we must discourage, and rightly put down, everything in the way of attempting to fraternise with the enemy. Never encourage it. Suppress it. Give the men to understand they are dealing with some human vermin they are going to eradicate.'[22]

In any case, other stories of trench exchanges show less amicable motivations. According to a soldier quoted by Gammage, 'An Anzac would shout something like, "Hello, Turk!" A Turk might reply "Hello, Australian." The Aussie would then ask how many on the Turkish side would like to share a tin of bully beef. "Thousands!" would reply the Turk, who somehow spoke English. "Well, divide that among you!" the Aussie would yell, tossing a grenade.'[23]

However, these stories, like all punchline comedy, should be taken with a touch of saltpetre, and it is likely that they are told by every army in every language about every stalemate in the First World War.

In October and November 1915, icy winds tore through Gallipoli, blowing snow into the trenches and freezing out the flies. In the

Turkish winter Hamilton saw parallels with, well, *The Iliad*, 'as when winter torrents flow down the mountains to a waters-meet and join their raging torrents through the deep ravine'.[24]

On December 19, under cover of night, the entire Dardanelles Army of the Mediterranean Expeditionary Force began to evacuate the peninsula. By morning, they were gone. In what is widely regarded as the best-planned operation of the campaign, they left without taking a single casualty. Sir Ian Hamilton later described the British retreat as 'the greatest moment in history since the Greeks evacuated Troy'.[25]

Near the Beach Cemetery, a memorial stone stands like a billboard, advertising Atatürk's words: 'Those heroes that shed their blood in this country! You are now lying in the soil of a friendly country. Therefore rest in peace. There is no difference between the Johnnies and the Mehmets to us, where they lie side by side in this country of ours . . . You mothers who sent your sons from faraway countries! Wipe away your tears. Your sons are now lying in our bosom and are in peace. After having lost their lives on this soil, they have become our sons as well.'

But there is no evidence that Atatürk ever said this. The words do not appear in his early biographies or his obituaries. No mention of the speech had even been made until 10 November 1953, the fifteenth anniversary of Atatürk's death, when his former interior minister, Sükrü Kaya, told a Turkish journalist that he himself had given the speech near the stately, forbidding Çanakkale martyrs' memorial, but that Atatürk had written the words. This speech is said to have been delivered on Martyrs' Day in 1934, but there is no record of Kaya making any speech about anything on that day, and no reason to believe he was in Gallipoli. A version of the words appeared in Turkish on the martyrs' memorial, which was opened in 1958, but it did not mention Johnnies, only Mehmets.

Kaya did give a speech at a monument to the Gallipoli dead in 1931. What he actually said then – in words that he attributed to Atatürk – was more or less the opposite of what are now taken to be Atatürk's words: 'Tomorrow, the history of civilization will judge those lying opposite each other and determine whose sacrifice was more just or humane and who to appreciate more: The monuments of the invaders, or the untouched traces of the heroes left here in the form of sacred stones and soil.'[26]

Kaya, channelling Atatürk, saw no equivalence between the invaders from the other side of the world and the defenders of their homeland. However, Kaya's later remembered version of his/Atatürk's words, transcribed from the memorial, appeared in a guidebook that came into the hands of Australian Gallipoli veteran Alan Johnston Campbell, of the Gallipoli Fountains of Honour Committee, which was involved in the planning of memorial fountains in Brisbane. Campbell added the reference to Johnnies lying beside the Mehmets, although he did first check his revised inscription with the Turkish Historical Society. The society put up no objection except to note that 'there are two minor errors in the inscription ... Atatürk's first name is not Kamel, but Kemal; secondly, the statement was made not in 1931, but in 1934'.[27]

Kamel!

During his later years as President of the Republic of Turkey, Atatürk did make several conciliatory remarks about the Anzacs, always in response to requests from Australian newspapers. Most notably, in a message received through 'the usual diplomatic channels' by the *Daily Mail* in 1930, Atatürk (described in the newspaper as 'the Turkish dictator' and 'the Mussolini of Turkey') offered lavish praise for the valour and 'spirit of the gladiators of old' embodied by the Anzacs. In recognition, he promised Australians that the Turks would always 'pay tribute on the soil where the majority of your dead sleep – the wind-swept wastes of Gallipoli, ever sacred to the memory of your heroes'.[28]

While the inscription on the memorial was meant largely for domestic consumption, the message in the *Mail* was composed for an Australian audience. And every victorious fighter pays tribute to the spirit and ability of their opponent, if only to show that they have defeated a worthy foe – and are therefore that much tougher themselves. When the *Mail*'s report of the statement was picked up by the *Observer*, it was augmented with a background piece headed 'Kemal, Himself A Fighter, Can Speak Of Courage'. This credited Atatürk with 'bravery and acumen' during the war and 'great statesmanship in reforming what was a decaying country' in the aftermath of the conflict.[29] Just as Atatürk helped construct the Anzac legend, Australians were instrumental in building Atatürk's reputation.

Australians cannot seem to leave Atatürk's words alone. In *Speeches that Reshaped the World*, a faintly desperate book published in 2008, editor Alan J. Whiticker's introduction to Atatürk's famous 'speech', has the original version acknowledging the 'heroes from England, France, Australia, New Zealand and India' who had shed their blood in the Dardanelles. This seems to be Whiticker's own contribution to the tradition, although he mysteriously omits Canada and Senegal from the roll of nations which left behind their dead.[30]

Atatürk's 'famous words' were hardly known in Australia before they were inscribed on the Gallipoli Fountains of Honour, which opened in Brisbane in March 1978, in time for Martyrs' Day. In 2008 the words found their way onto the Atatürk's Tribute monument in North Adelaide; then in 2015 to the curious Australian Turkish Friendship Memorial in Melbourne, and a plaque in Hyde Park in

Sydney. They were first raised in a prime-ministerial speech by Bob Hawke in 1990, then quoted by Kevin Rudd in 2008 and 2010. In 2012, Julia Gillard made the strange claim that the retreating Anzacs 'did not begrudge the victory of their enemy', and echoed the supposedly Kemalist idea that the Australian dead were treated as the sons of Turkey.[31] Gillard's successor, Tony Abbott, referenced the words again in 2015.

As historians have pointed out, the rise of Atatürk's words 'maps perfectly onto the idea of the second memory boom from the late 1970s, and more specifically to the contours of the Anzac revival'.[32] When everybody wanted to be an Anzac, they also wanted the Anzacs to be loved. And they loved the Turks, too.

Eric Bogle's 'And the Band Played Waltzing Matilda' lives on in the very beaches where it was not born (Bogle had never been to Gallipoli at the time he wrote the song). The idea in the song that Anzac Day would die off and one day no-one would march at all niggled at Gerard Henderson, who wrote in 2005 – just after it was announced that John Farnham would be excluded from the ceremony in Turkey – that 'the 90th anniversary of Anzac Day would be an appropriate time to dispatch Eric Bogle's message to the musical graveyard'. Henderson argued that Bogle's song carries the message that the casualties of the First World War died for no reason, and that this was a left-wing myth, as Australia was not fighting 'another nation's war', because 'Germany had possessions in the Pacific and a victory by the Kaiser would have had a deleterious effect on Australian security'. Henderson is my favourite conservative commentator, and perhaps the only Australian public intellectual willing to defend the concept that the First World War was a rational enterprise. His rather grandiose characterisation of the threat posed to Australia by

German New Guinea and German Samoa is more than made up for by the wonderful image of a 'musical graveyard'.[33]

As it happened, Bogle sang his ballad at Anzac Cove on the centenary of Anzac Day in 2015. But Henderson came gunning for the song again in 2019 when he wrote – with some justification – that it was not the military that had fuelled a perceived surge in 'Anzac Day nationalism' but that 'the evidence suggests that any "surge" in interest in Anzac Day reflects a growing fascination with genealogy, which has become more accessible because of the internet.' He suggested that Australians who 'in increasing numbers still march in honour of the First Australian Imperial Force' were 'defying Bogle'.[34] It was beginning to seem personal – and it was. Bogle had written 'And the Band Played Waltzing Matilda' in 1971 to highlight the futility of the Vietnam War, and Henderson, like John Howard, was never going to give up on that one.

Just as an earlier generation conflated the Gallipoli campaign with Homeric myth, the children of the 1960s (or, at least, the politically conscious minority among them) saw only bloody parallels with Vietnam. Sir Ian Hamilton, whose insistence on the equivalence of the Dardanelles campaign and the siege of Troy was at least consistent, also seems to have accurately predicted the Australian family-history boom. 'In another thousand years,' wrote Hamilton, 'the two legends will have blended and passages from the historians will be expounded in the schools as beautiful images of wicked happenings long ago; yet all the same, wicked or not, if that bald and toothless professor is able to trace his descent to a man who fell at the Dardanelles he will not fail to let his students know it.'[35]

Robin Prior dismisses the argument that the Gallipoli Campaign was of significance to anybody but the men who fought and died there and their friends and families back home. Even if the troops had attained their objective and reached Constantinople, he notes, the capital would have been defended with the same ferocity shown at Gallipoli. Even if Constantinople had fallen, the Ottomans could simply have moved their base elsewhere. Even if the Ottoman Empire had crumbled, it would have been a difficult task to unite the Baltic states with each other, let alone with the Entente. Even if the Baltic states had united, their armies were of generally poor quality and probably could not have achieved much against Austria-Hungary.

The campaign 'did not shorten the war by a single day', writes Prior, 'nor in reality did it ever have that prospect. As Churchill said (and then promptly forgot), "Germany is the foe & it is bad war to seek cheaper victories". As it happened, it did not even offer a cheap victory or in the end any kind of victory. But even if it had, the downfall of Turkey was of no relevance to the deadly contest being played out in France and Flanders.'[36]

But the last word belongs to Paul Keating, if for no other reason than Keating always had the last word. The former prime minister made his own definitive Gallipoli speech at a book launch in Canberra in October 2008, without ever having set foot in the Dardanelles. In Keating's analysis, Australians in 1915 believed that if their sons had to suffer and die, then at least their sacrifice would help prove their nation's worth.

'In some respects we are still at it – not at the suffering and the dying, but still turning up at Gallipoli, the place where Australia was needily redeemed,' he said. 'The truth is that Gallipoli was shocking for us. Dragged into service by the imperial government in an ill-conceived and poorly executed campaign, we were cut to ribbons and dispatched.

'And none of it in the defence of Australia. Without seeking to simplify the then bonds of empire and the implicit sense of obligation, or to diminish the bravery of our own men, we still go on as though the nation was born again or, even, was redeemed there. An utter and complete nonsense.

'For these reasons,' said Keating, 'I have never been to Gallipoli, and I never will.'[37]

The Myths of Monash and the Western Front

That General Sir John Monash won the First World War. That there was something odd about being a Jewish soldier in Australia. That the 1st AIF won the First World War. That the graves of the First World War dead will be maintained in perpetuity.

Before I talk about Sir John Monash, the highest-ranking Jewish soldier in modern diasporic history and the only Jewish commander of any national army in either of the two world wars, I will introduce another great Jewish soldier, Abraham Benjamin, who happens to be related to me.

Abraham Benjamin did not play a large role in my life. In fact, he had been dead for 102 years before I even learned that he had lived.

I had been told that my great-grandfather, Simon Benjamin, had fought in the British army during the Boer War, but had never found any military record to bear this out. All I possessed of Simon was a photograph of a soldier wearing a uniform with sergeant's stripes, and a moustache like two slugs kissing. It is a Boer War-era uniform, and I suspect Simon did go to South Africa, but British family historians are not nearly as fortunate as Australians: Boer War-era British soldiers did not have self-contained service records and their surviving documentation has to be assembled piecemeal and for a fee. Moreover thousands of service records were destroyed or damaged in the Blitz.

The Australian desire to have a First World War soldier for an ancestor always resembled past-lives therapy to me – until I found Abraham Benjamin, my great-grandfather's brother, and I came to understand the thrill of it all.

I had not been looking for Uncle Abe. I was trying to discover more about my Spanish(ish) great-grandmother, Simon's wife, to see if I might qualify for Spanish citizenship after Brexit. While googling genealogy websites, I found another photograph of my great-grandfather, still wearing the same moustaches, posed with two of his brothers, Abraham and Moses. All three men are in uniform, dressed for the trenches, not the veldt.

I still did not know if Simon went overseas in the First World War, but Abraham must have done, because he was recorded as having died in Flanders on 6 December 1914. More than a century later, I was able to pay my respects at his final resting place, courtesy of the Australian government.

In October 2017, the Honest History website published the news that the soon-to-open $100 million Sir John Monash Centre near Villers-Bretonneux had been visited by Paris-based media and two Australian journalists, who had been flown to France for the purpose. The media party would also explore the recently established Australian Remembrance Trail along the Western Front. Honest History had asked the Department of Veterans' Affairs for the objective and cost of this exercise, and was told in reply that the DVA 'has a partnership with Atout France, who is the official French Government travel bureau, to promote the Sir John Monash Centre and Australian Remembrance Trail in Australia. Your question should be directed to them.'[1]

Actually, their question should have been directed to me, since I was one of those two journalists (and I had also just contributed an essay to *The Honest History Book*). I have no idea of the cost of the whole operation, but the other journalist and I were flown business-class on Emirates from Sydney to Paris and put up in luxury accommodation, including the Pullman Paris Eiffel Tower hotel. Also along on this taxpayer-funded trip was the candid, personable and informed Director of the Office of Australian War Graves, Ken Corke.

It was a great experience, and I will be forever indebted to the Australian taxpayer, but we had very little to do with Atout France. By coincidence, I had been invited only a few weeks after I had found out about Abraham Benjamin. The DVA asked if the journalists on the trip had a relative who had fought on the Western Front, and suddenly I did. The department promised to discover more about him for me.

So I had a personal stake in the story – which, I guess, was the point of the exercise, the John Monash Centre and the whole Centenary of Anzac spectacle – when I took the DVA's shilling and flew to France. The trip had been arranged against a background of pride and controversy over the military and cultural legacy of Monash, a Melbourne-born civil engineer. The Liberal Prime Minister Tony Abbott had been a prime force behind the drive to establish the Sir John Monash Centre. The Monash family was supportive of the project but later angered by the self-styled 'Monash Forum', a grumble of right-wing MPs organised around the by-then-deposed Abbott, which had conscripted Monash's image to support its steampunk campaign for coal-fired power stations.

I spoke with Michael Monash Bennett, the great-grandson of the general, who said, 'We wish the name to be used for activities that we know John Monash would be proud of . . . [A]ll his support for his soldiers and the creation of the Shrine of Remembrance makes me feel he would greatly approve of a centre of remembrance in northern France.' However, Bennett was also party to a statement, signed by seven of Monash's direct descendants, lambasting the Monash Forum. 'I have seen other examples where a great name is used to hide the lack of intellectual underpinnings for whatever argument is put,' he said. 'This was an extraordinary example of this. Whilst we don't own the name, we expect those that wish to use it on the wider stage should at least enquire first as a matter of politeness. Most do just that. It, of course, didn't happen in this case.'

Like any dead soldier, Monash can be used to service pretty much any cause from pacifism to total war, although few are disturbed from their slumber by proponents of a particular means of electricity generation. But the civilian Monash had once been the head of the State Electricity Commission of Victoria and the family believed that their patriarch today would have been 'a proponent of the new technologies, e.g. wind and solar generation, rather than revert to the horse-and-buggy era'.

Myths plume like pipe smoke around the rather large head of Sir John Monash. In 2004, Roland Perry published a book entitled *Monash: The Outsider Who Won a War*, and ever since, many of Australia's more serious military historians have felt bound to point out that neither Monash nor the Australian army actually won the First World War. Academics were further riled by a later campaign, spearheaded by the former deputy prime minister Tim Fischer, to have Monash promoted to the rank of field marshal, a hundred years after his last command in the field. A pointless debate ensued about whether other dead people might be more worthy of posthumous promotion.

The idea that Monash might be an outsider comes from the fact that he was both a Jew of Prussian ancestry and a part-time soldier rather than a career military officer. As the author of the book *Jewish Anzacs*, I will deal only with the ethno-religious aspect which, I think, has not been properly understood in the context of the broader sweep of Jewish military history. Monash was not the first prominent Australian Jew in military affairs. That title, unwieldy though it may be, belongs to man who is all but forgotten but was well known throughout the British Empire during the Boer War. If his name, Walter Karri Davies, does not sound especially Jewish, it's because Karri is a nickname that became incorporated into his surname.

Western Australia-born Karri Davies arrived in the Transvaal in South Africa in 1893 to open new markets for his family's timber business. He took up arms in support of the Jameson Raid and the rebellion against the Boer government, for which he was sentenced to two years in jail. While his comrades were eventually released, Karri Davies and another man refused to appeal or guarantee they would not join another uprising, and stubbornly served their time.

When the Second Boer War broke out in 1899, Major Karri Davies helped raise the Imperial Light Horse. The seventy-three Jewish Australian soldiers in South Africa were joined by one Jewish Australian nurse, Rose Shappere from Victoria. Rose's brother, Lieutenant Harry Shappere, also came to South Africa with the British Royal Field Artillery. Harry, an expert horseman, quickly established himself as a '"daredevil" and rough rider', but the *Australian Jewish Herald* reported that 'for nerve and pluck, there are few that can equal and none that can surpass' his sister.

After Karri Davis had ridden alone, with no cover and under heavy fire, to rescue a squadron of the Light Horse from ambush, his commanding officer wanted to put him forward for a Victoria Cross. Karri Davies refused, as he had pledged to serve without reward. He was wounded during the siege of Ladysmith, where Rose Shappere nursed the casualties, and he was the first man to ride into town upon the relief of Mafeking. He was also one of the first into Johannesburg when that city fell.

The deeds of Karri Davies were widely known and celebrated in both Britain and Australia, but the fact that he was a Jew went broadly unreported. Karri Davies' younger brother, Frank Davies, and his nephew, Keith Levi, also fought in the Boer War. Rose Shappere was Mentioned In Dispatches and, when the Royal Military College of Australia opened at Duntroon in 1911, its first riding instructor was Lieutenant Harry Shappere. Even in its earliest days, Jews were not outsiders to the nascent Australian military tradition.[2]

The characterisation of Monash the Jew as an outsider, although well meant as an acknowledgement of anti-Semitism, plays to stereotypes of Jewish men as unmanly and unmilitary. In 1970, the State Electricity Commission of Victoria published a biography of Monash that traced his forebears back to a line of rabbis in Prussia, a publisher of Hebrew prayer brooks, and a businessman who emigrated to Australia. 'Within those traditions it was perhaps not surprising that John Monash was a student, an intellectual and University administrator, a distinguished engineer and successful businessman,' pronounced the author. 'But nothing in his family history suggested that he would be a soldier, and perhaps the greatest of his era.'[3] This final sentence is a myth.

Monash was born in Melbourne in 1865 to Prussian Jewish parents, and proportionately far more Prussian Jews than Australians went to war against foreign powers in the nineteenth century. The idea of Prussian militarism is virtually axiomatic, but the Jews of Prussia were not eligible for conscription until Jewish leaders successfully campaigned for their inclusion so that they might be considered full and faithful citizens. In 1845, the government of Prussia decreed that all Jewish men would perform compulsory military service, although they would not be eligible for commissions.

The Myths of Monash and the Western Front

About 4,700 Jews fought for the North German Confederation in the Franco-Prussian War of 1870. Their names were published in a memorial book, as was to become the custom in Jewish communities internationally. Works of this type were supposed to serve as a testimony to Jewish patriotism and valour, and protection against perennial charges of duplicity and disloyalty. My own *Jewish Anzacs* is a book in this tradition.

Monash attended Scotch College, where he became dux of the school, and graduated from Melbourne University with degrees in arts, law and engineering. He worked as a civil engineer, building railways and bridges, while he pursued a parallel career in the militia. Although Monash was a prodigy, there was little that was unusual about his career path for a European Jew. For example, in the early 1890s, Jews made up some 0.25 per cent of the population of France but 3 to 4 per cent of the students enrolled at the École Polytechnique, an elite military engineering academy; they also constituted about one per cent of students in officer training at the École Spéciale Militaire in Saint-Cyr. Estimates suggest that Jews comprised 3 to 4 per cent of artillery officers in the French army and up to 10 per cent of officers in the engineers.

In his choice of career and military service, Monash was very much a Jewish man of his time. He was an exemplar rather than an anomaly.

Where Monash differed from other martially minded Jews and gentiles, was in his lack of enthusiasm for the Boer War. The idea that a soldier had to passionately believe in the cause for which he fought has been tacked onto history to bash the past into the shape of the present, and make heroes from men who simply wanted to fight foreigners. As Don Watson has ably documented, in the nineteenth century it was perfectly respectable to go to war on grounds that you did not support, or even for a cause that you opposed.[4]

Monash, however, was unwilling to leave his business interests and risk his life on a military adventure with few consequences for Australia. 'This is certainly not an occasion where patriotism demands the making of any personal sacrifices,' he wrote to a junior officer who had asked whether he should volunteer.[5] By forbearing to go to South Africa, Monash knew that he might never get to war. Nevertheless, he rose to the rank of lieutenant colonel, in command of the Victorian section of the new Australian Intelligence Corps. In a militia awash with officers of dubious quality, he stood out for his uncompromising intellect and his commitment to soldiering as a science. In 1913, twenty-six years into his military career, Monash was finally made a full colonel, and Commander of the 13th Infantry Brigade.

As his biographer Geoffrey Serle is at pains to detail, Monash had become a pillar of Melbourne society, a consummate insider: 'He had bought a Toorak mansion and a luxurious motor car, with a chauffeur and other servants to match, and was the calm centre of his extended family. He lectured and examined in engineering at the university, became chairman of the graduates' association and president of the University Club, then from 1912 was elected to the university council and its more important committees. As president of the Victorian Institute of Engineers, in 1913 he gave a constructive radical critique of his profession and worked towards foundation of a national body. He was prominent in the Boy Scout movement.'[6]

Within weeks of the outbreak of the First World War, the 4th Infantry Brigade was raised, and command was given to Monash. Reverend Danglow of the St Kilda Hebrew Congregation wrote to congratulate him on his appointment. Monash, who was not then much given to making declamations about his Judaism, replied, 'With the help of many fine men who are going to serve under me

I hope to be able to sustain the honour of Australia, of British Armies and, not least, of the Jewish Community.'⁷

Monash arrived at Gallipoli on 26 April 1915. On August 6, the Anzacs stormed the hills of Chunuk Bair and Hill 971, in what became known as the Battle of Lone Pine. Anzac forces took the main Turkish trench line, which was their target, and defended it with countless gallons of their blood, but the broader offensive was ultimately a failure. Monash's 4th Brigade had been tasked with assaulting Hill 971 from the left, but they got hopelessly lost, arrived late to the battle and suffered heavy casualties. Monash was always willing to give credit where credit was due, particularly when he felt it was owed to himself. Now a brigadier general, he wrote home that, from his point of view, operations had 'been brilliantly successful, notwithstanding that the main object, the conquest of the whole mountain range, has not yet been achieved'.⁸ It never was. Most commentators (other than Monash) agree that his promising command proved disappointing in the Dardanelles.

The AIF's only Jewish recipient of the Victoria Cross, Leonard Maurice Keysor, was decorated for his actions at Lone Pine on 7 August when, according to his citation, he 'picked up two live bombs and threw them back at the enemy at great risk to his own life, and continued throwing bombs, although himself wounded, thereby saving a portion of the trench which it was most important to hold'. The next day, the wounded Keysor 'successfully bombed the enemy out of a position from which a temporary mastery of his own trench had been obtained, and was again wounded. Although marked for hospital he declined to leave, and volunteered to throw bombs for another company which had lost its bomb-throwers.'⁹

Karri Davies' nephew Keith Levi was shot through the head and killed on Gallipoli on August 23.

*

In June 1916 Monash moved to the Western Front, around Armentières in northern France. In July he was promoted to major general and given command of the 3rd Division, which he trained in England on Salisbury Plain and Lark Hill. The men of the 3rd went to France in November and played their part in the costly victory at Messines in June, after which the British and Australians pushed north towards Ypres, to relieve the French. The Allies eventually took Ypres from the Germans at the Battle of Passchendaele, where the Anzacs were among the forces that recaptured Passchendaele Ridge to the east of the town. At Broodseinde Ridge, they fought their most successful attack, after which Monash cabled Melbourne, 'All well. Division again brilliantly victorious in "greatest battle of war".' He wrote home, 'In using the words "greatest battle of war", I quote from a letter the Commander-in-Chief sent me yesterday.'[10] For all Monash's evident satisfactions, there were terrible frustrations, too. 'Our men are being put into the hottest fighting and are being sacrificed in hair-brained ventures, like Bullecourt and Passchendaele,' he wrote.'[11]

Monash had won respect for his abilities from the British High Command, and he was an obvious candidate for the new position of commander of a single Australian army corps. But casually anti-Semitic forces within the Australian establishment hissed against him. Even before the formation of the independent corps had been approved, the influential war correspondents Keith Murdoch and Charles Bean had cabled Prime Minister Billy Hughes to warn against appointing Monash as Australian commander-in-chief. Bean was, during the war years at least, snidely anti-Semitic, and his prejudice clouded his judgement of Monash and was a factor in his misguided campaign to have the general replaced by a lesser man.

It's fashionable to take our ancestors to task for the crime of growing up in an earlier era, and sensibilities differed from today

The Myths of Monash and the Western Front

even in the comparatively recent past. For example, the *John Monash* volume in the 'Great Australians' series, published in 1962, spoke of Monash's 'prominent Jewish nose' and the fact that he was 'rather overweight'. While the author notes that Monash 'shed his excess flesh' as the war went on, he makes no mention of the possible effects of combat on the size of his nose.[12]

But Charles Bean carried the moral corruption of his class, who believed they were born to rule the empire, and couldn't conceive of the son of a German-born Jewish store-holder succeeding in a military career through aptitude alone. 'We do not want Australia represented by men mainly because of their ability, natural and in-born among Jews, to push themselves,' wrote Bean.

The gentry felt ambition to be vulgar, because they had no use for it themselves. Like many Jews, Monash was credited by his detractors with dark and almost supernatural powers. Bean identified in him the mysterious 'Jewish capacity for worming silently into favour without seeming to take any steps towards it'.[13] Meanwhile, Will Dyson, Australia's first official war artist, and brother-in-law of the notoriously anti-Semitic Norman Lindsay, predicted that Monash would become commander-in-chief as 'he must always get there on time, on account of the qualities of his race; the Jew will always get there'.[14]

Monash did win command of the new corps, from 1 June. His Jewishness had, of course, worked against him rather than in his favour. His corps formed part of the Allied Fourth Army, which was under the overall command of British General Sir Henry Rawlinson, who later described Monash as 'not unlike ... a clever, slippery, creepy crawley jew who will always back you if he thinks you are winning and who have no scruples about sticking you in the back if he thinks you look like a loser ... intelligent but his knees knock together when trouble is about.'[15]

The Australian Corps under Monash charged on to victory. He was an original, independent military thinker who rarely felt bound to repeat the mistakes of the past. On the recapture of Villers-Bretonneux in April 1918, he wrote of his conviction that 'the true role of infantry was not to expend itself upon heroic physical effort, not to wither away under merciless machine-gun fire, not to impale itself on hostile bayonets, nor to tear itself to pieces in hostile entanglements' – he cited Pozières and Stormy Trench and Bullecourt – 'but on the contrary, to advance under the maximum possible protection of the maximum possible array of mechanical resources, in the form of guns, machine guns, tanks, mortars and aeroplanes; to advance with as little impediment as possible; to be relieved as far as possible of the obligation to fight their way forward'.[16]

For Monash, routing of the Germans at Hamel on 4 July 1918 was the perfect battle. He wrote that 'no battle within my previous experience ... passed off so smoothly, so exactly to timetable, or was so free from any kind of hitch. It was all over in ninety-three minutes. It was the perfection of team work. It attained all its objectives; and it yielded great results ... The attack was a complete surprise, and swept without check across the whole of the doomed territory. Vaire and Hamel Woods fell to the 4th Brigade, while the 11th Brigade, with its allotted Tanks, speedily mastered Hamel Village itself. The selected objective line was reached in the times prescribed for its various parts, and was speedily consolidated. It gave us possession of the whole of the Hamel Valley, and landed us on the forward or eastern slope of the last ridge, from which the enemy had been able to overlook any of the country held by us ... The Tanks fulfilled every expectation, and the suitability of the tactics employed was fully demonstrated. Of the sixty tanks utilised, only three were disabled, and even these three were taken back to their rallying points under their own power the very next night. Their moral effect was also proved, and, with the exception of a few enemy machine-gun teams, who bravely stood their ground to the very last, most of the enemy encountered by the tanks readily surrendered.[17]

On 11 August 1918 Monash was knighted in the field by King George V. He was the first man for 200 years to be honoured this way. In the months that followed, he established his headquarters at Menin Gate in the east of Ypres. The town, he wrote, 'once a marvel of medieval architectural beauty, lies all around us a stark, pitiable ruin'.[18] At Mont St Quentin in August and September, Monash fought a fluid, imaginative battle, reacting spontaneously to enemy movements and helping to turn the war to the Allies' favour.

The armistice was signed in November 1918, but the ultimate outcome had been clear for some months. The pervasiveness of establishment anti-Semitism and the flexibility of Bean's thinking had both been demonstrated in October 1918, when Bean urged Billy Hughes to give Monash command of the repatriation scheme. The prime minister described Monash to Bean as 'out for himself all the time; like a Jew, showy'. He did not know whether Monash was 'human enough' to take charge.[19] Once again, however, Monash won the position. As Director-General, Repatriation and Demobilisation of the Australian troops in Britain and Europe, he oversaw a system which ensured that those who had served overseas for the longest period would come home first. The Jewish Anzacs left in London with no enemy to fight were given the gift of the YMCA's Jewish Soldiers' Hut in the Strand, which was opened by Monash on 25 January 1919.

Much has been made about the anti-Semitism faced by Monash, although the more pertinent point might be the failure of anti-Semitism to derail his career – perhaps because the prejudice was not as venomous as the language in which it was couched.

During the first two years of the First World War, a proportionately larger number of Australian Jews than the general population enlisted in the armed forces. Throughout the course of the war, more than 1600 Jews, or about 11 per cent of the Jewish population, enlisted in armed forces, as compared with about 9.2 per cent of the general population. About 15 per cent of Jewish servicepeople were killed, as compared with 14 per cent of the general population.

It is important to know what Jews did in the First World War because of what happened to Jews in the Second World War, when the Nazis exploited the myth that large numbers of Jews had shirked frontline military service for Germany in 1914–18. If we need a reminder of the damage that military myths can cause in the real world, we need only look to the Holocaust.

But there has never been an explosion of violent anti-Semitism in Australia. On the contrary, after Monash was briefly considered for appointment as the first native-born governor-general of Australia in 1930, the position went to Sir Isaac Isaacs – another Jew.

Academic histories look for continuity and precedent and seek to show how the past can be used to explain the present. In popular histories, however, everyone and everything must be unprecedented, unparalleled, superlative, the best, worst or only example of its kind. So Monash cannot just be a great general, he has to be an outsider who won the war. By some accounts, he seems to have won the war with a single battle. 'Storian' Peter FitzSimons' 2018 volume, *Monash's Masterpiece*, is subtitled *The Battle of Le Hamel and the 93 Minutes that Changed the World*. This kind of bizarre judgement would not have been made in even the most commercial publications in the past. The State Electricity Commission's Monash biography warned that 'the part Monash played in breaking the Hindenburg Line must not be overstated. Sooner or later, it would have been broken, for the

Germans were reaching the end of their endurance in the field and at home.'[20] Even the *Monash* booklet given away with special packets of laundry detergents in 1969 stressed that 'the Australians did not win the war'.[21]

Brigadier Chris Roberts, author of the study *The Landing at Anzac*, spoke to me of a cynicism overseas about some strands of Australian military history. 'Part of the problem is that most of our military history – certainly the popular military history that we see on the bookshelves – is overly nationalistic, it's overly parochial, and it gives an impression of hubris and arrogance,' said Roberts. 'We also have a tendency to criticise the British unfairly and a very strong tendency to exaggerate our own achievements.'

Roberts argued for a more mature approach, not based on national insecurity but on fact. The AIF did 'a wonderful job' in the First World War, he said, but 'the claim that an Australian Corps commander won the war is just ludicrous. And it brings us into ridicule.' Peter Stanley said that Monash deserves his eminence. 'But in recent years that justified renown has been inflated. It's been pumped up by admirers who don't actually know a great deal about the First World War – certainly not about the non-Australian aspects of it. So there's been a lack of proportion about Monash. He's now regarded not just as the most prominent Australian soldier, but he's regarded as the genius who probably won the First World War.'

In fact, said Stanley, 'Monash was an innovator, in all sorts of ways. He was a very methodical trainer, a very methodical organiser. But he was also an adapter. He adapted and implemented things that had already been invented by other people. And that's one of the roots of the confusion about Monash.'

There is an idea that Monash pioneered the use of tanks.

'Yeah, well, that's nonsense!' said Stanley. 'Tanks became operational in the British service in September 1916. They were used with the Australians in Bullecourt in April 1917. And they were used right through Passchendaele – the third Ypres offensive – in late 1917. They were used in the huge Cambrai attack in November 1917. So tanks weren't anything new when Monash took over the command of the Australian Corps. The doctrine was still developing, but Monash didn't invent any doctrine ...

'Monash made sure that the infantry who were going to be fighting with the tanks got to know the tank crews who were going to operate the tanks, so that was quite clever of him, because in 1917 at Bullecourt the tanks had let the Australian infantry down badly. And the Australians remembered this. So Monash helped restore trust. The other thing he did was he made sure that tanks were used to bring up ammunition and supplies during the battle – supply tanks – which, again, I don't think he invented but he certainly incorporated into his plans.'

But Monash is credited with all kinds of ingenious methodology in planning the battle of Le Hamel.

'Hamel is regarded as the sort of apogee of Monash's success,' said Stanley, 'but Australians tend to focus on Hamel and think it's a great victory. Well, Hamel wasn't. It was sort of a big raid, a line-straightening raid. It involved ten battalions. It famously lasted an hour and a half. And it was there basically as a kind of advert for Monash to show what he and his corps could do. It had no greater significance than that ... It's not the war-winning, epoch-making victory that everyone presents it as.'

Chris Roberts said, 'Combined tactics have been part of military operations for centuries – the use of cavalry, infantry and artillery together and the way in which you use them. What changed in the Great War was the techniques. So we have the artillery bringing in the rolling barrage to support the infantry, and the infantry keeping close to that barrage as it goes forward. We also have the introduction of new weapons. We have the introduction of the use of machine guns in great numbers. We have the introduction of aviation. We have the introduction of tanks.'

But these things were not initiated by Monash. 'As early as 1915 the British are changing their machine-gun tactics; they're using aviation in conjunction with artillery for spotting and adjusting guns,' said Roberts.'When tanks come on the scene in 1916, the British are looking for ways in which infantry and tanks can work together. The French themselves in 1917 are developing infantry–tank cooperation.'

I asked Stanley where he thought the Monash legend had come from.

'Well, the short answer is it comes from Monash himself,' said Stanley. 'In 1921, Monash published his book called *The Australian Victories in France in 1918* and in it he extols the achievements of the Australian Corps. And remember, in 1918 the Australian Corps is part of the victorious Allied army. Not without cost. There are 34,000 Australians dead and wounded in that last year of the war – exactly the same number as Australians lost in 1916, which is one of the most terrible years of the war. So Monash isn't saving anyone's lives here, but he is part of that victorious command. And Monash writes a book about this, and it gets published twenty years before the official history gets published. Volume Six of Charles Bean's official history comes out in 1942. In the intervening twenty years, the picture of Australia's victories in France is Monash's. That's how the legend develops.'

Aaron Pegram of the Australian War Memorial agreed that Monash's book is incredibly self-congratulatory. 'It should've been called "My Victories in France"', he told me. 'Monash belts it out in two months, and that really sets the tone for Monash the War Winner. And perhaps that comes about because of his fractious relationship with Charles Bean. He doesn't think that Bean is worth his salt in celebrating the Australian victories.'

Stanley added, 'By say, 1966, there have already been twelve biographies of Monash published. From 1966, there's another twelve. That's about twenty-two more than any other general gets. So first of all, Monash kickstarts his own legend, and secondly the legend builds because people keep writing about and talking up his achievements. And they were not inconsiderable. I mean, this man is in charge of the Australian Corps in its most successful six months. The problem is that more and more honours and adulation gets loaded onto the legend, and it's at the point now where Monash is presented as not just the most effective Australian commander, but the commander who could easily have succeeded Douglas Haig as commander of the British Expeditionary Force. Well, where does that come from? The answer is, it comes from a throwaway line in the British prime minister Lloyd George's memoirs. Lloyd George wanted to denigrate Haig, and he hinted that Haig could have been, or should have been, succeeded by a very skilful dominion commander – by which he meant Monash. Where's the substantiation? Was Monash ever proposed for it? No. Was he ever in line for it? Well, no, because he was the most junior corps commander in the British Expeditionary Force. Was he likely to have leapfrogged over six corps commanders and half a dozen army commanders? No, of course he wasn't. So the Monash legend has just been ridiculously inflated.'

The campaign to posthumously promote Monash to field marshal was vigorously supported by former deputy prime minister Tim Fischer, author of *Maestro John Monash: Australia's Greatest Citizen General*, published in 2014 by (who else?) Monash University Press. It is not a good book. It is difficult to imagine that it would have been published professionally (let alone by a university press) if it had not been the work of a nationally known figure. It is illustrated with risible, naive sketches, apparently by Fischer. The drawing of Churchill meeting Monash is particularly absurd.

The Myths of Monash and the Western Front

I spoke with Fischer once or twice and he was a likeable man, although partial to complicated conspiracy theories. And the propagators of one myth tend to also spread others. So it is that in *Maestro John Monash* Fischer quotes the 'famous words' that Atatürk 'wrote' – and he can't leave poor Simpson and his donkey alone either. When Monash created the first Anzac Day in the field, writes Fischer, 'It was of course to remember many mates.' With an utterly baseless conviction that served him well in politics, Fischer adds, 'all ranks would have been thinking about the likes of Private Simpson and his donkey and thousands of other individuals'. Later, he disputes Paul Keating's 2013 characterisation of the First World War as 'devoid of any virtue', with a pained, 'Was there not virtue in the actions of Simpson with his donkey?'[22]

Like me, Tim Fischer visited the Sir John Monash Centre before it was completed. Wearing a hard hat and a hi-vis vest, he made a brief promotional video for the centre. 'Right here,' he said, 'is where the turning of a tide took place.'

The centre was built in Villers-Bretonneux in the department of Somme, widely known to Australians as 'VB'. The centre marks the end of the Australian Remembrance Trail, which runs for 250 kilometres through western Belgium and northern France. Travellers can begin an Anzac pilgrimage at Ypres in Belgium and follow the frontline as it stood in April 1917, through museums, cemeteries and memorials close to the battlefields of Passchendaele, Fromelles and Bullecourt, then trace the River Somme to VB and Amiens.

My DVA media trip was timed to coincide with a dawn service held for the centenary of the Battle of Polygon Wood, on 26 September 2017. One hundred years before, 5770 Anzac troops had been killed or wounded to the east of Ypres. The town was razed to the ground in three battles, culminating in the 1917 Battle of Passchendaele. Winston Churchill had wanted Ypres to be left as a ruin, a warning against war, but its majestic medieval and Renaissance streets were painstakingly reconstructed, and the cautionary monument is the Menin Gate memorial, whose soaring arches bear the names of almost 55,000 Commonwealth soldiers who died in the Ypres Salient and whose bodies have never been found. Every night at 8 pm, the gate is blocked to traffic and a bugler sounds the Last Post.

When we arrived in Ypres the evening before the dawn service, it was like walking into a gathering of ghosts. At a table outside Café Les Halles sat four beer-drinking Anzacs, dressed for the Western Front. For a moment, it seemed to me that the men who had fought here had climbed out of their graves. It was only when a middle-aged British bugler walked past, followed by a heavily bemedalled but anomalously youthful Chelsea pensioner, that I realised the centenary had drawn crowds of military re-enactors. Until then – James Brown's scorn for the costumed Anzac Day marchers aside – I had no idea there was anyone on earth who wanted to re-enact the First World War.

In the early hours of the next morning, I tramped in darkness through the wood to the site of the commemorations. Small stage sets had been built among the trees. A scream rose from a reimagined casualty clearing station, where a woman dressed as a nurse tended to men playing the wounded. At 3 am in Flanders, it all felt like a dream.

Other Anzac re-enactors smoked cigarettes as they manned a machine gun, or poked a rifle barrel through a gap between sandbags.

'Is it just me,' a corporal asked his sergeant, 'or is the shelling getting closer?'

On the German side of the line, German-speaking re-enactors manned a pillbox.

The Myths of Monash and the Western Front

Deeper into the woods, newsreel film danced on half-hidden screens, showing flickering, monochrome giants marching to their deaths with jerky, shuddering purpose. A parade of actual living soldiers and sailors headed past, and then the whole question of who was real became uncomfortably complex with the arrival of a group of Belgian military veterans. They were neither troops nor re-enactors – or perhaps they were both.

I found the display of re-enactment tableaus quietly puzzling. I love history, but I had never thought to dress up as it.

That night, when the Last Post was sounded at the Menin Gate, I spotted two Anzacs in the crowd and assumed they were among the morning's performers. They were not: they were Queenslanders Ben Fenner and Darren Abbott, and they did not take part in the official commemoration. They had arrived independently in Ypres as part of a ten-day tour of Western Front battlefields, and mainly wore their uniforms at night.

'We were hoping it would add a bit of character to the evenings,' said Abbott, a Toowoomba firearms and militaria dealer, 'and give people a bit of an idea what it was like when the place was full of diggers.'

They were not allowed to lay a wreath, as it was against the Menin Gate's regulations, but they were in high demand to appear in selfies with tourists. Fenner and Abbott belonged to the Emu Gully Field Volunteers military re-enactment group. Neither of them had served in the forces. Abbott tried to join the army twice but was turned down because of a back injury. The younger Fenner was only interested in the historical side. In Australia they stage the occasional mock battle scene, but not many people in Emu Gully want to be the Germans, and those who do are often of German heritage. 'In a typical re-enactment,' Fenner told me, 'we'll probably have ten to twenty Australians and maybe eight Germans.'

They sometimes set up camp at vintage-car days.

I asked what kind of things people say to them.

'In Australia,' said Fenner, 'they usually they say, "Aren't you hot in that?"' He thought for a moment. 'We had a campfire,' he said, 'and someone asked us if the fire was real.'

The First World War uniforms worn by re-enactors were all reproductions and mostly made in India. It cost about $2000 to outfit yourself as an Anzac from slouch hats to boots, with a tunic coming in at about $275 and pants at $175. Sales to fellow re-enactors made up a big slice of Abbott's militaria business.

The following day, I was walking through the war cemetery at Fromelles when I noticed an Anzac re-enactor in an officer's uniform also strolling between the tombstones. This was the most jarring dislocation of all. It was as if he had come back from the dead to visit his men.

There are actors dressed up as heroes at historical sites all over Europe. The Colosseum in Rome is ringed by modern gladiators on busking tours, and Hadrian's Wall in England is defended by accountants and engineers in Legionnaires' breastplates, but nobody could mistake them for the real thing. It is different with the Anzacs – in situ, in Ypres and Fromelles, they look like they belong.

Back in Australia, I asked Peter Stanley what he thought of Anzac re-enactors. Why is it that men like to dress up as soldiers rather than other important historical figures, such as, well, journalists? I was trying to be funny, but as luck would have it, Stanley is probably the only journalist re-enactor in Australia. While he was principal historian at the Australian War Memorial, the memorial held an open day. 'I went around dressed up as Charles Bean – God forgive me – in this war correspondent's uniform,' said Stanley. 'Because I wear glasses as well, it was very convincing. I don't think I actually did anything much. I just seemed to wander around.'

The Myths of Monash and the Western Front

Brad Manera, historian at the Anzac War Memorial in Sydney, is another enthusiastic re-enactor. Manera was at the Polygon Wood commemorations, escorting a group of school students who had won scholarships to attend.

'I was curious to see the group of Australians who'd gone over to dress up,' Manera told me. 'From my perspective, the ceremony could have done without it, because I'm old enough to remember when those blokes were still alive. An old next-door neighbour of mine was with the 16th Battalion at Polygon Wood. So to see somebody dressed up, and not dressed up 100 per cent accurately – they had overseas service chevrons; they had Anzac "A"s on their colour patches; the uniforms weren't all that good for September 1917 – and calling each other "Bluey" and saying "strewth"... it just grated a little bit. Whereas the students thought it was terrific and the teachers were really delighted with it.'

Manera thought re-enactment might be used to investigate the lived experience of the past but did not believe it belonged in solemn occasions. At the Menin Gate, he was 'disgusted' at the number of Australian re-enactors in First World War uniforms. 'I thought, Mate, where do you think you are? There're 55,000 names of those who have no known grave in this place. It's not for dress-ups.'

As well as the service at Ypres, the DVA party visited the village of Ploegsteert and the nearby Toronto Avenue Cemetery, the only all-Australian cemetery in Belgium. Deer roam the woods around the graveyard, and meaty mushrooms grow like cushions from the ground. Here, we made a diversion to the grave of my great-uncle, Abraham Benjamin, who lies in the London Rifle Brigade Cemetery just outside the village.

Pilgrims to a war grave are like buses: you wait for 102 years, then nine turn up at once. So it was when his great-grandnephew (that's me) arrived at his tombstone along with the cultural attaché to the Australian embassy in Paris; a project manager from the Australian embassy in Paris; two French bloggers; an Australian Instagrammer; a Belgian guide/historian; and the other Australian journalist, whose ancestor had died *on the way to* Gallipoli.

The guide/historian told me that Abraham had been shot while carrying sandbags – information he had gleaned from a unit diary. Abraham had enlisted in the 1st Rifle Brigade on 30 September 1914 at the age of seventeen and was killed on December 6 at the age of eighteen.

In the Jewish tradition, I laid a small stone on his grave. I noticed three other pebbles, and wondered who could possibly have left them, then I saw that there were three pebbles on every Jewish grave in the cemetery, so I guessed the same visitors had honoured them all.

Ken Corke of the Office of Australian War Graves later told me that puzzled gardeners used to clear the pebbles off Australian Jewish headstones, but now the practice is to bury them and make them a part of the grave.

I was pleased there was somebody looking after Abraham's grave, tending to the memory of a man who had been forgotten even by his own family. I felt that I understood the family-history thing at last. And I was fairly sure that having Abraham as an ancestor made me 20 per cent more interesting.

The DVA made a short film in which I talked about the experience of having a First World War casualty as a relative. I said that I thought a passing deer might have been the spirit of my ancestor, and they took me seriously.

*

The Myths of Monash and the Western Front

The Sir John Monash Centre was built as an extension of the Australian National Memorial, which has been on the site since 1938. Although the centre is named for the general, it was never intended to be solely about Monash. A spokesperson for the DVA told me the naming decision had been made by the federal government several years before, 'on the basis that General Sir John Monash was a meticulous planner and engineering genius, whose leadership broke the stalemate on the Western Front in 1918 – a victory that became the template for much larger operations that followed. Monash actively cared for his troops and coordinated military operations to minimise the loss of Australian lives.'

The centre offers a fashionably immersive experience, allowing visitors to follow the journeys of real people from the past. Unfortunately, when our party arrived there, it was incomplete, but we strode around Tim Fischer-style in our hard hats and hi-vis vests, staring at walls and pointing at things.

A number of Australian and international historians withdrew from the project before the opening of the centre. Among them was the Australian National University's Bruce Scates. 'We were asked to nominate historical content, and when the difficult historical content was being shed, that sent real warning signals to us,' Scates told me. Historians had been informed that the purpose of the centre was 'to make Australians feel proud about their role on the Western Front. They want Australians to go away with just a touch of sadness, but an overwhelming feeling of pride.'

The centre, he said, is 'there to valorise war service. It's there as a tribute to the men and women of the 1st AIF – which is not bad in itself, but what is bad is that there's no critical reflection on what that war service meant, either to them or the Australian community more generally. So for all those reasons, we felt it prudent to withdraw – not before, though, we had provided a lot of content to the centre.'

Unlike me, Scates visited the centre after it was opened. He came away questioning its museum-craft. 'There're very few artefacts on display,' he said. 'It's so technologically driven that whenever anything goes wrong with the technology – as it invariably does – the whole museum really has to shut down and reboot. I didn't realise the extent to which it would embrace that digital technology when I was first involved in advising the centre.' Scates borrowed historian Jay Winter's term, 'pornography of violence', to describe the museum's digital animations. There is, he says, 'a celebration of killing'. A display he found particularly worrying was 'like playing a computer game, where you stalk the enemy through the streets of Villers-Bretonneux and you kill him, you shoot him. When these memorials, these great cemeteries, were laid out, the idea was that they would be a reminder of the cost of war, the futility of war, and I think what we have is a re-enactment of the First World War.'

The story told at the centre, said Scates, is that Australia played a very significant role in winning that war. 'Now, we didn't play such a significant role in winning that war – nowhere near as crucial a role as the John Monash Centre makes out. I think we belittle the efforts of the other Allies, even the French. It's almost as if John Monash thought of the strategies and tactics that were going to win that war. And of course, it takes a long time to develop the most efficient ways of killing and maiming; I think attributing this to one general is wrong.'

Scates has attended many Anzac Day services overseas, and described the ceremony at Villers-Bretonneux for the 2018 opening of the centre as hilarious. 'It started to rain, so you had people who realised they could sit there in their DVA plastic ponchos and get wet and cold, or they could pretend to be part of a [re-enacting] party and nick out down the back. And that's exactly what happened.

The Myths of Monash and the Western Front

It was complete chaos. We don't even do the ceremonies well anymore. The recourse to re-enactors underlines that this is theatre, it's not commemoration.

'How do you recreate the terror, the horror of armed conflict?' he asked. 'You can't – not by putting on however realistic-looking uniform it might be.' Scates believes the displays at the Monash Centre are 'trivialising the experience of that war in so many ways'.

I guess it is inevitable that I first fully imagined the cemeteries of the Western Front when I heard Eric Bogle's ballad (yes, even I'm getting tired of this) 'The Green Fields of France' in England, but Australians remember the war on the Western Front differently from European nations. For the Belgians and French, the campaign represents an invasion that was only reversed when other nations came to their aid. For the Germans it was a terrible, historic defeat. For Australians, it was a war they crossed the world to join and help win. And while the European nations took many of their dead home to the lands where they were born, the Australians, like other Commonwealth troops, are buried where they fell.

Australia appears to be committed to maintain 'in perpetuity' the cemeteries that hold most of the more than 100,000 Australian servicepeople – and many other Commonwealth troops – who have died at war. I spoke about this with Ken Corke.

'What does "in perpetuity" really mean?' asked Corke. 'Clearly they're not going to be there forever. That just can't happen.' For Corke, the graves of the fallen of 1914–1918, in particular, would be looked after only for as long as governments felt the political imperative to do so. Therefore, it was vital to preserve and encourage public interest in, and knowledge of, their war. For this to happen, he said, the Department of War Graves had to 'make the bones talk'.

Corke hoped that the Monash centre would play its part in keeping the memories of the dead in the public mind.

But often the dead were not remembered the way they would have wanted to be remembered, or the way their families wanted them remembered. Even that small courtesy was denied to them, as if the military owned them in death. Every First World War headstone carries the Rising Sun badge with the crown of King George. Regulations dictated that every man, regardless of rank, had to have a headstone of the same size, carved from Portland stone and bearing an inscription of no more than 66 letters. At the start of the war, families were charged three-and-half-pence per letter for engraving a message to their son, but the charge was eventually rendered voluntary. The families were generally allowed nothing that could be construed as political or pacifist, or question the loss of life or the war – or even insult the Germans.

My great-uncle Abraham Benjamin's tombstone said only that he was mourned by his family and should rest in peace. But his service record said much more. I had found his file on a website before I went to France with the DVA, but it had been damaged, scorched by the fires of the Blitz and I had thought that the opening page was the only page. (I am guilty of calling out other historians for not knowing how to handle records, but I have made every mistake myself.) About a year passed before I returned to Abraham's service record and realised that it included copies of plaintive, heartbreaking, handwritten letters from his mother, begging the British army for information.

I had never before seen my great-grandmother Sarah Benjamin's handwriting. She had written: 'I have received two letters from my son's chums who were fighting in the front in France saying that my son [has] been killed in action on Dec 6. I am therefore writing to you asking you if you have heard anything about it. I last heard from my son on Dec 7 but the letter was posted some days before. I may say that I am a widow & he was my only son at home and my sole support.' She asked if she was entitled to a grant from the War Office, should the news be true. 'I am sorry to trouble you,' she wrote, 'but my plea must be I don't know what to do.'

When I read my great-grandmother's letters, I knew that the true story of the war was not Abraham's four months on the Western Front, but Sarah's lifetime of grief.

And that, I suspect, is the reason his name was never invoked in my family.

The Myths of the Emu War

That the Emu War was largely the initiative of martially minded soldier settlers. That the commander of the Australian army contingent at the Emu War is a mysterious figure whose name does not appear in official records. That the avian commander of the emu forces was male. That the media did not realise how ridiculous the whole thing was at the time, as people were much stupider before the internet.

It will come as a blessed relief to the reader that I did not learn of the Emu War of 1932 through a song written by Eric Bogle. I first heard of it from my son, who knew of it from a YouTube video. My son asked me if it was true that Australia had once declared war on emus.

'No,' I replied, with the unassailable confidence of perfect ignorance. 'Of course not.'

But it is a fact: Australia is the only nation on Earth ever to have fought against its national emblem. The veterans of the Emu War have all passed on – and, in truth, there were only three of them anyway – their glories lost. But the Emu War will never be forgotten, as long as there is an internet to make memes about it.

Many young people besides my son became aware of the Emu War through a ten-minute cartoon video, 'The Emu War – OverSimplified', which was posted on YouTube in November 2018.

It had gathered 24 million views at the time of writing. The video is the creation of US YouTuber Stuart Dempster, who somehow makes a living out of animated exaggerations of military conflicts.

Dempster's video plays the shooting war for laughs – and unkindly labels emus 'discount ostriches' – but sticks to the truth of the story as it was then understood. As Dempster oversimplifies, the roots of the Emu War lay in the stock market crash of 1929 and the Great Depression, which led the US to erect trade barriers. These brought down the price of wheat, which was a particularly hard blow for embattled Western Australian wheat growers, some of whom were returned soldiers from the First World War who had been granted farmland under a soldier-settlement scheme.

The source of the video would appear to be an interesting but hitherto obscure essay by the historian Murray Johnson, published in the *Journal of Australian Studies* in 2006. In his paper, Johnson explains that emus in Western Australia had been protected under the Game Act until reclassified as vermin in 1922, 'solely due to complaints made by wheat growers, including soldier settlers at the limits of cultivation, whose crops were regularly being devastated by migratory flocks'.[1]

The emus' irregular, drought-driven migration had led the birds into vast plains of recently planted wheat. They imperilled farmers' livelihoods by eating the heads of wheat, but destroyed much more of the harvest just by stamping about in it.

Describing the wheatbelt farmers as 'soldier settlers' places the Emu War more squarely in the mainstream of military history, and makes the whole farce a little funnier by attributing its genesis to returned men seeking martial solutions to civil conflict – but it is possibly inaccurate.

The soldier-settlement scheme in Western Australia was a three-year program that began in 1918. Under the *Discharged Soldiers Settlement Act*, the state-run Agricultural Bank of Western Australia allocated advances to about 9000 veterans to buy comparatively small blocks of land in the south and east of the state. The hope was that the men and their families would successfully engage in mixed farming – perhaps growing wheat and raising sheep – and push the borders of settlement deeper into the bush.

Australia, already beset with the idea that ex-bushmen made the best soldiers, had come to imagine that ex-soldiers might also make the best farmers. However, as historian Leigh Straw writes, 'Some veterans had no prior farming and agricultural experience but were being sent to live and work in outlying areas with few resources to depend on', and during the Depression 'many men and their families simply walked off the land'.[2]

As far as I can tell, there were never many soldier settlers in the eastern wheatbelt areas affected by the Emu War, and none at all in Campion where most of the shooting took place. The wheat growers' leadership included a couple of soldier settlers, but most of the agitators were lifelong civilians. Of those few returned men who were granted land in the Shire of Nungarin and the neighbouring Shire of Westonia – where the Number One Rabbit Proof Fence funnelled the migrating birds – an unknown number had abandoned their farms by 1932. The remaining growers were furious with the government, which had repeatedly promised them a fair and fixed price for their harvest but proved unable to push the necessary measures through parliament.

Angry farmers formed the Wheat Growers' Union of Western Australia, and I suspect the cause of the Emu War is rooted in union desperation and militancy rather than the imagined Freikorpsian reflexes of returned men. The WGU made plans to withdraw the harvest and allow the wheat to rot in the fields – a 'holdup' or 'wheat strike' – until members could be guaranteed a decent return. But the emus arrived first.[3]

Jocelyn Maddock's not very well known but stunningly comprehensive history of the Shire of Westonia painstakingly reconstructs the early years of the WGU and gives the names of almost every farmer associated with the union's policymaking and organisation. Maddock describes the wheat growers of Westonia as 'a mixed lot, most not from farming backgrounds and without the ingrained conservatism of farmers in older districts'. Some were former miners from Westonia mines with a strong trade union background. She believes that 'many' were returned soldiers 'who came from a variety of occupations, many with union affiliations'.[4] The founding committee of the WGU comprised nine members, of whom only the former Light Horseman Eugene Best Smalpage was a soldier settler (at Westonia). The majority of the executive held land at the regional centre of Merredin, while the union's founding secretary, Daniel J. O'Leary, was a farmer at Walgoolan to the east of the town.

Merredin was the heart of the wheat farmers' world. The union's newspaper, *The Wheatgrower*, whose title perfectly described its readership, suggested that the state capital should be moved to the town, where 'politicians could hardly fail to derive some knowledge of actual conditions in the country that they at present misgovern', and where public servants could be 'shown what constitutes a day's work in the country [and] be shamed into doing half a day's work themselves'.[5]

The Agricultural Bank's register of settlers records only 123 soldier settlers ever to have received grants in the region around Merredin and Westonia, and many would have already left by October 1932, when mobs of up to 20,000 emus advanced towards Merredin from the east.[6]

The birds were soon scattered by heavy rains, and farmers commissioned a truck to chase them towards the Number One Rabbit Proof Fence, while men rode on the running boards and struck them with sticks. Many emus were killed, but the survivors quickly learned to be wary of approaching trucks.

Fearing a looming emugeddon, the farmers sent a deputation to the state parliament in the form of J.M. Tapping and T. Dixon, who were introduced to Premier James Mitchell by George Lambert MLA. Neither Tapping nor Dixon were soldier settlers, although they later appear to have been represented as such.[7] The farmers pressed the premier to approach the Defence Department to lend them machine guns to eliminate the emus. The recently appointed WA Military Commandant, Brigadier Athelstan Markham Martyn, was not opposed to the idea, and he and the premier agreed to petition the federal Minister for Defence, Sir George Pearce, for arms.

Pearce refused to lend military equipment to anybody outside of the control of the Defence Department, 'whether they were required for the destruction of emu or any other purpose', but was prepared to send in suitably equipped troops if either the Western Australian government or the local authorities would meet their expenses.[8] The settlers agreed to feed and house the troops and pay the cost of their ammunition. Or, as Dempster's video describes it, 'Pearce made the farmers sign an agreement saying they would pay for the whole thing and Pearce wouldn't take any of the blame if the operation – that was clearly very stupid – turned out to indeed be stupid.'

Why did the Minister for Defence go along with a scheme that had nothing to do with defence? Pearce, described as 'no genius' by his biographer, had only recently regained his portfolio and had more pressing military matters on his mind, such as the urgent need to rearm against Japan.[9] A trope in the video has Pearce coveting an emu-feather hat (a reference to a request by the 1st Cavalry Division, New South Wales for a hundred emu skins to be sent out east for light horsemen's hats), but he probably just hoped to placate the farmers with a semblance of action.[10] And Australian politicians have regularly acted as if the best way to demonstrate seriousness of purpose is to send soldiers on missions unconnected with fighting wars, such as using the SAS to turn back refugees seeking asylum from the Taliban government of Afghanistan only months before deploying those same troops under that same commander to invade Afghanistan and overthrow that same government.

Pearce had authorised a spectacle rather than a solution. Back in the 1930s, machine guns remained closely associated with the 1929 St Valentine's Day Massacre in Chicago, when the gangster Al Capone organised the slaughter of a rival gang by gunmen disguised as police. A headline in the Perth *Daily News* foreshadowed 'Chicago Methods at Campion' above a story that told of a plan to mount a machine gun near the Number One Rabbit Proof Fence, and have a posse of settlers in cars and on horseback, directed by members of the local branch of the RSL, drive the emus towards the gun post to be mown down.[11]

It may have been the involvement of the RSL that led to the idea that the men of the district were largely soldier settlers. But every man and his kelpie, Bluey, was an armchair military strategist. Eyewitness reports of the farmers' early tactics were collected by Jocelyn Maddock. In Maddock's opinion, the best and most accurate account she heard was delivered by Agricultural Bank inspector Max Brinkworth, who told her of a cunning plan supposedly hatched by farmer Charlie Mann: 'The settlers caught a large emu, dressed it in a pair of men's trousers put on back to front and fastened over the top with a white stocking. The idea was that the dressed-up emu would try to rejoin his flock who, in fear, would run away, he would chase them and they would just disappear back from whence they came. For a brief while, the plan seemed to succeed but later the bird apparently divested itself of the clothing and rejoined the mob.'[12]

Union secretary Dan O'Leary claimed to have written to the government to ask for machine guns to fight off an earlier emu invasion in the late 1920s, and felt that his proposal had been treated as a joke. Now that Defence had apparently come around to his idea, he sought to up the ante and suggested that 'an aeroplane with a machine gun mounted on it should also be sent to the district'.[13]

It would seem particularly cruel to deploy aircraft against flightless birds, and the wheat growers, like the military, had to settle for the resources that were closest to hand. Brigadier Martyn later explained that this type of operation had called for his best men 'as there might have been a certain amount of danger attached to the proceedings'.[14] In the absence of the best, Martyn sent the best available: Sergeant McMurray and Gunner O'Halloran of the Seventh Heavy Battery of the Royal Australian Artillery, under the command of Major Gwynydd Purves Wynne Aubrey-Meredith, equipped with two Lewis guns of the kind used by the Anzacs against the Germans on the Western Front.

The Romanian Journal of Historical Studies is not the premier academic journal for research into Australian studies, and Nangkai University in Tianjin, China is not known for its contribution to Australian military history. However, two Tianjin academics, Richard J. Cook and Srđan M Jovanović, published a paper about the Emu War in the journal in 2019 and added a mystery that is not mysterious at all. Cook and Jovanović refer to primary sources about the Emu War as 'rare', when what they mean is they could not find them. They speculate that the lack of documentation is 'probably due to the humiliating defeat of the Royal Australian Army' but there is not, and never has been, an entity known as the Royal Australian Army. 'Questions about the Great Emu War remain unanswered,' they claim. 'The one most prominent gap that begs for filling centers on the figure of G.P.W. Meredith, the Major who led the operation ... [H]e could not be found in the records of the National Archives of Australia.'[15]

In the case of both the primary sources and Meredith's service record, it appears that Cook and Jovanović, er, entered the wrong search terms into the database. The NAA holds a 91-page file on 'Use of Machine Guns for Eradication of Emus in WA and Wild Horses in North Queensland', and three separate service records for Meredith. And there is no doubt that the Emu War would not be so gleefully remembered were it not for Meredith's breathless dispatches attributing military acuity and tactical thinking to a mob of birds. The emus were Meredith's Germans – and, as it would turn out, his Japanese (but not his North Koreans).

Meredith did not have a good Great War. Born in Tasmania in 1887, he was a career soldier, commissioned as a second lieutenant in the Victoria Scottish Regiment. A strapping young man of 191 centimetres, he joined the Royal Australian Artillery in 1910. Eighteen months after the outbreak of the First World War, he was posted to Thursday Island in the Torres Strait, where he remained until January 1918. Although there was a fortress and battery on Thursday Island, there was no extant threat. After the Australian invasion of German New Guinea in 1914, the Thursday Island garrison was not really defending anyone against anything – a situation with which Meredith would become grimly familiar.

A journalist who visited the garrison in November 1916 found a land of 'scenic beauty' with splendid views of the straits from the barracks. It was not, however, a sought-after military posting. 'Not one of the young soldiers of Thursday Island but chafes under the difficulties and delays of getting to the Front to prove his prowess,' he wrote, 'yet he should be mindful that someone has to do outpost duty.' Garrison life might be monotonous, but at least the men were well trained. If necessary, the journalist believed, 'The little army of Thursday Island could march to battle at a moment's notice.'

But it never did.[16] A portrait of the garrison's officers includes a modestly moustached Meredith, looking lanky and gangly and faintly self-conscious with his hands folded in his lap and his tunic perhaps pulled a little too far down his pants.[17]

Meredith finally set sail for England with the AIF in July 1918. He arrived in September, was hospitalised with mumps in October and returned to duty in November, whereupon the war promptly ended. That was the closest he had come to combat, until the emu menace stuck up its elongated neck and reared its unusually shaped head.

The Emu War involved elements of conscious mythmaking. Meredith and his men were accompanied to the wheatbelt by reporters from the *Daily News*, the *Sunday Times* and the *West Australian*, and even a Fox Movietone News camera crew. The *Sydney Morning Herald* published comment suggesting 'the fact pictures of the destruction of the birds by machine-guns were being taken for film purposes creates a suspicion that everything might not be quite as stated'.[18] There was an underlying suspicion that Pearce hoped the fruit of his decisive action would be recorded on celluloid for posterity and celebrated.

He was not to know that posterity had other ideas.

The mission to Campion was scheduled to begin in October, but was delayed by unexpected rains. On 1 November 1932, Meredith's party finally left Perth by rail for Burracoppin, whence the men were transported by truck to the Campion siding.

According to the *West Australian*, which seemed reluctant to take the operation seriously from the start, the emus had fattened on their plundered wheat and were 'ready to scatter headlong into the bush at the first alarm'. At Campion, the troops were disheartened to learn that 'the breaking-up of the big mob of emus would make it impossible to conduct the intended drive by several hundred beaters over a 20-mile front into the mouths of the guns'.

Instead, the hunt would have to take place on individual farms. The town of Campion 'welcomed Major Meredith and his men by a turnout of about 50 settlers, all very excited at the prospect of the anticipated slaughter', wrote the *West Australian*'s Special Correspondent. 'The presence of a Fox Movietone photographer added to the importance of the event.'

The Agricultural Bank had guaranteed the army £50 for the party's 10,000 rounds of ammunition. Dan O'Leary told the settlers that the cost of the bullets would 'probably be subscribed by various firms' – words that would return to haunt the formidable O'Leary in years to come.

Three newspaper journalists, the film crew, the Agricultural Bank inspector, and between fifty and one hundred settlers followed the gun party to an unfenced paddock near Campion, on the Yilgarn property of Ben Sands (who was not a soldier settler) where a flock of almost forty emus had been sighted. Although the small Australian force had not planned a full-scale attack, Sergeant McMurray fired upon the emus at long range and was reported as 'mowing down half a dozen on the run'.

The settlers were impressed.[19]

The war then adjourned for lunch on the property of Joe Joyce (who may have been the soldier settler Lawrence Stephen Joyce) where, according to the meticulous reportage of the *Merredin Mercury and Central Districts Index*, the gun party was treated to 'a sumptuous lunch served up in Joe's most hospitable style'. Joyce's land was established as the headquarters of the operation, from which the major undertook a tour of inspection of the district to discover that the settled land east of the Number One Rabbit Proof Fence was only partly cleared, heavily timbered and scrubby.

'After traversing miles of crops,' reported the *Mercury*, 'indications of the depredations of the pests were most evident, but for the moment none were to be seen, with the exception of one lone bird in the crop some 1500 yards away. A shot was fired at this one, but he moved away quickly and was soon lost to sight ... The gunners crept through the crop for some distance, whilst the rest of the party observed from motor trucks and boughs of trees. The enemy was not in large numbers, but it is possible about a dozen were accounted for.'[20]

The results were disappointing, and Meredith concluded that it was barely practicable for the gun party to take a truck through the dense scrub; in any case, the sight and sound of the vehicle would alert the emus to his intentions. 'I decided, therefore, that an ambush was the only way of dealing effectively with the situation,' he wrote in an after-action report. 'Accordingly, sites were selected [and] one gun crew was always on watch, catching the birds as they came out to feed at daylight and when they approached the dam for water at sundown.'[21]

Early indications that press coverage might not be going the way that Pearce had hoped came with the report of the day's activities in the Perth *Daily News*, under the headline 'Campion Emus' Strategy'. The paper judged that the emus of Campion were 'more than holding their own against the Defence Department's crack gunners'.[22]

The *West Australian*'s dramatic and speculative reportage continued apace. Its Special Correspondent may have been the first pressman to attribute tactical thinking as well as combatant status to the emus. He observed that the big mobs had broken up and scattered into small foraging parties of birds who were 'as quick-sighted as they are suspicious' and showed 'remarkable ability to maintain full use of cover to attain the shelter of timber'. He judged that the campaign had developed into guerilla warfare, 'with the quarry holding every advantage'.

Meredith's men set up a gun by the side of a dam where dozens of emus had been seen to gather. 'They are exceedingly curious,' wrote the Special Correspondent, 'and ironically enough, a red danger flag was raised to attract their attention. Soon a mob of over 100 birds appeared, but with extraordinary cunning they kept in the hollow about 300 yards away, and only a long row of craning heads was visible.

'Towards sundown they approached to within 100 yards and the gun opened fire. Feathers flew and dozens of birds jumped high in the air and fell dead. Many others were badly hit but kept going with amazing fortitude. In a moment the mob had scattered in all directions, and effective shooting was out of the question.

'The emus have proved that they are not so stupid as they are usually considered to be. Each mob has its leader, always an enormous black-plumed bird, standing fully six feet high, who keeps watch while his fellows busy themselves with the wheat. At the first suspicious sign, he gives the signal and dozens of heads stretch out of the crop. A few birds will take fright, starting a headlong stampede for the scrub, the leader always remaining until his followers have reached safety.'

The black emu had been revealed as the kind of leader that Meredith himself had perhaps hoped to be: tested by combat, he (or probably she, as it turns out) was not found wanting.

The gun party then mounted its weapon on a truck, which pursued a single emu for several kilometres along the Number One Rabbit Proof Fence until the bird unexpectedly faltered and was hit not by a bullet, but by the vehicle itself. Even in death, the emu frustrated its attackers, as its body 'became wedged in the steering gear of the truck, which swerved and demolished half a chain of fencing before it was halted'. This was just one of the depredations faced by a barrier that was never meant to keep out giant birds. More frequently, wrote the man from the *West Australian*, the emus broke down fences themselves as they charged madly into the wire. He observed 'bundles of feathers every few yards along the rabbit-proof fence [where] the wire has halted a mad career through the scrub'.[23]

Where the *West Australian*'s man on the spot had smiled wryly, the Perth *Daily Mirror*'s 'Special Correspondent at the front – Bar' fell off his stool laughing. The *Mirror*'s headline announced 'Birds' Air Force Weak', over a sketch that had the Anzacs once again fighting 'the Turkeys – or the emus', and a dying emu murmuring 'Kiss me major' as he fell before the machine gun. The birds were reported laying eggs. 'No more will we squirm under the emus' yolk!' cried a farmer. It was suggested that when the bullets ran out the army should attack the emus with peashooters, in the hope that they would catch the peas in their mouths, swallow them and gorge themselves to death.[24]

'It was unfortunate that the Press should have seen fit to give the matter so much publicity,' wrote Brigadier Martyn later, 'and that some of the papers should have ridiculed the idea and have made it the subject of humorous articles and sketches, as the farmers of the district failed to see the jokes and the use of machine guns was a serious experiment.'[25]

The *West Australian* awoke in the war zone and continued to trudge after the troops, although its correspondent had to make his own decision about which way to go. The expedition split into two parties: Meredith went out with one Lewis gun, and O'Halloran took the other. O'Halloran, accompanied by a party of armed settlers, lay in ambush at a waterhole, where the gunner was finally rewarded with the sighting of a huge mob of about 1000 birds. The correspondent watched with anthropomorphic anticipation: 'The hunters kept motionless behind the high walls of the dam, and their suspicions lulled, the birds approached with long graceful strides to within a few hundred yards. Then with a common impulse, they halted in a long line with heads raised inquiringly. Some warning came with the wind, and just as the guns came into action they stampeded in all directions, raising great clouds of dust as their feet pounded the crop and earth.' For the first time, a large number of birds came within point-blank range of O'Halloran's weapon: 'They made an almost perfect target for the Lewis gunners. Perhaps a dozen birds fell at the first burst of fire, and then ... the Lewis gun jammed.'

And that was that.

The story was headlined 'A Thousand Birds in Luck: Machine Gun Jams'.

Meredith told the pressmen, 'If we had a military division with the bullet-carrying capacity of these birds, it would face any army in the world. They could face machine guns with the invulnerability of tanks. They are like Zulus, whom even dum dum bullets would not stop.'[26]

In one of his increasingly bizarre after-action reports, he admitted that 2350 rounds had been expended to slaughter only about 300 birds, but noted that the gun party had suffered no casualties in return and that 'the emu is an amazingly hard bird to kill outright, many carry mortal wounds up to a distance of half a mile (an actual observation)'.[27]

Animal lovers throughout Australia were disturbed by the prospect of the industrial slaughter of the national bird. The Royal Society for the Prevention of Cruelty to Animals became involved in attempts to mitigate the suffering of the injured. But when Inspector Arthur Austin of the RSPCA turned up on the scene with a rifle and knife, Meredith asked him how fast he could run as 'he would have to better Peter Pan to catch wounded emus'.[28]

The Myths of the Emu War

One minute of the Fox Movietone footage survives. The title 'Western Australia Makes War on Emus' wobbles on the screen, as if dancing nervously to the military march that plays in the background. There's a shot of the 'unfortunate farmers', followed by footage of a machine gun, at first lying in the bed of a truck then mounted precariously on the roof of the vehicle's cabin. 'They've never used this sort of scarifier before,' says the plummy, mock-jolly announcer, 'but things are desperate, and it's war to the finish this time.

'The scouts of the advancing army have keen eyesight,' says the announcer, as emus are pictured ambling through the scrub, 'and our lads have to do some real stalking . . . The focus shifts to armed men padding after the birds . . . with the enemy watching events through their periscopes.'

The 'periscopes' in question are the emus' long and sparsely feathered necks 'raised up over the heads of corn'.

Two men fire a machine gun at the emus, which beat a hasty retreat. 'Now they're retiring,' says the announcer, excitedly, 'off at 40 miles an hour.'

The abandoned ground is littered with the corpses of emus. 'Well, instead of the birds ruining the farmers, it seems the tables are turned and there'll be no more damage here for many a day to come,' concludes the announcer.

The implication is that the emus have been routed.

On November 8, the matter of the Emu War was raised in federal parliament. Rowley James, the Labor member for Hunter, New South Wales, asked, 'Is a medal to be struck for the war?' Albert Ernest Green, Labor member for Kalgoorlie, Western Australia, and a former Minister for Defence, said that the emus had 'won every round so far'.[29] In a debate in the Senate, Labor's James Dunn, who had served in the Middle East and France with the AIF, called Pearce 'the minister for the Emu War' and told him to 'get back to his emus'.[30]

It was announced that the government had approved the gun party's proceeding to Walgoolan but then, as the *Daily News* noted, 'military operations against the emu tribes ceased with dramatic suddenness and [all was] quiet on the Campion front'.[31] Brigadier Martyn had received an order from the Defence Department instructing that Meredith and his men be withdrawn. Labor's George Lambert complained, 'It is all very well for the city "pussy-foots" in the House of Representatives to make little of the attempt to eradicate emus with machine guns, and I can quite appreciate the attitude of the "brass-hats" in Melbourne in killing an attempt to do anything useful with the equipment of the military, which they consider should be held sacred to less worthy purposes.'[32]

The army's withdrawal from Campion via the Kalgoorlie Express was covered by the *Daily News*. 'Ironically, Campion emus appeared in huge flocks along the road that led the Lewis gunners home, as if to give a mocking farewell,' wrote the correspondent.[33]

The settlers were, as ever, livid.

A mass meeting was held to demand the return of the gun party, which the locals thought had done a decent job. The premier received a telegram from a farmer named King, who styled himself as the chairman of the North Walgoolan Emu Destruction Committee (and who was not a soldier settler), conveying his urgent desire to have the army come back immediately to prevent 'an enormous number of emus doing untold damage to standing crops'.[34]

But evidence of the birds' martial fortitude continued to emerge: 'Their capacity for lead-carrying was amply verified when Mr. A. E. Johnson ran one down in his truck,' reported the *West Australian*, 'and on examination found five bullets in the bird, some of which had evidently been there since the first operations.'[35]

The Myths of the Emu War

The *Daily News* noted the ceasefire but reminded readers that 'the emus remain in possession of disputed territory' and warned that 'regular military operations will be followed by guerilla warfare, which may continue for years and may be accompanied by stories of horrible atrocities'. The newspaper noted that 'the emu commander is maintaining a studied silence as to his future plans, but it is understood that he is much impressed with the capacity for resistance shown by raw troops and confident that they will continue to uphold the best traditions of the race.'[36]

However, no sooner had the party returned to base than it was sent back out in response to the farmers' protests. In the second campaign of the Emu War, operations were extended as far as North Campion and South Walgoolan. Major Meredith submitted the most curious of all his after-action reports from Campion Siding on November 18. He wrote of a foot patrol he had taken with a settler – the two men armed only with rifles – during which they engaged and routed the enemy: 'We got into one mob of about 30 and killed three outright, wounded many more. The last seen of the survivors was a cloud of dust at the rabbit fence about 3 miles north. Later in the afternoon I got 2 of a mob or 4 for certain and others wounded.' A couple of days later, Meredith and O'Halloran staged an ambush alongside the dam on another property at Campion Siding: 'We had a good day, buried 19 corpses and many others wounded.' In his finest anthropomorphic flourish, Meredith reported, 'The gunners are at last getting the upper hand over the enemy, many of which have been killed or are carrying lead. The rest, apparently considering discretion the better part of valour, are gradually sneaking off.'

In attributing to emus both the application of prudence and the potential for bravery, Meredith appeared to have lost his mind.

He later claimed the operation had been 'most successful' and offered extraordinarily unlikely statistics – based on a mixture of speculation and unverifiable observation – intended to show that the ammunition expended had accounted for 3486 birds, the majority of which had wandered off wounded and died in the bush. The men had received invaluable machine-gun practice and the only casualty to the army was a broken extractor and return spring.[37]

The gun party returned to Fremantle for the final time on December 10.

It is often difficult to separate the sober from the satirical in the nascent field of Emu War studies, but Pattrice Jones's essay 'Provocations from the Field – Derangement and Resistance: Reflections from Under the Glare of an Angry Emu' is meant as a serious contribution. And Jones, who seems to have spent a lot of time among emus, does shed some light on the reports of black-plumed emu leadership in the field.

'Emu females tend to be larger than the males,' she writes, 'so the enormous leaders seen by the soldier probably were female. And they probably weren't leaders or even designated lookouts ... emus collaboratively alternate between eating and keeping watch while others eat.'

Jones adds, 'Here we can see how human ideas about gender and hierarchy can lead to "observations" that confirm stereotypes.'

When I first read this, I wondered where Jones could possibly be going.

'For a long time, the only emu sex that people had witnessed and recorded was homosexual,' writes Jones. 'Which brings us to emu queerness.'

Ah, of course.

'We can say that emus are "queer" both in the sense of confounding our categories and in the sense that they are among the hundreds of species in which same-sex affection, parenting, and sex are common,' writes Jones. 'The females are the fighters. The males hatch eggs and raise chicks, as single parents or in co-parenting relationships with other males; some male emus enjoy sexual relations with other males, and those relations tend to be marked by more gestures of affection than heterosexual matings.'[38]

Although I had not considered queering the Emu War, I have become ever more interested in inventing spurious parallels between the Emu War and the Vietnam War, largely to bang on about points that I have made many times before. The currently accepted mythology of the Vietnam War bizarrely instructs us that the postwar experience of returned men is more important than the war itself. It seems that the veterans of the Emu War were recognised as such, if only as a bit of a joke. Although little is publicly known of the subsequent career of Gunner O'Halloran, Major and Mrs Meredith were reported as hosting the Royal Australian Artillery's invitation dance at Fremantle barracks in 1933, where Sergeant McMurray, described in the *Daily News* as a 'veteran of the great Emu War', was assisted by his wife with the catering.[39] McMurray later became secretary of the North East Fremantle sub-branch of the RSL, which suggests that veterans of the Emu War were neither refused entry to the RSL nor damned by older members with the calumny that they had not served in a proper war (although, to be fair, his artillery service in the First World War may have eased his acceptance).[40]

Then, of course, there is the ubiquitous spectre of PTSD. Jones states she has 'spent enough time with roosters used in cockfighting to know that repeated extreme terror can lead to an avian equivalent of Post-Traumatic Stress Disorder'. Emus, she speculates, might be particularly prone as they have few natural predators.[41]

After a war come questions of war debt and reparations, and in November 1933, almost a year since the cessation of hostilities,

Dan O'Leary received a demand from the Agricultural Bank for the payment of £24 for the gun party's ammunition. The bank offered to settle the matter by accepting an order on the proceeds of his crop. However, wrote O'Leary, the bank was 'slightly in error in stating that I had guaranteed the amount, because I had done nothing of the kind, and furthermore that I had not the slightest intention of paying it'.

The bank responded by reducing the bill, and helpfully enclosing an application form for a special advance of the money from the Finance and Development Board. In reply, O'Leary presented the bank with a bill of his own: his itemised invoice included £9 for victualling His Majesty's troops; £10 for 'transport of same'; £5 for 'damage to transport equipment during conveyance of troops to front line' (since, 'as Napoleon's ideas are now quite obsolete, the army engaged in the campaign did not march on its stomach, but in my motor car, the well-fed condition of the troops being responsible for the breakage of the chassis of that vehicle'); and £900 for 6000 bushels of wheat (which was 'not consumed by the troops, but was destroyed on my property by the enemy, during the delay in commencing operations, occasioned by the necessary war conference between the bank and the Minister of Defence, to determine who should pay the sum of £24, the estimated cost of the ammunition to be used in the campaign in this sector'), making a total of £924.

O'Leary indicated that, in recognition of the bank's own generous offer, he was prepared to allow the bank to pay him in wheat, too. 'I am particularly desirous of avoiding any rupture of diplomatic relations,' he wrote, 'but [I] am not prepared to consider any suggestion for a conference to discuss the cancellation of emu war debts. In view of my consideration in not including any charge for trench rents, or for the bashing out of the brains of such of the enemy wounded as could be found after each engagement, may I ask that the required amount of wheat be delivered to me without delay.'[42]

O'Leary's letter had the unlikely effect of bringing international fame to its author when it was reproduced in newspapers in the eastern states, the UK and the US. O'Leary's cause was taken up in federal parliament, where Country Party Senator Bertie Johnston asked the Minister for Defence, 'In view of the low price of wheat, is it proposed to hold a conference or take other steps to secure the cancellation of the Emu War Debt?'[43]

George Pearce kept his seat until November 1937. The political instincts that had arguably let him down when he allowed the Fox Movietone crew to trail Meredith's gun party saw him retire as the longest-serving senator in the Parliament of Australia.

Colonel Gwynydd Purves Wynne Audrey Meredith volunteered for the 2nd AIF but did not receive an overseas posting until September 1945, by which time the Second World War was over. He arrived in New Guinea (from Thursday Island, as it happened) just after the Japanese surrender, fell sick and was evacuated to Australia eight days later. He returned to New Guinea but was sent back home after three days.

By the end of his Australian military career, Meredith had served in two world wars but fired shots in anger only against emus.

So he travelled to Japan. As a civilian support worker for the US army, he eventually took charge of the small-arms section of the Tokyo arsenal. In 1952, he went to Korea as a civilian chief inspector of ammunition and explosives and finally saw frontline service. He remained in that position – which had been created especially for him – until the Korean ceasefire in 1953, then stayed on for several years to train the Korean army in gunnery. In 1957 he received two military service medals from the Korean government, but was not permitted to wear them on his uniform on ceremonial occasions, since Korean awards for service in Korea were only officially recognised in Australia as 'souvenirs'.

'I shall in all probability never again wear uniform,' Meredith declared furiously in April 1961. 'When medals and decorations are worn I shall wear plain clothes and my decorations.'[44]

He died in Sydney in 1975, aged eighty-eight, the only man in history to have served in both world wars, the Korean War and the Emu War.

But is it even possible to have a war in which one side lacks the cognitive ability to conceive of organised conflict? Jones insists that emus do know they are in a war, one that has 'simmered for sixty thousand years and has been raging for the past two hundred. Emus today may be unable to imagine any other way of being in the world other than perpetual battle with human beings.' Jones also holds that a form of sovereignty was at stake during the Emu War, as 'emus did not cede their inherent entitlement to peaceably occupy the lands in which they evolved'.[45]

Although Jones is the first academic to have tried to see the war through the yellowy eyes of the emus, several fiction writers have attempted something similar. Just as at least three books have examined the Gallipoli campaign from the point of view of Simpson's donkey, there are at least two self-published works looking at the Emu War from an exclusively avian perspective. Bryden and Park's *Letters from the Emu War* is dedicated to those 'brave emus' who 'lacked the opposable thumbs needed to record their historic achievement'.[46]

Murray Johnson, whose pioneering essay set the template for everything that followed, characterises the conflict as an 'environmental war', fought to determine who or what would dominate the land. I suspect it should be seen as a militarised wildlife-management program, accompanied by a misguided propaganda campaign and commanded by an officer with frustrated dreams of martial glory.

But were the emus victorious? As Meredith pointed out, the birds inflicted no casualties upon the Australian army beyond the broken extractor and return spring, but 'I still think the emus did win,' Johnson told me. 'I've been asked over the years to talk about it, but more since the YouTube. I was surprised how the YouTube took off.'

And what did he think of the video when he saw it?

'I haven't seen it, to be honest,' said Johnson. 'I'll have to Google it up.'

The Emu War, the first of two planned movies about the events of November 1932, premiered at Monsterfest in Melbourne on 22 October 2023, a few weeks after I missed the first deadline for this book. The second movie, *The Great Emu Wars*, co-written by British comedian John Cleese, is due to start shooting in 2024.

To put this in perspective, that is two more movies than have ever been made about Australia's part in the Korean War, one more than has been made about the Boer War, and half the number of Australian feature films about the Vietnam War.

I guessed that the battlefields of the Emu War would quickly become sites of pilgrimage – or at least tourism – and I determined to get in first. I had long planned a research trip to the eastern wheatbelt, although I had repeatedly been told there was nothing to mark the passing of the Emu War in Merredin or Campion. I thought I might be able to find something others had missed; I had particularly high hopes for Merredin Regional Library, whose librarian, Wendy Porter, had been interviewed for a short ABC video about the conflict.

I'd spoken on the phone to Porter and knew that she had compiled a dossier about the Emu War. While we were discussing soldier settlers, a voice in the background called out that there had not been many soldier settlers in the area – most ex-servicemen had been granted land further north. Porter offered to check the names of settlers in contemporary news reports against the inscriptions on tombstones in the local cemetery, which would always mention any service in the AIF.

The drive from Perth to Merredin follows the Golden Pipeline Trail, a niche tourist attraction that might excite travellers with an interest in water-supply infrastructure. There is also a Public Silo Trail ('bringing world-class murals to grain silos'), which is attractive but intermittent. My partner and I arrived at Merredin at midday and drove past the cenotaph – which remembers the dead of two world wars, but not the Emu War – to the regional library, where I was lucky to find Porter, as I had forgotten to remind her that I was coming. She said that most of the settlers appeared not to have been soldiers.

Then my partner showed me the Register of Settlers, and it became clear that there were no soldier settlers in Campion at all.[47]

From the library, we checked into a motel and then headed out to the battlefields. At first, we followed what may one day be known as the 'Emu War Logistics Trail' to Burracoppin, where Meredith and his men had disembarked the train from Perth. Burracoppin (population: 114) is a town of redbrick, rust, timber and dust. Some of the more rickety homes look like they were owner-built from found materials.

From Burracoppin, the troops had boarded a truck to the Campion Siding. I, too, followed the saddle-brown road through a level landscape that comes to yellow with bristling wheat. Blue-tongued lizards watched our hire car pass. Pink galahs, green parrots and magpies fly close to the ground, as if the sky starts lower out here. Lakes of sunlight make aqueous patches on the graded dirt.

The Number One Rabbit Proof Fence, a very long fine-mesh fence with rusty fencepoles and oxidised barbed-wire trim, has collapsed in several places. My partner was becoming impatient now, repeatedly questioning the point of the journey.

Then suddenly, as if by a miracle, we were sent a sign. Not a sign from heaven, but an actual sign. Mounted on poles, framed in steel, and embedded in the roadside was a placard bearing the legend 'Emu War 1932' with an image of an emu on either side.

After jubilantly photographing every aspect of the sign (okay, so there aren't many) we turned around and drove back towards Merredin, when my partner spotted in the distance – two emus standing sentinel in a field of wheat!

It was as if they were paying tribute to their fallen comrades, on the very ground where they had met their end.

I returned to town, elated. I needed to revisit Merredin Regional Library and find out the origin of the sign. The baffled Wendy Porter suggested I ring Nungarin Shire Council, where the works manager assured the administrator that he had not erected the sign. The administrator recommended I call the Nungarin military museum, because it sounded like the kind of thing that they might do. A volunteer at the military museum advised me to contact Mukinbudin Shire Council, where a woman called Hilda told me, 'Our CEO went for a drive through there yesterday, and he assumed Nungarin had put up the sign.'

Interestingly, nobody I spoke with thought it at all unusual that private citizens might independently erect memorial signage by the side of a public road.

The redoubtable Hilda promised to investigate, and called me back a few minutes later with the phone number of a man named Ralph English.

I phoned Ralph and told him I was trying to discover who had erected the sign.

'I did,' he said. 'About ten days ago.'

I felt like the archaeologist Howard Carter when he rediscovered Tutankhamen's tomb, or myself when I finally acquired documents proving that not every national serviceman who was sent to Vietnam had volunteered for overseas service. Ralph was not to know this, however. He continued to answer my excited questions in slow, measured tones.

'I've had the sign for about a month,' he said, 'but I've been waiting for the steelworks to make a frame to mount it on, because I was worried that somebody might nick it. So I made it so nobody was able to pinch it, and I took it out there and put it in the ground.'

But why?

'For people that're interested, like yourself, when they drive through there,' said Ralph.

Were there many of us?

'It's a bit mystifying, really,' said Ralph. 'It seems to have been made more public in the last eighteen months and everyone seems to be getting on the bandwagon. Some of the things I've seen on YouTube are just a big mockery of the army.'

Ralph felt this was inaccurate and unfair. 'I did an interview with the ABC,' he said. 'A guy came out here, but he had his own agenda. He was more interested in getting into Merredin and having a chat with the librarian.' Ralph told me his father had been 'out there when that Emu War happened. He went there in 1923 when it was virgin country.'

Ralph's father, Jim English, was not a soldier settler. He and his brother had been given a land grant and sent to Campion. 'I wish they had've got sent to Wongan Hills or somewhere where it's a bit safer,' said Ralph. 'The eastern edge of the farm was where the Number One Rabbit Proof Fence goes through.'

That was the site Ralph had chosen for his sign.

'I don't know if you know emus,' said Ralph, 'but they're pretty hard to shoot.'

The Myths of the Emu War

I told him I had seen emus on a farm earlier in the day.

'There's the odd little pocket of them here and there,' said Ralph, 'but they don't seem to do much damage.'

Apparently Jim English, not unlike Vietnam veterans, had been reluctant to speak about what he had seen in the war. 'I don't know why,' said Ralph, 'but he was one of these blokes that you had to pump him to get him to tell you anything.'

The Emu War was not a war to end all wars. It was not even a war to end all emu wars. The wheat growers continued to request military intervention whenever there was a large emu migration. In 1943, the government issued wheatbelt farmers with free ammunition so they could turn their own guns on the emus. But the problem was finally solved in the late 1950s by gentler and more Australian means, when emu-proof fences were built to contain the birds northwest of the wheatbelt.

The Emu War has been mythologised and mocked and dismembered by millennials for memes, with the message that government is stupid, the army is stupid, everyone in the past was stupider than everyone today, and even funny-looking animals are superior to self-important people. It's all a bit nihilistic and solipsistic, but it's also kind of funny.

Unless you happen to be an emu.

The Myths of the POWs

That Changi was a hell camp. That the bridge on the River Kwai is the Bridge on the River Kwai. That seventy prisoners were beaten to death at Hellfire Pass. That Weary Dunlop was the surgeon of the Burma Railway. That Australian prisoners survived better than the British or the Dutch.

The tragedy of Australian POWs in Southeast Asia began eighteen months into the Second World War, at Changi in eastern Singapore, where about 87,000 defeated Allied soldiers were imprisoned after the Japanese invasion of the Dutch East Indies and British Malaya and Singapore. 'Fortress Singapore' was supposed to hold off any Japanese advance towards Australia and deny the Japanese navy command of the sea, and when the Straits Settlements fell on 15 February 1942, after only seventy days of fighting on the Malay peninsula, British Prime Minister Winston Churchill called it the 'worst disaster' in British military history. The British commander, Lieutenant-General Arthur Percival, unconditionally surrendered on behalf of all Allied troops, and nearly 15,000 Australians – most of whom had not fired a shot – were captured. The entire 8th Division, a host of Alfs and Berts and big men called 'Tiny' and redheads named 'Blue', disappeared behind barbed wire. The Japanese had never planned to take so many prisoners, and at first had no idea what to do with them, so they simply herded the Australians into the old British Army Selarang Barracks in the Changi Garrison. Some POWs and many Allied civilians were also interned in nearby Changi Prison.

In Australia, Changi has a reputation as an outpost of Hell, a concentration camp where Japanese guards ruthlessly committed acts of sadism on hungry and helpless prisoners. This picture was repainted for the new millennium in the six-part TV miniseries *Changi*, written by comedian John ('Rampaging Roy Slaven') Doyle and first broadcast by the ABC in 2001.

In Doyle's *Changi*, POWs were beaten, starved, mutilated and ultimately murdered by their captors, whereas the actual Changi 'in many ways could have been called a P.O.W.s' paradise', according to former Changi inmate Kenneth Harrison.[1]

At different points in the war, Australian prisoners were taken from Changi and dispatched to build a military airfield at Sandakan in Borneo while their officers and NCOs were held in Kuching; sent to work in factories and coal mines in Japan; and, most famously, used as slave labour to construct a railway between Thailand and Burma.

I had been interested in Changi and the Burma Railway ever since I first visited Singapore and Thailand as a backpacker tortoising my way through Southeast Asia in the late 1980s. When I discussed Changi with Peter Stanley on my radio show, Stanley said, 'Although Australians are obsessed with their military history, there are aspects which have eroded in public knowledge, and I think POWs of the Japanese is one of them. In 1947, if you went into the main street and said, "What do you know about Sandakan?" "What do you know about Kuching?" or "What do you know about Japan?" people would be able to tell you that this place was different to that place. Seventy-odd years on, that knowledge has eroded, so now the word "Changi" has come to encompass the whole prisoner-of-war experience. A lot of people I'm sure think the Burma–Thailand railway was somewhere near Changi: they have no concept that it was actually several hundred miles away. And that television drama from 2001 has not helped in this because it was called *Changi* but it was actually a completely fictitious and imaginary, exaggerated portrayal of the POW experience. So, as time goes on, people know less and less about the specifics.'

The idea of Changi as a place of horror is 'quite odd in a way', said Kevin Blackburn, an expert in POW history at the University of Singapore. In fact, only 850 men (fewer than one per cent of those captured) died in Changi, the running of which was left largely to the Allies. There were Japanese guards around, particularly to escort working parties, but it would have been possible for some prisoners to spend months in Changi and not see a Japanese face.

Blackburn thought the camp's reputation came in part from photos of ruined, skeletal bodies taken in Changi after the war.

'This type of visual image was enshrined in the national consciousness of Australians in particular,' he said. 'There were, of course, tropical diseases and unfortunate experiences in Changi, especially towards the end when the food became scarce.' But many of the POWs photographed in Changi had actually been abused and starved on the Burma Railway.

Discipline in Changi was maintained by Australian officers. The commander of the Australian prisoners, Lieutenant Colonel Frederick Gallagher 'Black Jack' Galleghan, wrote, 'Discipline was regarded as of paramount importance. Not only did the camp function more smoothly, but a high standard was necessary to prevent any gradual slipping in control of troops and performance of duty (e.g. hygiene) which may well cost lives. Discipline again saved many men from the illogical temper and brutality of the Japanese and from infringement of Japanese orders which would not only have resulted in Japanese punishment to the individual, but also in collective punishments upon the whole camp.'[2]

In other words, Australian officers ensured that Australian prisoners followed Japanese orders. The officers even had their own provosts patrolling the camps and keeping order among the men. According to former Changi inmate David Griffin, Galleghan's 'strict orders – thought by some to border on the absurd for a prisoner-of-war camp – saved countless lives', although it is not clear that the 1500 Australian civilian detainees of the Japanese in Singapore, most of whom survived the war, suffered and died disproportionately as a consequence of not being under Australian military command.[3]

Cultural life in Changi was surprisingly rich and, like the rest of their generation but more so, the POWs made their own entertainment. Sports were extremely popular. Among themselves, prisoners boxed (until boxing was banned) and played tennis, and organised teams to play Australian Rules Football, cricket, rugby union, baseball, basketball and soccer. But sport was not confined to the inmates. In his book *The Sportsmen of Changi*, Kevin Blackburn points out that 'Japanese guards refereed POW boxing matches and Japanese commanders gave prizes to the winners of bouts. A soccer-loving Japanese guard played in a team alongside the POWs in Changi's soccer league. The winners of the Changi baseball series, the Australians, led by cricketer Ben Barnett, faced and beat a team of Japanese. A basketball team of Korean guards was also soundly beaten – by the Australian team that went on to win the Changi competition.'[4] This is a difficult reality to square with the myth. Prisoners at Changi were (slightly) more likely to play sport with Japanese soldiers than be beaten to death by them.

Many of the more educated prisoners took the opportunity to teach, and others found they suddenly had the time to learn at

'Changi University'. 'So high were the qualifications of the tutors and instructors at Changi University, that we were told that any awards and diplomas granted at Changi would be recognised by any outside university,' wrote Kenneth Harrison.[5] He remembered 'courses on bookkeeping and the Theory of Music; lying on the grass in the moonlight listening to Der Rosenkavalier; evening meetings when we discussed every subject under the sun and solved all the ills of the world', but also 'lectures from medical men who assured us that if we were not released within twelve months, we would be either sterile or mad'.[6]

John Doyle was the first to admit that *Changi* was not representative of historical reality. In his introduction to the published screenplays for the show, he wrote that it was originally conceived as a situation comedy that would 'do to Japan what *Hogan's Heroes* had done to Germany'. Doyle's Changi 'bears little resemblance to the real Changi [which] was more or less a holding camp from which men were taken to various locations to work as slaves,' he wrote. 'In this context, Changi was seen as a holiday camp.'

Doyle was most heavily criticised – by Peter Stanley, in particular – for the final episode of *Changi*, which is set at the end of the war, when the prisoners are told they will all be killed the next morning. Come daylight, they are rounded up and shot, the wounded are bayoneted to death and the luckiest flee while the camp records burn.

In real life, writes Blackburn, 'The POWs and the guards simply waited for the Allies to return. The Japanese at Changi ... made no official announcement of the surrender. The POWs knew from their secret wireless sets that the war was over. Instead of shooting the POWs, the Japanese merely handed over to them the large number of Red Cross food packages and clothing supplies that they had denied them for years.'[7]

But Doyle was not trying to recount history and he had no obligation to stick to the facts. Arguably, as a writer, he had a duty to make things up to serve his higher artistic purpose and illuminate a deeper truth, which was, as he put it, that 'Australian humour and mateship allowed Australians to survive in greater numbers than other groups of prisoners'.

The problem is it did not, and they did not.

Before Doyle's miniseries, the best-known dramatic representation of POW life in Changi was the American movie of James Clavell's 1962 novel, *King Rat*. Some of the more famous photographs of Changi show listless skeletal men with sunken eyes, dressed in rags like concentration camp survivors, obvious victims of starvation and deprivation. However, the majority of these men lost their health and vigour on the Thai–Burma Railway and actually came to Changi to recover. For those men who had slaved on the hammer and tap in Hellfire Pass, Changi was a place where they could put on weight, rest and recuperate. It was only after 1944 that food in Changi itself fell into very short supply, and those are the desperate days that form the backdrop to *King Rat*. The movie caused controversy when it was released in Australia in 1965, because of its depiction of Australians as the camp's most accomplished criminals and black marketeers.

King Rat's American hero, Corporal King, comes up with a scheme for the prisoners to breed rats to sell as food to their officers. He approaches the shady Australian prisoner-crook Gurbels and says, 'You Australian thieves are the only thieves who can supply in bulk. I'll tell you what I'm prepared to offer. You can buy all the cages we need, and whatever the profit is, we'll cut you in for 50 per cent of the action. Interested?'

The Myths of the POWs

'Well, yeah,' says Gurbels, 'it sounds like a proposition.'

An angry question was tabled in federal parliament by the Country Party member for Mallee and former POW Winton George Turnbull. He asked 'whether the film *King Rat* currently being screened in Australia is a true record of events in Changi prison camp, Singapore, or a money-making project to the detriment of the reputation of many Australians and others who served in Malaya and who were imprisoned in Changi'.

King Rat is virtually forgotten in Australia today – although Blackburn still shows extracts to his students in Singapore – but the thrust of the movie continued to pain the wonderful journalist Martin Flanagan as late as 2005. Flanagan, whose father was a POW at Changi and on the Burma Railway, wrote that he was concerned about what *King Rat* 'obscured in the popular imagination', which was 'a vitally important Australian experience'.

Flanagan's father had spoken often of the POW leader and surgeon Edward 'Weary' Dunlop, an unimpeachable war hero who was repeatedly beaten and tortured by the Japanese for insisting that his sickest and most vulnerable men should not be put to work, and who persuaded sometimes reluctant Australian officers to contribute funds to buy medical supplies for the other ranks.

'Basically,' wrote Flanagan, 'the Weary Dunlop story is the opposite of *King Rat*. What Dunlop demonstrated was that in the most barbaric circumstances civilised standards can still be maintained, the sick can be cared for, the strong can help the weak, the rich (or those with any money at all) can help the poor', whereas in the world of *King Rat*, 'the man who best looks after himself is king'.[8]

Australian prisoners of war of the Japanese were different, said Prime Minister John Howard at Kanchanaburi War Cemetery in Thailand on Anzac Day 1998. They were different because they had mates: 'Mates,' he said, 'who would carry a man's pack or his body when pain or fatigue became too much. Mates who would break all the rules or give up their own meagre rations to a friend in need. Mates who listened to last words whispered from dying lips... Mates who contained their fear but freely showed their courage and strength.'

John Howard was always keen on mateship, which struck me as a bit odd since he seemed like the Australian prime minister who was least likely to have any mates. It's hard to imagine Howard rocking up at the local RSL at the end of a thirsty day's speechmaking and slipping into a school with the boys at the bar – let alone breaking 'all the rules' like the diggers in the camps.

Howard was addressing, rhetorically, a question which he claimed had been posed at an unspecified time in an unknown place by an unnamed English officer, who was amazed to see exhausted Australian prisoners trudging back to camp from a day of back-breaking slave labour, *singing*. In the rain.

'Just what is it that these Australians have?' the officer supposedly asked.

'The answer,' Howard revealed, 'was each other.'

And as we saw during the First World War, the English – particularly English officers – have never understood Australian soldiers, and were not the kind of men who might sing together or have mates.

I first visited Kanchanaburi about a decade before John Howard, and this is perhaps the only time that Howard might be described as having followed in my footsteps. Kanchanaburi is the town at the Thai end of the Thailand–Burma Railway, and the home of the Bridge on the River Kwai. I remembered watching David Lean's classic 1957 war movie *The Bridge on the River Kwai* when I was a child, and I saw it again in Kanchanaburi, because *The Bridge on the River Kwai* played every night in every budget guesthouse. I visited

The Myths of the POWs

the town's World War II Museum with its horrific diorama of an unknown war crime: the massacre of Australian and British POWs, herded by their Japanese captors onto the bridge on the river as it was about to be bombed by Allied planes. Plaster figures of naked men lie bleeding and tormented in brackish water as friendly bombs rain upon their skeletal bodies. It is as if the dead have been dragged to Hell to be murdered again.

I never forgot the awfulness of what I saw. It stuck in my head, occasionally crying out to me, and many years later it re-emerged as my second novel, *Spirit House*. Before I finished the novel, I went back to Kanchanaburi and the World War II Museum. I looked again at the exhibit that showed the prisoners strafed by their own air force. Captions on the cabinet described the tragedy: 'They waved their hands stopping the said aircraft from going to bomb the bridge ... in vain ... The bridge got broken into pieces in a twinkle of the eye, together with the lives of those hundreds of prisoners of war who suddenly rank [*sic*] and disappeared in the torrent ... The whole of the river turned red with the blood gushing forth from the bodies of those prisoners of war ... The water of the River Kwai turned non-potable for several days because of the stench of the corpses.'

No Japanese soldier was ever brought to justice for these killings on the Kwai. This used to sadden and anger me, but it does not anymore.

Because the killings never happened. Pretty much the whole museum is a fraud.

Elsewhere in the galleries rest the remains of '104 of the prisoners who worked on [*sic*] labourers in World War Two', including two reconstructed skeletons. Their bones used to be dressed in Allied uniforms, until protests forced their removal because the bodies did not belong to Allied POWs. They were the skeletons of Asian 'coolies' – probably Tamils – who died in much greater numbers than the POWs, but never wore a uniform except in death. Their bodies were found in a mass grave near Kanchanaburi Town Hall in 1990 and their bones were purchased by the World War II Museum's Thai owners.

The museum is like a pardoner's reliquary, stuffed with fraudulent bones. It is an affront to the intelligence, an insult to the fallen, and no help at all to the pilgrims who come to Kanchanaburi to honour the Allied war dead.

Whereas the Japanese occupation of Singapore is studied in Singaporean schools, the Japanese domination of Thailand 'doesn't really feature in their national history at all', said Blackburn. The Burma Railway is 'seen as something that's just for tourists'. And this had led to the grotesque distortion of the POW story in the World War II Museum, the farcical trade in nearby markets where stalls sell stills from Lean's film passed off as photos from the prison camp, and a road sign pointing to the war cemetery that promises a 'feel *goood* journey'.

Northwest of the river, beside the graveyard where the remains of 7000 Allied POWs are buried, is the Thailand–Burma Railway Centre, whose Australian founder, Rod Beattie, once managed the cemetery for the Commonwealth War Graves Commission. An engineer by profession, Beattie is acknowledged by both academics and ex-POWs as one of the world's foremost experts on the railway. He said the World War II Museum is 'just awful . . . absolute rubbish'.

Most of what people think they know about the Thailand–Burma Railway and the bridge on the River Kwai is mistaken. The problem with Lean's work is that it seems like a true story. Protests from British ex-POWs preceded the film's opening in London. They feared the public would accept the drama as fact, and they were right. Foreigners came to believe there was a bridge on the River Kwai, so the Thais, rather than build a new bridge, renamed an old river. The bridge at Kanchanaburi actually straddled the River Mae Klong, not the Kwai. The stretch of the Mae Klong that runs through Kanchanaburi was arbitrarily made a part of the Kwai in the 1960s to please tourists who came to the area looking for the site of the movie, which was filmed in Sri Lanka.

The movie, in which British officer Colonel Nicholson, played by Alec Guinness, collaborates with his Japanese captors to build a better bridge, was based on a novel by Pierre Boulle. During the war, Boulle was a French secret agent captured and imprisoned in Indochina. His memoir of the period is entitled *My Own River Kwai*. Boulle's own River Kwai was actually the River Nam-na, down which he tried to raft to Hanoi, until he was apprehended by Vichy loyalists in Lai Châu in Vietnam.

The Bridge on the River Kwai won seven Academy Awards. Boulle won an Oscar for Best Adapted Screenplay, despite the fact that he did not write the script and could not even speak English. Drafts of the screenplay were actually authored by Michael Wilson and Carl Foreman, who were both blacklisted as Communist sympathisers and therefore could not take a screen credit in Hollywood.

In 1994, Rod Beattie was working as a gem dealer in Kanchanaburi when he heard that somebody was needed to clear the pathway to Hellfire Pass – a notoriously gruelling section of the railway where, according to the official Australian war history, sixty-nine Australian POWs were beaten to death by their guards – in advance of a visit by then PM Paul Keating. The maintenance of Hellfire Pass was nominally handled by the Australian-Thai Chamber of Commerce but it had 'just about fallen back into jungle', Beattie told me. As a private individual, he organised workers to clean up the trail. Spurred by a mix of expat's ennui, an amateur archaeologist's enthusiasm, and a technical interest in railways, Beattie took to looking after the path himself, and eventually became the official project manager of Hellfire Pass memorial work, paid by the Australian government.

He also independently set out to find the remains of dozens of jungle work camps that stretched from Kanchanaburi to the Burmese border, where the Thai side of the railway met a POW-built line from Thanbyuzayat, southeast of Rangoon. He did this clearing in his own time, at his own expense, fascinated by both the horror of the POW experience and the engineering achievement of the railway.

Before the war, the idea of a Thai–Burma railway had been canvassed by British, German and Japanese engineers, who had all discounted it because even with modern tools the jungle, the monsoons, tropical diseases, and the almost impassable terrain would make the job impossible without vast expense and huge loss of life. But tens of thousands of diseased, abused and starved POWs, and hundreds of thousands of coolies, began the project in June 1942 and finished it in sixteen months, largely with implements that wouldn't have looked modern in the Iron Age. And they died in large numbers. They died of cholera, of beri-beri, of malaria, of malnutrition and dysentery. What did not kill them, by and large, was the sadism of individual guards. According to Beattie, it is a widely held fallacy – first quoted in Lionel Wigmore's official history, *The Japanese Thrust*, and regularly cited since – that sixty-nine men were beaten to death at Hellfire Pass. In 1998, John Howard put the number at sixty-eight.[9]

'The true figure,' said Beattie, 'is one.'

Kanchanaburi gets a lot of tourists, most of them on short package excursions from Bangkok. They might get ten minutes in the cemetery, a boat ride under the bridge, and a baffling tour of

The Myths of the POWs

the World War II Museum (or the sincere but clumsy JEATH War Museum) before they are whisked off on an elephant trek or a visit to a tiger temple. Some come to see the graves of their fathers or grandfathers, to find out a little about how they lived and died, but local guides tend to know little and care less.

Beattie knows because, on his own initiative and using his own funds, he has consolidated death records, hospital records and military records held throughout the world, and has discovered exactly how and where every single Australian casualty of the railway met his death.

Most families of POWs have only a hazy idea of their relatives' experiences during the war, and their impressions are usually wrong. Many men believed to be murdered by the Japanese on the Burma Railway never even worked on the railway, Beattie told me. They were POWs elsewhere in Asia. Besides, he said, 'There were very few men beaten to death on the entire railway project.'

At the end of the war, a combined Australian, Dutch and British war-graves party had gone to Thailand and taken all the death records that had been compiled by soldiers, and, said Beattie, 'The Australian government made a decision in 1945 that the families would never be told what their relatives had died of.' In some archives, the death records have actually been stripped out. 'A lot of families believe these men were up here for three-and-a-half years, building a railway,' he said. 'No, they weren't. There were men here for five or six months ... and they were returned to Singapore as soon as they were fit to face the train trip.'

Beattie, an intense, compact man, energetic even in the tropical heat, had spoken to hundreds of veterans, travelled the world examining archives, entered material from countless handwritten documents into his own database, to try to reconstruct the death records – and, to an extent, the life stories – of every man on the railway. The vast majority died of disease. Dysentery was the biggest killer. Most of the men could have been cured with a handful of pills and cleaner living conditions, but the Japanese refused to help them.

They died from the brutality of neglect.

The most accomplished memoir written by an Australian former POW is Russell Braddon's *The Naked Island*, in which Braddon rails against both the cruelty of the Japanese and the petty militarism of Galleghan (who later commented that 'Russell Braddon's idea of how to run that camp was that it was to be like a town council, of which the mayor would be elected and all the rest of it. After all Russell Braddon was a private.')[10]

'Russell Braddon's book is one of the classics,' said Beattie, 'but if you believe Braddon, every POW got flogged every day of his existence. No, they didn't. If you meet enough of them, a lot of them will quite happily admit – once they know that you know a bit – that they were never beaten by the Japanese during their captivity, apart from a bit of face slapping. Or if they were, it was because they did something wrong and were caught. The vast majority of the prisoners were not beaten. The vast majority of the Japanese did not carry out beatings.'

Beattie used a tight definition of beating, and a generous characterisation of face slapping, but Blackburn supports his conclusions. 'Very few were bashed to death,' Blackburn agreed, 'but the Japanese were extremely negligent in looking after these men, and making men work who were unfit to work and eventually killing them through that process. When the Japanese talk about this and whitewash it, they say, "The men all died of tropical diseases." I think, "What? You couldn't do anything about the tropical diseases?"'

Beattie was particularly dismissive of the myth of the bridge, which gives Kanchanaburi its tourist cachet. There were two river bridges in the town, one made of timber, the other of steel. Some

3500 POWs built them over eight months, and only nine men died, due largely to the intelligent and careful leadership of the commander of the Allied prisoners, Philip Toosey, who came to consider his reputation unfairly damaged by Lean's film and a public identification of his own character with the fictional Nicholson.

Both bridges were destroyed by Allied bombing, although there were no prisoners standing on either at the time. (Some POWs were accidentally killed, however, when bombs hit their camp.) That which is now the bridge over that which is now the River Kwai is, like so much else, a postwar reconstruction, repaired by the Japanese with rectangular spans where the original bridge was curved. 'It looks nothing like it,' said Beattie.

When Beattie began his work, there were many more ex-POWs still alive: twenty men might turn up in Kanchanaburi on Anzac Day alone. Now they are all gone.

The story of the Burma Railway in Thailand is more British than Australian. The great sweep of line on the Thai side, from Kanchanaburi to Tarsao, was largely built by British prisoners. Kanchanaburi catered for British tourists in a miserable strip of bars. The Cheers Bar offered free pool, whereas the Candy Bar next door, either by accident or design, promised 'free pull'. A makeshift food stall sold chip butties and kebabs. When I was there, Beattie's Thailand–Burma Railway Centre was one of the few foreign businesses with any apparent integrity, and the majority of its visitors were Dutch.

About 18,000 Dutch POWs helped to build the Thailand–Burma Railway and more than 2700 died. *The Bridge on the River Kwai* was a huge hit in the Netherlands, even though it shows nothing of the Dutch experience. The Dutch prisoners tended to be judged harshly by Australians. The Australian journalist Tony Wright wrote that the leadership of Weary Dunlop and the forty-three other Australian POW doctors who worked on the railway is 'credited with Australians experiencing the least-dreadful proportional death toll of all the nationalities – British, Dutch and Southeast Asian, principally – who were forced into slavery in the jungles of Burma (now Myanmar) and Thailand ... Dunlop insisted that Australian officers pool the little money they possessed to purchase medicine and fresh food on the black market along the River Khwae Noi, unlike many British officers who stood aloof from ordinary soldiers.'[11]

Tony Wright is a better journalist than me, but he is mistaken about the comparative death toll of the different nationalities on the railway and overly generous to Australian officers. 'The old myth is that the Australians survived far better than anyone else,' said Beattie. '"The Poms, oh, their officers were hopeless, they were dirty, and they died like flies. And the Dutch, they were just so despicable" ... The reality is the British and Australian death rates are almost identical, and the Dutch survived far better than either. The British and Australians died of cholera in large numbers. On the entire railway, we had seventeen Dutch die of cholera. Tropical ulcers took out huge numbers of Australian and British, and almost no Dutch. Why? Because they knew of local conditions, were experienced in tropical medicine. Many of the Dutch troops on the railway were of mixed blood, they were Eurasian soldiers who'd lived their entire lives in the Far East. They knew how to eat, survive, behave and treat their people. The British didn't and the Australians didn't.'

In fact, if the tremendous death rate of one party sent from Changi is taken out of the calculation – the mixed-nationality F Force, in which one-third of the British contingent was already sick – then for the rest of the railway, the British survival rate was far better than the Australian.

Survival on the railway often depended on when you arrived, where you were, and who was in charge of your camp. 'You had good Australian officers and bad Australian officers, good and bad Brits,' said Beattie. All the Australian POW autobiographies talk about the importance of mateship to the diggers' survival. 'But the British had mates,' said Beattie, 'the Dutch had mates, and they all wrote about their mates. You had to have a mate to survive, regardless of nationality.'

Joan Beaumont argues that rank made an enormous difference to an Australian's experience of captivity. 'This doesn't sit well with Australian mythology and belief in the value of egalitarianism,' she told me. 'Nor does it fit with what most people think about the Japanese respect or disrespect for international law. There were indeed many provisions of the Geneva Convention that the Japanese didn't observe, but one that they did observe – generally – was not forcing officers to do manual work. The film *Bridge on the River Kwai* would lead you to believe that was not the case, and there were places along the railway where officers, in small numbers, *were* forced to do manual labour, but in most other camps they were not. And it's clear that very few officers, if any, died of disease and malnutrition. Even in the worst camps. And I think that's because – and I'm not suggesting they were having a good time, or that conditions were at all tolerable – they didn't have to go out to do manual labour. And at the height of the building of the Burma Railway, some POWs were working very long hours, eighteen hours a day, walking back in the dark to their camp, hardly getting any food, and suffering, of course, tropical diseases, leg ulcers and so on. I think it's probably fair to say that to work or not having to work was the difference between life or death. And the officers, because they didn't have to go and do that work, survived. And I was struck, when looking at the records of F Force, that very few officers actually offered to take the place of the men in the work gangs. But it might have made a lot of difference to some of those men if they'd been given three or four days off the very ghastly and exhausting working conditions.'

A handwritten memoir by Private Alexander Hatton Drummond of the 2nd/29th Australian Infantry Battalion survives in the archives of the Australian War Memorial, along with a fat, transcribed diary of Drummond's POW years. The author, who had worked in the publishing department of the Melbourne *Truth* newspaper, relentlessly and furiously attacks Australian POW officers who, in his view, consistently and cravenly put their own interests ahead of the welfare of their men. He calls his book *The Naked Truth*, in contrast to Braddon's *The Naked Island*.

In Drummond's eyes, the officers were often little better than looters and collaborators, and the regime which they created and maintained was responsible for some of the worst hardships suffered by the men. He claims that Galleghan's attitude towards the Japanese seemed to be 'If you can't beat them, join them' and that, encouraged by Galleghan's example, 'the majority of officers . . . took the attitude that if the Japs gave them privilege and licence to exploit they were only too happy to do so'. Many POW memoirs include the insulting nicknames given by the prisoners to their Japanese guards. Drummond's memoir extends to the post-years, when a 2nd/29th reunion bestowed similar sobriquets on their own former officers: 'Mongrel Mal', 'Greedy Guts', 'Poison Bottle' and 'Satan's Shit'.

Drummond was particularly angry about the petty and sometimes brutal punishments doled out to hungry, sick and wretched soldiers in order to maintain a ragged parody of military discipline. He wrote that 'the A.I.F. Admin went to extremes in instituting punishment for any trivial offence [and] any criticism of the abuses being carried out by many officers and senior NCO[s] brought reprisals in an attempt to squash it'. The Australian military maintained its own jail within the POW camp. Drummond lists the offences of the doubly incarcerated Australian troops as including 'having a shirt button undone', 'smoking in a prohibited area', 'hanging washing on the line during prohibited hours', 'playing two-up', and injuring a pair of boots.[12]

Despite his contacts in the media, Drummond was unable to find a publisher for his work. However, he felt vindicated when, in 1946, the newspaper *Smith's Weekly* revealed the ultimately substantiated allegations made against POW officers of Gull Force, which had been deployed to Indonesia and incarcerated in Ambon and Hainan Island in China after the fall of Singapore. Prisoners in Ambon suffered the highest death rate of any cohort of Australian POWs, under the command of Lieutenant Colonel William John Scott, a former member of the proto-fascist New Guard. A postwar investigation made known that Scott had handed over his own men for punishment by the Japanese, who had obliged by flogging them with pickaxe handles and convulsing them with electric shocks. In October 1944 an Australian prisoner had been beaten unconscious by the Japanese then hung by his hands to sustain a further bashing. Prior to his punishment, the sick prisoner had been hospitalised while his offence had been 'investigated' by his own officers, and he had to be returned to hospital for a further seventeen days to 'recover' from the beating, which had caused his lower back to bruise brown and swell to twice its normal size.[13]

The diary of a junior officer was presented to the inquiry. It recorded the prisoner's offence as 'insolence to an officer ... a particularly bad case [which] to make matters worse ... occurred in the sight and hearing of a Japanese guard'.

The shattered POW's crime had been to use the officers' bathroom.[14]

Martin Flanagan had worried that there was 'no movie about Weary Dunlop', and wrote that his father feared that Dunlop would be forgotten. For Flanagan, any culture that could produce a man such as Dunlop had great cause for pride – and he was right, but Dunlop's contribution to the surgical care of the men of the railway has also been greatly exaggerated. A plaque at Hellfire Pass marks the spot where Dunlop's ashes were scattered and names him as 'SURGEON OF THE JUNGLE', which he was not and never claimed to be. Dunlop's *War Diaries* make mention of fewer than twenty surgical operations carried out in the field, not all of them successful. As the amateur historian Major M.D. Cobcroft has written, Dunlop's outstanding contribution to POW welfare on the Burma Railway lay in his talent as an administrator but, perhaps unfairly, 'MEDICAL ADMINISTRATOR OF THE JUNGLE fails to stir the heart anywhere near the extent that SURGEON does'.

The finest doctor on the Burma Railway was Albert Coates, senior surgeon to the AIF, who became chief medical officer of a 10,000-bed POW hospital in Thailand, where his patients included Dunlop himself. Coates is said to have amputated 120 gangrenous legs.[15] Cobcroft speculated as to why Dunlop is nationally feted but Coates, whose statue stands in his hometown of Ballarat, remains barely known. He pointed out that Dunlop's distinctive nickname, 'Weary', sticks in the mind whereas Coates's 'Bertie' is simply generic; that Coates worked on the Burma side of the railway while the majority of Australian POWs laboured on the Thai side; that Coates was older, shorter and introspective while Dunlop was younger, taller and an outstanding sportsman; and that Coates died in 1977 but Dunlop survived until 1993. 'Back in 1977,' he wrote in 2004, 'there was not the collective nostalgia for our national heritage that there is today.'[16]

Sometimes, the mechanics of mythmaking are not very complicated at all.

The Myth of No Poofters

That there were no poofters in 1914. That there were no poofters in 1942. That there were no poofters in Vietnam. That Bruce Ruxton could smell a poofter.

As we have seen, Anzac Day has been contested from every angle for more than a century, and you would have to be wilfully ignorant of history – or a Liberal minister with oversight of the history curriculum – to suggest otherwise. In the early 1980s, one of the gentler challenges to Anzac Day orthodoxy came from the Gay Ex-Services Association, a small group of pioneering activists led by RAAF Vietnam veteran Max Campbell.

The opposition to GESA was personified by Bruce Ruxton, a former soldier who was president of the Victorian Returned and Services League.

In 1982, GESA asked to lay a wreath at Melbourne's Shrine of Remembrance on Anzac Day.

'We won't have a bar of them,' said Ruxton.

We won't have a bar of them.

'In 1942,' said Ruxton, 'there were none.'[1]

Ruxton told *The Age*, 'I don't mind poofters on the march, but they must march with their units. We didn't want them to lay a wreath because we didn't want to have anything to do with them. We certainly don't recognise them and they are just another start to the denigration of Anzac Day.'² He had earlier speculated, 'Maybe they're too frightened to march with their old groups, maybe they're afraid they'll get raped.'³

By straight men.

At the Anzac Day service, Ruxton and others were photographed physically blocking GESA members from reaching the shrine.

The following year, GESA did succeed in laying a wreath, but in 1984 Campbell and his comrades were once again refused permission to honour their 'gay brothers and sisters'. Campbell said, 'We didn't want any hassle ... But the first reaction was just part of thinking that poofters don't join up and that they don't serve their countries overseas.'⁴

In 1982, Ruxton had declared that other troops would have been immediately aware of gay servicemen in the ranks. 'You know as well as I do they couldn't hide themselves,' he said. 'The men would get onto it straight away.'

In 1984, it was revealed that the previous president of the Victorian RSL, former RAAF officer Colin Keon-Cohen, had lived the last ten years of his life with his male lover, Alasdair Cameron.

By 1985, Campbell claimed thirty members for GESA, but expressed dismay that little had changed for gay people in the military. Brigadier Ross Buchan, Director-General of Service Personnel Policy, responded that there was 'evidence to prove that a practising homosexual in a group of servicemen helped reduce the group's cohesion and combat effectiveness'.⁵

GESA seems to have folded in 1986 'for fear of infiltration by those wishing to identify homosexuals still serving'. The next year, the ADF's Surgeon General was reported to have said that it could be necessary to uncover and remove homosexuals from the military because under stress they 'break down and try to hop in bed with someone else'.[6]

There were, of course, plenty of queer soldiers in the Australian army in 1942 (although Ruxton could not have known this, as he was still at school). There were queer Anzacs in the First World War, despite an assurance in the Official History that there was no significant evidence of 'moral perversion' or homosexuality in the 1st AIF or in Australia generally; hence the records could provide 'no contribution to the place of the homosexual in a total war effort'.[7] But queer soldiers were identified in Peter Stanley's book *Bad Characters: Sex, Crime, Mutiny, Murder and the Australian Imperial Force*, even though homosexual acts were illegal in Australia and prohibited in the army under rules against 'conduct prejudicial to good order and discipline'. Stanley found his evidence in disciplinary files. He wrote, 'The reports of the AIF's Egyptian provosts show a small stream of men charged with sodomy: in June 1918, five men in one month ... Local court records show at least two AIF men convicted of "feloniously committing the abominable crime of buggery" in bucolic Wiltshire.'[8]

And in fact, contrary to Ruxton's assertion, 1942–1943 could almost be seen as peak years for queer men in the Australian army. First came the fall of Singapore, which saw almost 15,000 surrendered diggers imprisoned among other Allied servicemen in Changi and other jails. As we know, Changi quickly became a centre of creativity, education and experimentation. An anonymous former Changi prisoner wrote lovingly of the ingenuity that powered the evolution of the drag aesthetic in Changi, as practised by the entertainers and musicians of the Changi Concert Party: 'Wigs ... were produced – blonde, brunette and redhead; sophisticated and lifelike, from the highly improbable raw materials of surgical hemp and the discarded sporrans of the excessively virile Scots. Make-up was non-existent and ersatz products, such as flesh tints made out of powdered clay and mosquito cream and eye shadow made out of chinagraph pencils, were applied with vicious effects upon the faces of artists until the pathology lab, in sympathy, went mad and produced results that Max Factor might have envied.'[9]

The actor, musician and Concert Party stalwart Slim de Grey remembered: 'As time went by in Changi the female impersonators became more and more conscientious about their make-up and they would not burlesque the thing. After a while you looked upon them as women. You knew that they weren't, but in that particular show you'd accept them. You'd say, well, that's the girl. You wouldn't laugh at her and she would look rather attractive.'[10]

Russell Braddon's biographer, Nigel Starck, wrote that 'on the Railway, and on the subsequent return to Changi, Braddon's emerging identification with homosexuality saw him mix increasingly with . . . "the arty crowd"' in the concert party, among whom he 'plainly felt comfortable'. Another of Braddon's POW mates, Jack Garrett, told Starck that Braddon had a boyfriend in Changi, as did 'most of the concert party chaps'. Starck asked Garrett how he could tell that Braddon was gay. 'You saw him kissing blokes,' said Garrett.[11]

Other POWs in Changi were disturbed by the stirrings of unfamiliar urges. 'I had always considered myself the normal male,' wrote Kenneth Harrison, 'and it was with a sense of shock that . . . I found in myself certain homosexual tendencies.' While Harrison felt no physical attraction to his mates, 'there was the urge for the companionship of one of my fellow men and the desire to be of service and share all things with him'.

Luckily, these aberrant desires were confined to soft, unmanly Changi. 'I was gratified and relieved to find that this temporary aberration vanished completely once we resumed the normal, hard P.O.W. work life,' Harrison wrote.[12]

Phew.

This type of occupational conversion therapy was apparently endorsed by the Allied officers who constituted the camp authorities. POW provost Eric Bailey said he was tasked with night-time vice patrols, as 'couples were known to be going to particular spots and indulging in homosexuality'.

He remembered: 'I was supposed to break it up, tell them to get back to their separate bunks or huts et cetera. On one occasion, it seemed to be getting so bad that the officers went to the Japanese and asked them would they give the soldiers some trenches to dig, some great long trenches ... and nobody was told what they were for. In actual fact they worked just to get rid of some of their energy. Others had to fill the trenches within a week or so, and then the men had to dig more trenches, and this was in an effort to stop this type of business.'[13]

Alexander Drummond wrote that the 'Changi Lovelies' used to meet in a car park around the chassis of a truck. 'With glorious long curly locks, dressed immaculately in female attire down to the last unmentionable, they minced about on their romantic missions ... Norma, Judy the Garland, Moonlight Aggie, Flossie the Flirt and many others won their way into the hearts of willing swains ... That they were not always kindly of nature showed out when they had tantrums. Norma, displeased at the ensemble the dressmaker made for him-her, stamped his-her feet in the approved female manner and with vibrant hatred exclaimed, "You beastly man/You are nothing but a cloth-butcher."'[14]

The largest known community of queer Australian servicemen in the Second World War was in Port Moresby in New Guinea. The men – who called themselves 'girls' – came to the attention of the Commander of New Guinea Force Lieutenant General Sir Leslie Morshead when the US army passed on the information that Australian troops routinely engaged in 'the female side of homosexual intercourse' with their US counterparts. It was thought that up to fifty Australians were involved and, since the US army had just identified and evacuated queer elements in its own ranks, a situation might soon arise where 'the perverted desires of American soldiers' were 'satisfied mainly or wholly by "girls" from the Australian forces'.

It was decided that other suspects should be watched and interrogated, but disciplined rather than discharged – otherwise straight men might pretend to be queer to get out of the army. Records of extended interviews with eighteen of the 'girls' who surrendered themselves – in effect, outed themselves – survive in a file in the National Archives of Australia and offer a detailed picture of queer life in a place and time where it might otherwise have remained hidden. The file forms much of the Australian basis of Yorick Smaal's fascinating study *Sex, Soldiers and the South Pacific, 1939–1945*.

The surnames of the interviewees have been expunged, lending an oddly infantilised air to their accounts. On investigation, the Australian command had discovered that some men had become 'addicted' to homosexuality. One interviewee, 'Pete', tried over and again to give up sex with men, but it turned out he could not stop himself. Another, 'Ken', was unable to resist the urge to have sex with other soldiers, if they approached him first.

It seemed easy to find partners in New Guinea. One man discovered 'very early on that the opportunities were better and more consistent than before'. 'Gerard' cruised the US Red Cross canteen for sex. 'Jack' favoured the troops' canteen and the Sergeants' Club. Another man asked for a transfer because the company of other gay soldiers was interfering with his work: 'I was right in the middle of it in Moresby,' he said. 'It was impossible to keep away from the Kamp crowd, or to avoid going out with them and the Australian or American soldiers who picked them up.' Then there were 'truck parties' where the 'girls' had sex with groups of nominally heterosexual men, on the beach or in the bush; 'Eric' might have five or six men in one night.

'Girls' were always 'passive' ('bitches' rather than 'butches') and, according to 'Charlie', never had sex with each other. ('Charlie' himself preferred straight men.) 'Gerard' revealed that some Australian troops were bisexual while others 'just take us on to see what it is like, or because they can't get a woman'. There was, he said, only 'a sprinkling' of butches in New Guinea.[15]

In 1982, the year Ruxton denied the existence of queer soldiers in 1942, Queensland MP Bob Katter Sr, chairman of the Government Parties Ex-Servicemen's Commission, revealed that there had been none in 1972 either. In the last year of Australia's involvement in the Vietnam War, Katter had served a brief and undistinguished term as Minister for the Army in the brief and undistinguished government of William McMahon. During his ten months as minister, Katter claimed, he was 'advised on background character information' about Australian Vietnam veterans 'and he was able to 'give an unqualified assurance to the Australian people that it would have been very difficult indeed to find any soldier with homosexual inclinations'.[16]

But it was the experience of gay national servicemen in the Vietnam War that prompted my interest in LGBTIQA+ people and the military. I sought out gay veterans for my study *The Nashos' War* because I was absorbed by the sociology of military life at Nui Dat and Vung Tau, and I wondered how gay men might have fitted in. Despite Katter's 'unqualified assurance' to the contrary, it was easy to find them.

Australia first sent an Australian Army Training Team into Vietnam in August 1962. The RAAF established a small presence southeast of Saigon in Vung Tau, in August 1964. In December 1964, mindful of the looming threat to the Australian protectorate of Papua from President Sukarno's Indonesia, Prime Minister Robert Menzies introduced selective conscription to quickly increase the size of the Australian army. Potential national servicemen were chosen for consideration by a birthday ballot, which was unkindly dubbed the 'lottery of death' once it became clear that the threat from Sukarno had passed and the 'nashos' might instead be sent to Vietnam.

It was pretended that South Vietnam had asked for Australian assistance against the local Viet Cong guerillas and the People's Army of North Vietnam, and that communist aggression could translate into a direct threat to Australia. In fact, Menzies' primary goal was to encourage the US to remain involved in the defence of Southeast Asia after the British had left the region.

In 1965, an Australian infantry battalion, 1RAR, was dispatched to join US troops in Biên Hòa. It was made up entirely of regular soldiers. Every subsequent Australian battalion sent to Vietnam was based at the 1st Australian Task Force in Nui Dat, Phuoc Tuy province, and comprised about 50 per cent national servicemen and 50 per cent regular soldiers. Logistics and support troops built their camp in Vung Tau, beside the RAAF. Vung Tau was also a centre for in-country leave, known as R&C (rest and convalescence), for the Australian military. The Royal Australian Navy's involvement in Vietnam consisted primarily of ferrying troops from Australia to Vung Tau on HMAS *Sydney*.

There should not have been any gay servicemen in Vietnam, since homosexual behaviour had become a specific, dischargeable offence in the army in 1944 – and yet there was. And, as gay men, they were in Vietnam voluntarily because, like so many straight men, they wanted to fight a war.

There is a popular picture of the horrors of Vietnam: isolated platoons of inexperienced soldiers hacking through rainforest, always in danger of stepping on a mine or activating a punji trap, never certain if the local people are their allies or their enemies. Unwilling conscripts were forced to fight alongside hard-bitten regular soldiers, every man counting down the days until he could return safely to his loved ones back home.

However, some men had a very different experience.

'Nui Dat was paradise for a gay man,' wrote David Bradford, a young doctor who served in Vietnam from 1967 to 1968 as a regimental medical officer with the Artillery. 'Good-looking, well-built young men were everywhere, mostly wearing very little during day-light hours – just shapeless Army shorts, socks and boots. There were no women, and it was always hot and airless under the rubber trees. During the day, few soldiers or junior officers ever wore shirts ... Some gunners vied with each other to develop the best "all-over" sun tan. On a medical visit, I might arrive at a gun site to find gunners lying totally naked in the sunshine. It was distracting, but I couldn't help being inwardly delighted.'[17]

I spoke to Bradford, who said he was religious and a virgin when he joined the army. But he knew he was gay. 'And I have to say that that played quite a big part in my thinking,' he said. 'Looking after young soldiers did really appeal to me. And because I was an evangelical Christian at the time and because homosexuality was anathema to anyone who was a committed Christian, I felt that perhaps one way I could sublimate these urges that I didn't seem to have a lot of control over would be to spend my time looking after the people who I found most attractive. It was a kind of mental gymnastics reaching this conclusion but, for the time, it seemed to help me.'

An openly gay soldier would have had an unpromising future in the Australian army in the 1960s. If a man was caught having sex with another man and he did not respond to medical treatment aimed at 'curing' his 'problem', he would most likely be given a pragmatic discharge on medical grounds.

'I thought, Well, I'm not acting on it,' said Bradford. 'I'm not going around saying I'm gay. I'm not in any way indicating to any of the soldiers that I'm looking after that I'm gay. And if you don't talk about it, and don't tell anyone – and hardly admit it to yourself – I thought, Well, the army's not probably going to be very interested. Which, indeed, proved to be the case.'

Noah Riseman, co-author of *Serving in Silence?: Australian LGBT Servicemen and Women*, interviewed about a dozen gay or bisexual men who had served in Vietnam; he also found one transgender woman, who declined to participate in his study. While researching our respective books, both Riseman and I heard of several other gay Vietnam veterans.

'The Air Force seems to have been attractive to gay and bisexual men, historically and in the present day,' Riseman told me. 'I still, for the life of me, cannot tell you why that's the case. For army men – and army men posted at Nui Dat especially, [it was] very rare that there'd be sexual opportunities. The Navy guys? They certainly had opportunities on the ships. Sometimes with other sailors. Sometimes with soldiers who they were transporting to Vietnam.

'One Navy veteran, Wally Cowin, talks about being able to use the Oh-you're-going-off-into-a-warzone-and-you've-never-had-sex-before as a way to entice some men into it,' said Riseman. 'So it varied across the services and it had a lot to do with where you were posted and also, a little bit, with your rank. Officers would have a bit more privacy so officers would have a bit more opportunity.'

Riseman had interviewed Brian McFarlane, a queer career infantry officer who grew up in a religious Catholic family in Sydney and whose time at Nui Dat overlapped with David Bradford's. From June 1966, Major McFarlane commanded C Company, 6RAR, elements of which were involved on the fringes of the Battle of Long Tan. He told Riseman that he could name nine other gay officers who served in Southeast Asia during the war. 'Most people thought I was gay,' said McFarlane, 'and also thought I had a fair bit of money, and a lot of contacts. In a lot of ways, that probably helped ... But overall, on the gay thing, I didn't want to be put upon, so I just toughed it out and said to myself, "Well up yours, I don't give a stuff what you think."'

On the whole, McFarlane was more concerned with shooting other men than making love to them. 'I believe that the Defence Force is there to kill the enemy, and keep Australia safe,' he said, and his vocation was more important to him than his sexuality throughout his career.[18]

Riseman put me in touch with Leon Fry, who had served in Vietnam with 9th Squadron RAAF. Fry told me that he'd had his first gay sexual experience at thirteen. He knew homosexual behaviour was an offence in the services and yet he joined without qualms. 'I was gay,' he said, 'I knew that, I couldn't change that, and I wanted to be in the Air Force. So I chose to try and live with it. I wanted to be in Vietnam, I wanted to be a returned guy and march down the street.'

At Vung Tau, 'You ate, lived and shat together,' said Fry, 'so people saw everything that went on. It was very lonely for a gay guy. I became very insular. But I tried to maintain a friendly, outgoing facade for the other people. It was quite difficult, but it was a matter of life preservation for me.'

There was a documented gay scene among US troops in Vietnam. 'I ran into it once,' said Fry. 'I was in a club one night – because they were on the same base as I was – and this guy latched on to me and I thought, Mm, very nice. And he said, "I'll get in touch with you, and we might have a night out one night." I said, "That sounds pretty good." He contacted me a couple of weeks later and he said he'd pick me up by the time I finished work on Saturday night.

'He had a jeep, there were two other friends with him. They were in uniform because the Yanks had to always wear uniform and no civvies. I was in civvies.' The Americans had booked into a hotel in Vung Tau, and Fry 'went in there expecting just to be with this guy and I found out the situation was totally different, and I was the trick for the night and I was trapped. I resisted what was going on, had a few drinks, and eventually they took it in hand and I was raped by the three of them. And then he took me back and dumped me back at the base.

'It affected my life badly,' said Fry. 'I came back that night and I got absolutely plastered. The next day I did too, to try and forget what had happened, because there was no way I could tell anybody or do anything without exposing myself. I had to learn to live with it.'

The need to conceal their sexuality had repercussions in all areas of the lives of gay men who had volunteered to put their country before themselves. The threat of discharge meant that Fry could not report his rape to his officers. The double life he led meant he could not even tell his mates.

There were no national servicemen in the Navy or the Air Force during the Vietnam War, but about one-third of Australian soldiers who served in Vietnam were conscripts, including an unquantifiable number of gay men. This is problematic for those who believe nashos were reluctant soldiers, as any man could avoid conscription if he could convince the doctors he was queer. In 1968, the Draft Resisters' Union published a short pamphlet entitled 'How Not to Join the Army'. One of its recommendations was 'BE GAY':

The Myth of No Poofters

'Play the homosexual bit ... Wear white slacks ... [This, of course, was a sure sign of homosexuality.] Have your hair cut rather camp, wear a charm. Visit a couple of camp pubs and study homosexuals. Learn the gestures, the wrist movements. And the delicate body movements, how to touch the fellow you're talking to suggestively, how to smoke a cigarette. Be a little pathetic, talk melodically, act embarrassed in front of other inductees when you undress.'[19]

As everyone knows, the history of any war – with the possible exception of the Emu War – is most likely to be told by the winners, and a curious consensus has arisen in Australia that the winner of the Vietnam War was the anti-war movement. So we tend to see the war through the eyes of those who opposed it, and we've come to believe that national service was despised and that young men would go to any length to avoid it. In fact, many were happy – even anxious – to be taken into the army.

There's a further complication when it comes to remembering gay servicemen in Vietnam, particularly those who were enthusiastic about the war: Australia's gay liberation movement, which took off in the 1970s, borrowed at least some of its organisational cues from the anti-war movement. Its most prominent early leaders included anti-war activists. To them, national service and militarism were part of the same oppressive system as racism, sexism and homophobia. Other gay men sometimes saw things differently. For them, the army offered a chance to learn or grow, or simply get out of a rut.

The first gay nasho I found was David Collyer, a public servant from Melbourne who was both actively queer and actively Christian. Collyer was drafted in 1969 and served briefly with 2RAR in Vietnam in 1970. He later published a short memoir, in which he recalled the day in recruit training when he had to strip his rifle blindfolded and was told to love it 'more than a woman'. 'Well, that bit wasn't too hard for me,' he wrote.[20] His infantry training took place in Townsville, where he found no gay men in the army. 'Mind you,' he told me, 'I did make full use of the uniform – only when I was off duty.'

He wrote, 'The others probably thought I was off to a Prayer Meeting or Bible Study. And sometimes I was. But more often than not, I'd get dolled up in my finest and head off down to The Strand in Townsville and simply take my choice of the passing parade of meat ... No-one back at Lavarack ever knew that one of my pairs of trousers had the bottom neatly cut out of the pockets. This made things very simple for someone I fancied to simply slip his hand in my pocket to sample what was on offer. Then it was a very short walk either down onto the beach or in among the aerial roots of the banyan trees to get down to real business. Others were always welcome to join in too if they wished.'[21]

Collyer was preceded in Vietnam by the colourful Lorenzo Montesini, a conscript lance-corporal in the Medical Corps, who found the love of his life in Vung Tau, where he served in the 8th Field Ambulance and met Robert Straub, a national serviceman with the Royal Australian Army Dental corps. In basic training, Montesini had shared a hut with a man who cleaned all his gear naked, and there had been, he said, 'this feeling there was nothing wrong with that. We had certain *pruder*, as the French say, you wrap a towel or something. No, it was perfectly natural. It was also, for a gay, disconcerting.'

Montesini had planned to suppress his sexuality in pursuit of a kind of military-aesthetic ideal that would have him emerge from the war as a warrior poet. 'Then I had my ground taken out from my feet when this creature appeared and it was a sort of self-shattering,' he told me.

The 'creature' was Straub. 'Robert was in a sister unit – a brother unit, I should say,' Montesini told me. 'And I had seen him a few times and Rob was very attractive. I mean, as a male he was strong, good-looking in a strange sort of way, and he was a suburban boy who was engaged at the time. He had appeared three months after our arrival and there was something about him which arrested you. You meet hundreds of people, but someone stays with you.' A group of soldiers went into town for a drink, and Montesini sat next to Straub on the truck that took them back to base. 'I was a virgin at the time, in terms of male companionship,' said Montesini, 'and I was very aware of this presence beside me. Of course, we'd all fantasised – presumably – but this was different. I was aware that he was focusing on me.

'After that night, there was kind of a compact, a connection between us. And we were about to leave, and three days' before, one of the units gave a truck full of beer to our unit, because some of us were going home, and we of course demolished the beer. We were drinking and drinking, and we got drunk, and then we started playing hide-and-seek around the perimeter, in the sand – this was sand dunes – and Rob and I were together somehow, hiding, and I could feel this thing . . .' Montesini decided to go for a swim. 'I dove into the water and he came after me and we just played around, and before you know it, we were caught in this wave and we ended up in each other's arms. And in some ways we never left each other from that time on.'

So it was that for some soldiers, the Vietnam War and its aftermath was not a nightmarish orgy of death, destruction, genetic mutation and mental illness, but a gentle gay love story.

'Most people couldn't understand that killer thing in Robert,' said Montesini. 'In the gay world, he was supreme. He was an alpha. Mainly because of certain attributes of his, which are very important in the gay world. In the gay world, the phallus is the primal object of obsession, and he was Herculean. But it wasn't just that. He was very special . . . a damaged person but very special.'

I asked Montesini what he thought he had taken back from his national service experience. 'I took my own practical sexuality back,' he said, 'and I took Robert back, in some ways. Instead of sublimating it and becoming someone, I turned inwards, and we became small people. The adventure became an inward journey rather than an outward journey. We had a very interesting life.'

Montesini lived with Straub until Straub died in 1995. Major Brian McFarlane, after he left the army, lived for many years with a former RAN officer who was also a gay Vietnam veteran. David Collyer attended regular reunions and was accepted by his fellow veterans. 'They always shout, "Backs to the wall, it's Collyer!" when I come into the room,' he told me. 'They don't realise it's not their arses I'm after, it's their cocks ...'

But it's easy to see why Australia's gay Vietnam veterans have not been widely recognised. They do not fit into Ruxton's No Poofters school of historical thinking, which probably exists to make the point that gay men did not fight and die for their freedom in the same way as straight men – and therefore should be accepted only on sufferance, and not be encouraged to flaunt their sexuality in front of their betters. Ruxton was also expressing a wariness about modernity, and the hunch that all this homosexuality was little more than a fad, since it had not been around in the hyper-real days of 1942.

Nor can gay Vietnam veterans be eased into a narrative of gay liberation rising from opposition to the Vietnam War, since they were enthusiastic participants in that war. They do not fit into reductionist theories of intersectionality; they saw no commonality between themselves and the anti-colonialist Vietnamese.

I asked Riseman what the point of studying gay servicemen was for him.

'Because they've been forgotten,' he said. 'They haven't been recognised. And many of them were kicked out of the defence force because they were gay, and I think it's a shameful part of our past. But also it's a way of trying to reconceptualise our understanding of LGBTI history but also of Australia's military history, where the stereotype of the digger or the Anzac is of a white, bronzed, fit-looking, heterosexual cisgender male. My research is trying to point out, that's not true of all of them: there's actually a lot more complexity. But also this intersects with other parts of Australian history and by learning about their experiences in the Defence Force, we're also learning about their experiences in other parts of history. In the 1980s, David Bradford was running Melbourne's sexual health clinic at the time that AIDS appeared on the scene. He was one of a very small number of doctors in Melbourne in the 1980s who was treating AIDS patients. He was fighting it on the front line. And a lot of that he links back to his Vietnam service. Because it was in Vietnam he first was exposed to '*a lot* of venereal disease . . .'

In November 1992, the ADF dropped its ban on openly gay recruits. In 2022, the exhibition 'Defending with Pride: Stories of LGBTQ+ Service' opened at the Shrine of Remembrance, where GESA had twice been forbidden to pay its respects. Feted at the opening was RAAF veteran Phil Neil, the last surviving member of GESA's wreath-laying party of 1982. Today, the website of the New South Wales RSL expresses its backing for the Defence LGBTI Information Service, which advocates for and offers support to LGBTIQA+ servicepeople.

Soon open homophobia will become as socially unthinkable as open homosexuality used to be, and nobody will admit to ever having harboured the kind of violent and visceral anti-gay feeling that was commonplace as recently as the 1990s. But, like the queer soldiers themselves, it was there – and history makes little sense if it is overlooked.

The Myths of Victimised Veterans

That Vietnam veterans were spat upon (by women). That Vietnam veterans faced demonstrations when they returned to Sydney Airport. That Vietnam veterans were told not to wear their uniforms in the street for fear of antagonising protesters. That protesters attacked soldiers. That Vietnam veterans were not welcomed home until 1987. That postal strikes against the war delayed soldiers' mail in Vietnam.

Everybody knows that when Australian troops returned home from the Vietnam War, they were greeted by demonstrations at Sydney Airport, where they were spat on by women and branded as 'baby killers'.

Like many things that everybody knows, this is not true.

Everybody knows that the freshly returned veterans were human timebombs, irreparably damaged by the terrible things they had seen and done in the jungles of Southeast Asia, unable to readjust to civilian life and apt to explode into homicidal rages at the pop of an exhaust.

Because it stands to reason, doesn't it? Waging war wounds the warrior. A rifle (or a herbicide sprayer) has a victim at both ends. If we can all agree on that, then surely we will never again go to war.

Unless it's, like, absolutely necessary.

I first became interested in military mythology while writing *The Nashos' War*, a history of the national service scheme during the Vietnam era. I had read about attacks on veterans by protesters and I wondered how they might have been organised.

The story that interested me most of all – because it was the most dramatic and violent, and would have required the highest level of planning and commitment – was published first in a collection of veterans' writings to mark the National Reunion and Welcome Home Parade in 1987, and more widely showcased in Paul Ham's bestselling *Vietnam: The Australian War in* 2007.

The story is credited to 'Mike' from Perth, a national serviceman who served in the Royal Australian Artillery and flew home, relieved, in January 1970. 'At Mascot, the relief turned to anger,' wrote Mike. 'We were pelted with tomatoes and spat on. But we got our satisfaction afterwards – 150 toey, angry lads from Vietnam versus 400 demonstrators – they didn't stand a chance. The cops were very good about it. They seemed to be otherwise occupied for a while. It's impossible to describe what it feels like to have been away at war for your country and come home to that kind of treatment. It's something you never forget. Feeling as I do now about the whole thing I guess I could have been on the opposite side of the fence. But to be spat on and treated like shit, that's something else.'[1]

As well as never forgetting this incident, Mike never remembered it – because it did not happen. Mike's essay came out of a veterans' creative-writing class, whose participants were invited to create either fiction or memoir. Mike's story is fiction. A riot involving 550 people would have been one of the worst incidences of political violence in post-war Australian history, and the only time a large number of returned soldiers ever fought with demonstrators – at the country's major international airport, no less. Mike's story received no coverage in any newspaper, and nor did any story remotely like it. It is not mentioned in any history or memoir of the left. There is no trace of the organisation behind the demonstration, the logistics of which would have been fantastically difficult, given that the flight arrived last thing at night in the presence of military police. No other veteran has ever claimed to have been involved. The Qantas flight crews who manned the returning aircraft do not remember the battle. The official historian of Sydney Airport has never heard of it. There is no record of any participant having been arrested or injured.[2]

But the mechanics of the myth are less important than its meaning. In a few short lines, Mike's story encapsulates the majority of popular untruths about the anti-war movement and presents their sum as a cautionary tale. We read that returned men were pelted with food (they were not, but certain anti-war demonstrators were); that they were spat on (they were not, but certain anti-war demonstrators were); that there were demonstrations against returning soldiers at airports (there were not, ever, anywhere in the world); that the anti-war movement in Sydney had the capacity to secretly mobilise 400 demonstrators last thing at night to confront troops in a security area (it never tried); that demonstrators blamed the troops for the war (they did not); and that returned men took revenge upon demonstrators by beating them up in a massive brawl (they did not, although soldiers who had not yet been to Vietnam once attacked a peaceful protest in Adelaide).

What lies beneath Mike's unreliable narrative is the idea that the anti-war movement was much larger, more militant and more logistically capable than contemporary reports suggest, and that its target was returned men. His story also addresses the central problem with the spitting myth – that spat-upon soldiers would have been likely to batter their spitters into cracks in the ground: in this revenge fantasy, they do just that.

During my research for two books, a doctorate and a handful of magazine stories, I interviewed hundreds of Vietnam veterans and at least two men pretending to be Vietnam veterans (both of whom claimed service in the SAS). Almost to a man, the genuine veterans were thoughtful, generous, philosophical and humblingly perceptive. There were left-wingers and right-wingers, militarists and pacificists, nashos and regs. The nashos, in particular, were the cream of their generation (which is why they were selected for the army in the first place). They were dispatched by Coalition governments to a traumatising war, and their experience was later brazenly exploited by those governments' ideological heirs. I visited Vietnam three times, in what was to become, for me, a customary quest for insight into the past in places that had long since changed and moved on. Vietnam presented special difficulties. As soon as the Second World War ended, diggers returned to the battlefields and POW camps to retrieve makeshift crosses and small memorials, lost keepsakes and buried memories. But after the fall of Saigon in 1975, Vietnam closed its borders to the non-communist world, and it was impossible for an Australian veteran to go back for the things he'd left behind. The pilgrimages of former soldiers did not start until the late 1980s, when the Vietnamese government began cautiously to relax its restrictions on tourism.

By that time, there was almost nothing left of the veterans' war. Today, there is only a scattering of roads and wells, foundations and stones at the former base at Nui Dat; a replica cross at Long Tan; and the flickers of ghosts in the milky eyes of old men. What was once the faded and unlovely beach resort of Vung Tau – known to the Australians, inevitably, as 'Vungers' – a garrison town of camp followers and conmen, hand-job parlours, blow-job bars and brothels, is now an oil town, popular with riggers on their breaks, and a weekend destination for locals. It's also home, for at least part of the year, to perhaps a hundred Australian veterans who have married much younger Vietnamese women. They drink at bars such as Lucy's Sports Bar, Tommy's and Ned Kelly's, and relive their youth in both word and deed.

On a visit to the city, I spoke with Glenn Nolan, who owned three local bars and ran tours of Australian battlefields. 'It's a great little place,' he said, 'but we get people here for the wrong reasons: cheap beer and young girls.' He complained of pensioners 'brawling in the streets'.

Jimmy Thompson, a historian of Australia's combat engineers, or 'tunnel rats', has organised several veterans' tours to Nui Dat. The first time he went, he told me, he met an Australian former soldier, now resident in Vietnam, who was making his own nostalgic journey back to the base.

'They treat me better here than they did when I came back home,' he told Thompson.

Back then, I thought I knew what he meant.

The foundation myths of victimised Vietnam veterans in Australia were born, like so many other myths, out of Hollywood movies. The pivotal role of two particular films in helping to form the imagined memory of US veterans was first identified by the sociologist and Vietnam veteran Jerry Lembcke. When Lembcke returned from Vietnam, he joined Vietnam Veterans Against the War, an organisation probably best known for an action in April 1971, when it mustered 800 US veterans to throw their medals onto the steps of the Capitol building in Washington DC. Among the apparent medal throwers was future US politician John Kerry, who later claimed to have only tossed his ribbons.[3]

In Lembcke's book, *The Spitting Image: Myth, Memory and the Legacy of Vietnam*, he traces the idea that Vietnam veterans were spat upon back to the slurring invective of the fictitious John Rambo, played by Sylvester Stallone in the 1982 movie *First Blood*; and he ascribes the notion of airport demonstrations against returning soldiers to the 1978 Jane Fonda movie, *Coming Home*. In a later book, Lembcke argued that Hollywood movies 'made Vietnam veterans into political props for slandering the anti-war movement', and that the diagnosis of PTSD was formulated to pathologise dissident veterans. (*Look at those long-haired soldiers throwing away their medals! They must be mad!*)[4]

In Australia, there was no real movement of anti-war Vietnam veterans. While activists in the US attended demonstrations in military uniform, some Australian veterans have complained that they could not wear their uniforms in Australian streets for fear of being attacked by protesters, often women. And this did happen, but only once, in June 1966, when 21-year-old Nadine Jensen, a typist from Campbelltown in New South Wales, doused herself in red paint and kerosene and ran at the leaders of a homecoming march for 1RAR in Sydney, smearing two officers with ersatz blood. An estimated 300,000 Sydneysiders had turned out to cheer on the battalion, and only Jensen and a handful of banner-wavers in the crowd protested what was at the time a very popular war. Jensen, who belonged to no political party and was acting alone, was thought to be insignificant if not insane.

'My action was not so much against the soldiers but against authority itself,' she told a court. 'My action may have been wrong in that it should have been protesting against the Australian attitude of complacency.'

The Myths of Victimised Veterans

Jensen was fined £6, then disappeared from history for perhaps two decades. I cannot say for certain – as there may well be items I have missed, and there are many newspaper archives still to explore – but it is possible that Jensen was never again mentioned in a major Australian newspaper or magazine at any time during the Vietnam War. Although there was never another photographed demonstration at any one of the next fifteen welcome-home parades, nor one single verified account of veterans being accosted by protesters during the war itself, Jensen's actions later became seen as representative of the anti-war movement.

According to Gary McKay, a decorated veteran who has written a dizzying number of books on Australia's Vietnam War, 'The wearing of military uniform in Canberra was actually stopped for a long period of time when it was felt that the presence of uniforms in public would invite violence or embarrassing demonstrations against service personnel.'[5] McKay is wrong. It was not felt that the uniforms might 'incite violence', although officers were encouraged to come to work in suits since they were not permitted to wear uniform outside an army base in a social or commercial setting, and they might want to stop off for a drink on the way home, for example.

As for the idea that veterans might be spat upon, Lembcke ascribes it to a closing scene of *First Blood*, when former Green Beret John Rambo, holed up after his spree of justified vengeful violence, is cornered by his former commanding officer Colonel Troutman, who tells him, 'It's over, Johnny. It's over!'

'Nothing is over!' replies Rambo. After the war, he says, 'I came back to the world and I see all those maggots at the airport. Protesting me. Spitting. Calling me baby killer, and all kinds of vile crap. Who are they to protest me, huh?'

The last Australian troops came home from Vietnam in 1973. The first Rambo movie, *First Blood*, was released in 1982. There was not one single reported, recorded or otherwise publicly aired comment or complaint about an Australian veteran being spat upon until 1982. But that says nothing special about the Vietnam War. As we have seen, the movie *Gallipoli* transformed memories of Gallipoli in the minds of some First World War veterans. *The Bridge on the River Kwai* actually changed the accepted history and geography of Kanchanaburi in order to harmonise with the film. The TV show *Changi* helped fix the comparatively mild Changi prison camp as a Hell camp in Australian public memory.

But where did Rambo get the idea that there were demonstrations against Vietnam veterans at airports? None were ever reported in the US until the movie *Coming Home*, in which Bruce Dern plays a paraplegic veteran coming home (in this case) from the airport with his wife, played by Jane Fonda.

'Where's all the demonstrators?' he asks. 'An asshole on the plane told us there was going be a bunch of flowerheads out here.'

'Well, there are some kids out there,' says his wife, 'but they can't come on the base.'

Meanwhile, a small group of anti-war protesters circle the gate, chanting, 'One. Two. Three. Four, we don't want your rotten war.'

There were no reports of demonstrations at Australian airports until 1982, either, four years after the release of *Coming Home*.

Just to make myself clear – because I am sometimes thought to be using the wrong words by people who do not make much of an effort to choose their own – I am not saying that no Vietnam veteran *today* claims to have been spat on or demonstrated against at any airport during the war, because they do. I *am* saying that there is no record of these allegations being made in Australia in newspapers, in broadcasts, in letters, in diaries, in airline records, in Qantas records or in police records at any time between the beginning of Australia's

The Myths of Victimised Veterans

Vietnam commitment in 1964 until the local release of *First Blood* in 1982. Then the spit gates opened.

The spitting stories multiplied around the period of the National Reunion and Welcome Home Parade in October 1987, when about 22,000 men marched through Sydney to the respect and applause of a crowd estimated at 100,000–110,000. The stories were collected by Paul Ham in *Vietnam: The Australian War* in 2007 and presented as if they were more than the sum of their parts. History had already been turned on its head in the reporting of the 1987 parade. According to a *Canberra Times* correspondent, 'Fourteen years after the last Australian soldier returned from Vietnam, the Australian community finally gave veterans of the war the welcome home they had been waiting for.' It was as if there had been no previous parades or, if there had, they had been attended largely by protesters.

In fact, a total of about 11,000 soldiers had marched in the sixteen battalion welcome-home parades during the war years, and the turnout at the 1987 reunion was only a little more than one-third of the size of the crowd that had supported the famous 1RAR parade in 1966 – and only about one-fifth of the half a million people who had cheered for 7RAR in Sydney in 1968.

While several Vietnam veterans had expressed grievances in print before the publication of *Vietnam: The Australian War*, Ham's book rolled all the various complaints into a single package, which was then used as reference by other authors and journalists. One product of this process was the 2009 book, *Bomber: From Vietnam to Hell and Back*, a kind of augmented autobiography of former Australian army engineer Tony 'Bomber' Bower-Miles.

According to *Bomber*, when Bower-Miles and his cohort left Sydney for Saigon in October 1969, 'they boarded the plane in the middle of the night to avoid the protesters', although there were never any protests against troops leaving from Sydney Airport (even the idea had barely been suggested before) and the Qantas flight to Vietnam did not leave in the middle of the night (the idea that it did directly contradicts the more prevalent furphy that it *arrived* in the middle of the night).[6] While searching bunkers in the Long Hai mountains, Bower-Miles found 'medical supplies from Monash University' and 'he had no doubt that they'd been sent by campus radicals to the enemy'.[7] He made this confident assertion even though there would have been no way to tell who had paid for a medical kit, and even though no money had been raised at Monash for medical aid to the National Liberation Front since 1967.

Bower-Miles had only been in-country for a couple of months when Christmas came around and, as described in *Bomber*, 'The mood was sombre. The Mail hadn't arrived. The posties were on strike protesting the war. Letters from home were a cherished item, so there was no better way to hurt the soldiers than by cutting them off. And the posties were trying to hurt the soldiers.'[8]

In fact, there was no postal workers' strike in 1969, or at any time during Bower-Miles' tour of Vietnam. While there had been a postal workers' strike in 1968, it was not at Christmas and it had nothing to do with the Vietnam War. Postal workers never went on strike against the war, and when they took action over pay and conditions, inconveniencing businesses and the general public, they explicitly put into place measures to ensure that mail to the troops was unaffected. Delays to delivery were a perennial issue. Second-class mail and parcels had to be carried on service courier aircraft, as there was no direct commercial shipping between Australia and Vietnam. The Secretary for Army had suggested that many early holdups were caused by incorrect addressing of envelopes.[9]

When Bower-Miles came back from Vietnam in October 1970, the world had changed. There had been moratorium marches in the US and Australia, and the story of the massacre at My Lai had

The Myths of Victimised Veterans

broken: US troops had gang-raped, tortured, mutilated, robbed and murdered hundreds of unarmed civilians in two hamlets in Quang Ngai province in South Vietnam (although the full extent and pornographic detail of the carnage was not revealed until years later). After the murders at My Lai, according to Bower-Miles, Australian troops had 'suddenly' become known as 'baby killers' and 'that's why their mail wasn't getting through'.[10]

In fact, My Lai had nothing to do with why soldiers' mail was not getting through – if, indeed, it was not – and there is no evidence that Australian troops 'suddenly' became known as 'baby killers', and certainly not during the war itself. More civilians were killed in four hours at My Lai (504) than Australian servicemen were killed in battle (426) during the entire Vietnam War, and yet veterans' memoirs such as *Bomber* make the slaughter at that hamlet seem like something that happened to Australian troops, rather than something that was done to Vietnamese old men, women and children.

Later in *Bomber*, Bower-Miles' mate, fellow sapper Gerry Lyall, tells a strange story about his homecoming. When he returned to Brisbane, 'he was told that he shouldn't go into town wearing his uniform'. Determined that no-one was going to tell him what to do, 'he went to Town Hall Square and found himself in the middle of a moratorium demonstration'. According to the story, 'He was walking down the road, minding his own business, when he heard someone say, "There's one!" Next minute it seemed like the whole street had filled up with people running after him. He sprinted off like a member of the Beatles, but those long-hairs weren't throwing underwear at him. He ran into Rose Arcade on Adelaide Street, turned into a barbershop, took off his slouch hat and jumped into a chair. "For God sake, cover me up," he said to the barber. The mob ran rabidly by.'[11]

Aside from the fact that this appears to be a scene from some half-forgotten movie, the moratorium demonstrations in Queensland were extremely heavily policed. It is almost unthinkable that a group could break away to attack a lone soldier, unlikely they would even want to, and amazing the incident didn't reach the newspapers. More tellingly, Lyall arrived home from Vietnam on 29 October 1970, and the moratorium demonstrations had taken place the previous month, in September.

Some of Bower-Miles's assertions are so puzzling as to defy explanation. He speaks of his mate Rod Hubble being 'buried outside the war cemetery because Vietnam wasn't a war', when in fact Rod Noel Hubble, an engineer who was killed by a landmine in the Long Hai mountains on 22 February 1970, is buried in Perth War Cemetery, plot X, row D, grave 1.[12]

By the time *Bomber* was published in 2009, the first eight volumes of the magisterial 'Official History of Australia's Involvement in Southeast Asian Conflicts 1948–1975' were already on library shelves, but two of the handful of footnotes in *Bomber* refer to Ham's popular work and none reference the Official History.

At first, I felt that the reason some veterans believed they had been regularly attacked by female demonstrators was that the Nadine Jensen provocation served as a typical flesh-to-feeling story: the veterans felt under attack socially and ideologically, so they used the only substantiated incidence of physical assault to describe the roots of their mental trauma in a way that could be easily understood. Later, I realised that the protests the veterans came to 'remember' after 1987 were not the wartime moratorium marches (nor, as they sometimes seem to have been semi-reconstructed, the acts of the Save Our Sons movement), but the feminist mobilisations against rape in war that disrupted Anzac Day parades after the Vietnam War.

The Myths of Victimised Veterans

Although these protests were never specifically targeted at Vietnam veterans, Vietnam was slowly becoming known as a rapists' war, and Australian veterans have sometimes complained of being called rapists after My Lai. The first demonstrations against rape in war appear to have taken place in Sydney on Anzac Day 1977, when a small group of women held banners bearing slogans including 'U.S. SOLDIERS ADMIT TO MASS RAPE IN VIETNAM' and 'WAR IS THE BIGGEST GANG RAPE OF ALL'. In Perth, a woman was arrested at the dawn service in Kings Park when she attempted to lay a wreath 'to commemorate all those women raped by soldiers'. On Anzac Day 1978, there were anti-rape protests in Sydney, Canberra, Brisbane and Perth. In 1979, black-robed members of Women Against Rape picketed the Melbourne Anzac Day service under the slogan 'Remember Women Raped in the War', prompting the reliably moronic Bruce Ruxton to comment, 'When I look at them on television, I wonder how rape would be possible.'[13] (This stood in ambiguous contrast to Ruxton's later quip that gay ex-servicemen might be frightened of getting raped on Anzac Day.)

In 1981, sixty-four anti-rape protesters were arrested when they attempted to break through police lines and join the Anzac Day procession in Canberra. The next year, more than 500 women in Canberra staged their own march against rape in war before the official Anzac Day parade began.[14] In 1983, 168 women organised by the Sydney Women Against Rape collective were arrested for trying to march on Anzac Day in Sydney.[15] On Anzac Day 1984, seventeen anti-rape protesters were arrested in Melbourne, while others protested in Brisbane, Adelaide, Canberra and Perth; in Sydney, a woman styled as the 'Unknown Victim of Rape' was paraded on a stretcher in an elaborate ceremony supported by about 350 women.

On Anzac Day 1985, there were three arrests of members of Women Against Rape in Sydney, and in Melbourne a photograph on the front page of *The Age* showed a Vietnam veteran who had jumped on a truck carrying women from the Anti-Anzac Day Collective, unstrapped his artificial leg and thrown it at them. According to the report, the women shouted, 'You haven't got a leg to stand on,' which, if true, demonstrates that punchline comedy occasionally does play out in real life.[16] In 1986, a protest of about eighty women was hemmed in by police and mocked by spectators shouting taunts such as, 'Who'd want to rape you anyway?'[17] In 1987, *The Age* reported that women marching under an 'Abolish Anzac Day' banner were confronted by 'another group', and as the women with 'cropped and often dyed hair' sang 'One, two, three, four ... Anzac glorifies their war', their antagonists chanted, 'Kick all dykes to the floor!'[18]

It was the familiar story of women's initiatives being met with threats of violence from angry, contemptuous men. And while the various anti-rape and anti-Anzac campaigners are remembered (although not, obviously, by Alan Tudge) in the literature of feminism and Anzac Day, I have never seen another mention of those would-be dyke-kickers at the Melbourne march. Who were they? What did they do before and afterwards? Does the history of Anzac Day make sense without reference to the attitudes they embodied? Could queer history be better understood if they were included? Did the people who opposed the anti-rape demonstrators support the anti-anti-rape demonstrators? Or were the homophobes no more than an irrelevant sideshow, representing nothing and nobody but themselves in a particular moment? Whatever the case, the anti-rape demonstrations ended in the year of the National Reunion and Welcome Home Parade, leaving their memory fresh in the minds of veterans at the very point in time when veterans found both a national voice and a receptive audience.

The Myths of Victimised Veterans

The reactions to the demonstrations against rape in war offer a modicum of an idea of what would have happened if this type of protest had actually occurred in Australia *during time of war*. The demonstrations were reported in detail by major newspapers, often on the front page. Large numbers of women were arrested for simply disturbing, rather than assaulting, former servicemen, and both police and politicians responded to the women's protests with a vigour that would be unimaginable today. In the ACT special legislation was gazetted in 1981 to thwart the marchers; in New South Wales the police were granted a Supreme Court injunction in 1983 to prevent an anti-rape march, and Special Branch and the elite Tactical Response Group were deployed when the demonstration went ahead. And the fact that a 1RAR Vietnam veteran told his local newspaper in 2010 that 'someone from Women Against Rape in War threw red paint all over our commanding officer' in 1966 suggests that the rape protests and Nadine Jensen's action have merged in some veterans' recollections.[19]

While Women Against Rape helped return Jensen's stunt to the public memory, a larger role may have been played by the popular Australian TV miniseries *Sword of Honour*, which first aired on Channel Seven in October 1986, one year before the National Reunion and Welcome Home Parade. The show competently articulated a conservative view of the war for primetime television, and offered a right-wing hero in angry Duntroon graduate Tony Lawrence. The second episode opens with Lawrence marching proudly in his battalion's welcome home parade in 1967, applauded by a small crowd of respectable spectators and harangued by what appears to be an equal number of anti-war protesters. A nervous and deranged-looking man slips out of the crowd and hurls a bucket of viscous red liquid, which splatters the face of Lawrence, who falters but marches on as police brawl with the demonstrators. The bucketer looks far more like Peter Kocan, whom we shall meet later, than Nadine Jensen. He is not a woman, but he is doing women's work.

Fighting to the Finish, the final volume of the 'The Official History of Australia's Involvement in Southeast Asian Conflicts 1948–1975', was published in 2012, but surprisingly there was more to come. Perhaps the most remarkable fact about Peter Yule's 2020 work, *The Long Shadow: Australia's Vietnam Veterans Since the War*, is that a book published by the Australian War Memorial, and written specifically to ensure that 'the voices of veterans are heard', would reach such a comprehensively damning verdict on the war. The Australian commitment to Vietnam was based 'on an assortment of unproven assumptions and half-truths', writes Yule. 'Our armed forces were sent to fight in support of a corrupt military regime [which] received solid support only from the Catholic minority [and] the small landowning class. Few fought willingly for the regime.'[20]

It was once important to many Vietnam veterans that they should be recognised as having fought a just war, but Yule's characterisation of the conflict passed without comment at a time when the conduct of the war mattered less to veterans than its consequences.

The Long Shadow was a significant new episode in the history of the writing of the history of Australia's Vietnam War. Until then, there had been two distinct strands to that history – the academic and the popular. The former was best represented by the forensic, meticulous Official History – 'official' because its authors were allowed access to government archives – which takes pains to analyse and explain command decisions and public policy. The popular thread included partly folkloric life stories, oral histories and journalistic accounts. It described the war from the point of view of the grunt on the ground, who tended to see little but malicious, ill-informed incompetence in the actions of politicians and senior officers.

Academic histories generally shy from the biographies of individual 'ordinary' soldiers – each of which, obviously, is unique. The great flaw of the popular histories is that they often present spectacular statements as fact, simply because somebody once said them. *The Long Shadow* marks the point where these two strands met. It was researched and composed with academic rigour and free use of government documents, and at the same time showcases the uncorroborated, unmediated nature of many veterans' testimonies. Men describe events without giving them dates. They talk about others in their unit without using their names. One man offers a mortality rate for his infantry company with no indication of how the figure was calculated.

The *Long Shadow* has its own long history. It was written largely in response to the rejection by organised, activist veterans of the essay 'Agent Orange: The Australian Aftermath' by Professor E.B. Smith, which appears in the third volume of the Official History, *Medicine at War*, published in 1994. Smith's essay supported what Yule calls 'the official narrative': that is, the veterans were wrongheaded to pursue their claims about chemical poisoning – in particular, the ingestion of carcinogenic substances through the US defoliant popularly known as Agent Orange – because most Australian servicepeople were never exposed to Agent Orange and there is no proven link between other chemicals and the cancers and birth defects sometimes held to plague Vietnam veterans and their families. Moreover, those same cancers and birth defects are no more prevalent among Vietnam veterans than in the general population.

Many vocal veterans – whose campaigning was channelled through the Vietnam Veterans' Association of Australia and, later, the Vietnam Veterans Federation of Australia – were infuriated both by

Smith's conclusions and the language in which they were couched. They agitated to have the Official History rewritten to better reflect their own experiences, because some veterans did have cancers, and some of their children do suffer birth defects, and they desperately sought ways to understand their intimate tragedies and invest them with a wider meaning.

Veterans' leaders were further incensed by a plaque at the Australian War Memorial that endorsed the major finding of the Evatt Royal Commission on the Use and Effects of Chemical Agents on Australian Personnel in Vietnam – that Agent Orange was 'not guilty'. One activist veteran described this as 'a most devious, treacherous, and certainly a maliciously crafted exhibition of contrived falsification of fact and bloody reality by the AWM's Council'.[21] The charge seems to have stung the council and ultimately prompted it to commission Yule to write about the 'medical legacies' of the war.

'Whatever the rights and wrongs of the arguments about Agent Orange, any study of the post-war experiences of Vietnam veterans should have attempted to understand the sources of the feelings of anger and injustice that were widespread among many Vietnam veterans,' writes Yule.[22]

Is that the purpose of a medical volume of an official history? I'm not sure that it is, but it is certainly the overriding purpose of *The Long Shadow*.

The notion that Australian troops in Vietnam were poisoned by American chemicals has a delicious poetry for the left. Anti-war campaigners embraced the idea that the defoliant used by the US military to strip life from the jungles also left a legacy of devastation, disease and genetic mutation, not only in Vietnam, but in the bodies and minds of the hapless young men dispatched by heartless governments to fight an amoral war. Many former radicals hoped and believed that the case against Agent Orange would be proven at the Royal Commission. But the veterans faced a bottomlessly funded offensive by the US chemical company Monsanto, which enabled extravagantly paid corporate lawyers to tear shreds off the motley collection of sometimes inexpert experts assembled against them.

Commissioner Justice Phillip Evatt, who had begun the inquiry predisposed to the veterans' argument, eventually hit up against the science, which at that time could not be interpreted to support the Australian veterans' claims against Agent Orange.

Evatt saw tragic allegory in the veterans' case. He said, 'We sent the cream of our youth, with strong value systems and a belief in themselves and those values, to Vietnam. We trained them to kill men ... When they returned to Australia they were ostracized by many and any sense of purpose in the sacrifice evaporated. Is it any wonder they felt poisoned?'[23]

Reputable studies have repeatedly shown that the biggest medical issue disproportionately affecting Vietnam veterans – and which is indisputably, distinctly and uniquely linked to their war service – is not chemical-related cancers or birth defects, it is post-traumatic stress disorder. Objectively, it does not matter whether the veterans' problems are caused by enemy fire, American chemicals or army-encouraged alcohol dependence. But the guilt of Agent Orange was, essentially, a case for the left. In the absence of Agent Orange, what tends to emerge is a case against the left. Many Australians in Vietnam never saw combat, and yet support troops seem to suffer from similar levels of PTSD to fighting men. So what was it that traumatised the POGOs (Persons on Garrison Operations), as they were unkindly nicknamed by fighting men? The hunt for the root of their suffering often ends at the 'homecoming'.

'For many Vietnam veterans,' Yule writes, 'the rejection of their service has played as great a role as the trauma of war in their subsequent mental health struggles'. While Yule bravely discounts the airport-demonstration stories, he quotes a veteran who said, 'You wouldn't go anywhere near the pubs near the university. Women would spit on you. I've lost count of the amount of women that spat on me.'[24]

This is peak spit.

These stories now have nowhere else to go.

I doubt whether Yule believes that any veteran genuinely lost count of the number of times he was spat upon, but what does it mean that he feels obliged to include the claim? In a sense, he has no choice. He cannot offer a voice to the veterans and then ignore one of their most colourful complaints. *The Long Shadow* also reprints an anonymous, easily disproved anecdote about protesters throwing food at veterans. Again, this is something that several former soldiers believed to have occurred. However, it is not history, because it did not happen.

And things that do not happen cannot cause other things to happen.

When veterans' psychological malaise is blamed on anti-war demonstrations as much as exposure to combat, then protest against the war takes on the moral (and martial) equivalence of shooting at soldiers. But this can only be true if the rejection was real. If the incidents generally held to express the rejection were not real, but the *perception that they were real* was real, and if this perception has contributed to veterans' PTSD, then the responsibility for that trauma must surely fall upon those who have propagated the myths that veterans were spat upon and so on.

But the spitting stories are poetry for the right. They help supporters of the war blame opponents of the war for the war wounds of warriors.

*

The Myths of Victimised Veterans

While I was writing *Lest*, I laboured under the pleasant – and highly motivating – delusion that I had at least put to bed the myths of demonstration confrontations and airport protests. But then came Fitz.

In the lead-up to the commemoration of the fiftieth anniversary of the end of Australia's commitment to Vietnam, the journalist and 'storian' Peter FitzSimons interviewed an SAS veteran who served in Vietnam for nine months in 1971, in a question-and-answer session presented as an 'opinion' piece. FitzSimons asked the veteran about the anti-war protests before he left, and the veteran claimed that he had read in the paper of a 'big demonstration' about to happen in Sydney, so he and a few mates made the journey into town: 'We turned up in uniform, so it was red-rag-to-a-bull stuff, and they were yelling at us in Martin Place and Angel Place. We deliberately placed ourselves in front of them, I guess, to provoke them. And we got into a bit of a rumble, a bit of biff, and the police were there and they broke it up.'

There is no report of an incident anything like this occurring in Sydney in 1970, 1971 or any other time. And it would have been front-page news if the SAS – the *SAS!* – had blocked and attacked a street march in Martin Place: not only in the middle of the city but in front of the police.

Later, FitzSimons asked the veteran about the homecoming, and he said he was flown back to Sydney via Darwin on a flight for US troops taking R&R in Australia. His mother and father were waiting for him at the airport, and he kissed his mum. FitzSimons pushed the point: 'The story always goes that Vietnam vets were often greeted by protesters calling them "baby killers",' he said. 'Was that your experience?'

'Well, there was a hardcore of protesters at the airport when I got there,' the veteran replied, 'shouting abuse, even though it was one o'clock in the morning.'

But Sydney Airport was not even open at one o'clock in the morning. No flights ever arrived at that time. No protests were reported at Sydney Airport on 6, 7 or 8 October 1971 or any other date. The steam had gone out of the anti-war movement as well as the war by then, and there is no conceivable reason why peace protesters should demonstrate against the final withdrawal of troops, or why the press would not report on their bizarre and eccentric behaviour if they did. And even if protesters had chosen to turn up – for the first and only time – they would not have had access to the schedule for Pan-Am's R&R flights and would not have known there would be troops in the airport. Which was closed.

'Some of those protesters at the airport and at Angel Place, all those years ago, are likely reading this,' said FitzSimons to his interviewee. 'What do you say to them?'

This is one of the stranger questions in journalistic history: asking a third party to address people who do not exist about something that did not happen.

'Well, we live in a democracy and you're allowed to demonstrate,' said the veteran to nobody, 'but I think you had it wrong. You don't demonstrate and throw abuse at the soldiers or the servicemen. You throw abuse and demonstrate against the government.'[25]

By the 1960s, veterans of the Second World War could be ridiculed by the young as old, drunk and out of touch. Fifteen years after 1945, the playwright Alan Seymour was able to portray them as sodden pathetic caricatures in his drama *The One Day of the Year*, about which much has been made by historians. But Vietnam veterans have experienced this process backwards. There is no doubt that in the years after the war they were mocked and ignored by some people, and thought of as gullible and culpable by others. But by the Sydney welcome-home march in 1987, fifteen years after Australia's withdrawal from Vietnam, the veterans were widely accepted as misunderstood, brave, honest men. This is a tribute to the strength of the narrative they have collectively evolved. They have become a victim group – their claims need not be verified, their truth should not be questioned. Today, they are not the rapists, but the raped.

The swift and comprehensive public rehabilitation of Vietnam veterans had a knock-on effect for other groups of returned men. According to Bob Hawke's defence minister, Kim Beazley, one of the reasons the Hawke government felt able to invest $10 million of taxpayers' money on returning Dardanelles veterans to Gallipoli in 1990 was a feeling that the Vietnam cohort had 'been very harshly handled as a result of the controversy surrounding the war and that political dispute had been unfairly imposed on the fighting men and women'. As it happens, there were never any Australian women 'fighting' in Vietnam, but that is by the by. 'Honouring them,' said Beazley, 'gave the government a sense of the scale of these sorts of enterprises which, again, contributed to a willingness to be big on the 75th anniversary of the landing.'[26]

So, a myth that had begun as the marginal viewpoint of a militant minority of Vietnam veterans had become entrenched as a truth, which in its turn enabled a Labor government to breathe new life into one of our oldest military myths – that the beaches at Gallipoli saw the birth of the Australian nation and the original Anzacs were its midwives.

Equally unpredictably, another group of maligned veterans also came to benefit from the Vietnam veterans' public-relations triumph, and they too were recast in an accepted and even venerated role in Australian military history. The thousands of unfortunate Second World War prisoners of the Japanese had no immediately obvious place in the Anzac tradition, not least because they had surrendered. I spoke about this with Christina Twomey, the author of a study of the postwar lives of the POWs. She told me that immediately after the war there had been 'a great sadness that so many Australian service people had been through quite a devastating experience. But the returned prisoner was also an ambivalent figure in some ways, because they were contrary to many aspects of the Anzac mythology of being strong, good fighters, representatives of the Australian race.

'People didn't quite know how to respond to that,' said Twomey, 'and the army and the Defence Force themselves had a very ambivalent attitude towards prisoners of war. They weren't interested in commemorating them. They don't want people to make heroes of prisoners of war [who] had spent the war confined in a camp and controlled by the enemy.'

Attitudes changed during the 1980s when some public focus began to shift towards victims of conflict. 'And, initially, that's civilians, women and children,' said Twomey, 'but ultimately the veterans themselves start stepping into that space – of being people who can be victims of war too. After that moment of increasing interest in victimhood and suffering, and the transference of that to the veterans themselves, then attention starts to settle on the prisoners of war as people who have endured a very hard war and do embody, in some senses, the suffering of war. So a focus on prisoners is, post-Vietnam, almost a safe way of commemorating suffering.'

So, a myth may be a dubiously inspired, unthinkingly promoted ahistorical fabrication, and yet still have some beneficial effects in the real world.

Which, I guess, accounts for the continued prevalence of religion.

I am not sure how it took me so long to understand this, because I suspect it is one of those things that everyone else knows to be true.

The Myths of Vietnam Veterans, Anzac Day and the RSL

That Vietnam veterans were not allowed to march on Anzac Day. That the RSL regularly rejected Vietnam veterans. That the RSL had magical powers, which it used to prevent HMAS Sydney *from docking in its home port. That Second World War veterans physically assaulted Vietnam veterans.*

On 18 April 2016, I was interviewed by Richard Glover on ABC Radio 702. To my surprise, Glover opened up the phone lines. After a call from a veteran's son about the RSL, which organises the nation's Anzac Day marches, came a message from a woman named Jenny who suggested that Vietnam veterans were not allowed to march on Anzac Day during the Vietnam War. I lost my temper and said, 'That's nonsense, Jenny.'

The truth is that Vietnam 'veterans' had been marching in Anzac Day parades even before an Australian battalion had come home from Vietnam. Alone in the history of 'returned' soldiers, some men bound for the Vietnam War had marched in Anzac Day parades before they were sent overseas. Vietnam veterans marched regularly, proudly and conspicuously, and their presence was generally highlighted in the press, along with the fact that they received a warm reception from onlookers.

The myth that Vietnam veterans did not march on Anzac Day seems to have its roots in three interconnected ideas: first, that Vietnam veterans were not integrated into the Anzac tradition; second, that Vietnam veterans had no support from the wider public; and third, that the RSL was institutionally hostile to Vietnam veterans.

None of these ideas existed during the war itself.

The RSL was formed in June 1916, as the Returned Sailors and Soldiers Imperial League of Australia, to pressure for better conditions and repatriation benefits for returned and serving military personnel. It is not a government organisation, it has no official status, it is not a part of the military and it does not have magical powers. While it is Australia's largest ex-servicepeople's organisation, it never quite managed to recruit even half the survivors of the 1st AIF. There is no essential reason why the RSL should have become Australia's guardian of remembrance – in Britain, that role was played by war widows – but the league grew as commemoration blossomed, and Anzac Day and its attendant parades came to 'belong' to the RSL.

In 2007, author Paul Ham made the extravagant claim that, historically, 'most – although not all – RSL branches either refused or discouraged admission and membership to Vietnam veterans'.[1] He offered no statistics to support this, but his position became the received wisdom. Its theory goes that the RSL did not consider Vietnam 'a real war'. While this might have been true of some individual RSL members in some clubs, the RSL nationally first sent Christmas parcels to Vietnam in 1963, when there were no more than a hundred Australian servicemen in the country. Although these Australians were in Vietnam as instructors, and ostensibly not

The Myths of Vietnam Veterans, Anzac Day and the RSL

taking part in the fighting, the RSL recognised that they worked under 'conditions of great hardship with a considerable element of danger'.[2] The RSL had sent similar packages to Malaya during the Emergency but discontinued them when the Emergency was officially declared over, even though there were still Australian troops stationed in Malaya.

In fact, the RSL judged Australians in Vietnam to be involved in a 'real war' more than a year before the Australian government officially committed fighting troops to Vietnam.

The first Australian battalion to serve in Vietnam, 1RAR, was dispatched in June 1965. In January 1966, two RSL officials embarked on a fact-finding visit to Vietnam and Malaysia and came home determined to press the government to award a distinct decoration to Australian troops in South Vietnam. 'Our troops in Vietnam are probably the finest we have ever committed to action,' said Victorian RSL State President W. H. Hall. 'There is no feeling of security anywhere in South Vietnam. I don't think there has ever been a war as desperate as this.'[3]

The first Anzac Day for Australian fighting troops in Vietnam fell on 25 April 1966, when Prime Minister Harold Holt addressed Australian and New Zealand troops at a parade in Bien Hoa and told them, 'You may have written another chapter in the history of Anzac. Anzac Day has taken on a deeper significance here today. On another field of battle, remote from our countries, Anzacs are together again fighting for freedom.'

The headline of *The Australian*'s front-page coverage of the 1966 Anzac Day parade in Sydney was 'Vietnam veterans join march'. Even though the main body of 1RAR was still in Vietnam, the press noted twelve Vietnam veterans – including two army officers, an RAAF warrant officer and nine other ranks – at the head of the contingent of troops from the Korean, Malayan and Borneo campaigns. The *Sydney*

Morning Herald reported that they received 'a special cheer from the crowd', and wrote that at the end of the march, 'old soldiers broke their ranks to shake hands with the young Vietnam veterans'. One veteran asked a group of teenage spectators 'with long hair and duffel coats', 'Why aren't you demonstrating today?'

There were no conscripts fighting in Vietnam on 25 April 1966, but three national servicemen were permitted to take part in the Perth parade as they had completed their training and were scheduled to leave for Vietnam in the coming months.[4]

On 27 April 1966, a soldier reported to be the first Vietnam veteran to be admitted to the RSL joined the ACT branch. When Private Noel O'Halloran of 1RAR was presented with his badge by the ACT branch president, a photograph of the men together was printed in the *Canberra Times*.[5]

In Vietnam, 1RAR was replaced by 5RAR and 6RAR. In 1967, members of 5RAR's advance party, who had returned by air before the majority of the battalion came home by sea, marched in Sydney on Anzac Day, and veterans marched in Melbourne, too. The *Sydney Morning Herald* headlined its front-page report, 'Vietnam gives new meaning to Anzac', and described how 'a wave of applause ran along the streets of Sydney in tribute to young veterans of Vietnam [who] looked tanned and tough, big youngsters in their prime. They were a small contingent ... but they drew the loudest recognition. It came from youth [whose] strongest acknowledgement was for their own generation – the young Regulars and National Servicemen.'

The Vietnam veterans marched near the end of the parade with the returned men from Korea and Malaysia, but New South Wales RSL president Sir William Yeo said he would have preferred to see them marching separately – as an honour. Vietnam veterans also marched with the Korean and South East Asia Forces Association in Melbourne. The following year in Melbourne, it was announced

The Myths of Vietnam Veterans, Anzac Day and the RSL

that the troops from Vietnam had been set a place near the head of the march, in front of KSEAFA and just behind the survivors of the 1st AIF.

Far from habitually rejecting Vietnam veterans, the RSL had officially feted them. In January 1968 the magazine of the New South Wales state branch of the league, *Reveille*, featured a poignant photograph of a man wearing striped hospital pyjamas with one leg bared to display an artificial limb. Standing with the aid of crutches between two smiling nurses was Private Denis Enright, a national serviceman who had lost his left foot, right leg and some of his fingers while serving with 2RAR in Vietnam. According to the story, the severely wounded man 'had one important thing to do shortly after he returned to Australia with multiple injuries ... join the RSL'. So North Bondi sub-branch officials went to the hospital to present him with his badge.[6]

There is overwhelming contemporary evidence that the RSL supported Vietnam veterans on Anzac Day during the war years, and no evidence whatsoever that it did not. But the contempt of some commentators for historical sources is perhaps best illustrated in the story of 7RAR, which ended its one-year tour of duty and shipped out of Vung Tau on HMAS *Sydney* on 9 April 1968.

As the battalion's intelligence officer and historian Michael O'Brien has noted, the *Sydney*'s return home was delayed when the ship was required to sail back to Australia via Thailand to pick up a signals squadron that had been taking part in a Southeast Asia Treaty Organization exercise; a soldier then contracted peritonitis and had to be flown to hospital in Singapore.

The author Gerard Windsor has written that the *Sydney* had been scheduled to dock in Sydney early on Anzac Day morning but did not do so because 'that would have meant the men would have to march in the Anzac Day Parade, and the RSL didn't want that'.

Furthermore, 'The charitable interpretation of the request/order was that the Vietnam veterans deserved their own individual march. The more common belief was that the RSL didn't regard them as having fought in a real war and therefore they were not eligible for the Anzac Day March.' With baffling confidence, Windsor concluded, 'The latter is the more likely interpretation.'[7]

Windsor did not at first cite any foundation for his assertion that the *Sydney* should have docked on the morning of 25 April. The ship's recent previous trips back to Sydney from Vung Tau had lasted twelve days (in June 1966) and thirteen days (February 1968), which would have had the men home on 21 or 22 April respectively.[8] Nor has Windsor ever endeavoured to suggest by what means, or at what level, the RSL might have been able to make a 'request/order' to the Australian army and the Royal Australian Navy, or why the military would have agreed to a petty, insulting entreaty that would, in effect, cost thousands of dollars in wasted sea time and lost shore time.

As it was, 100,000 people turned out to watch the Anzac Day parade in Sydney in 1968. Once again, the *Sydney Morning Herald* noted that young people cheered the most, 'particularly for those nearest their own age group – the recently returned Vietnam veterans'. The paper further reported that 'as the young Vietnam veterans came along, near the end of the parade, they [were joined] behind the barriers, by other excited young people – girlfriends, brothers, sisters, even a few of the younger mums – in a way never before seen at an Anzac march'.[9]

In 2019, in response to my criticism of Windsor's attack on the RSL, Windsor revealed a source: 'I rang a former 7RAR platoon commander,' he wrote. 'He assured me HMAS *Sydney* slowed very noticeably as it came down the Queensland coast.' Against the amassed data of the SEATO operation, the hospitalised soldier and the log of the *Sydney*'s previous trips, Windsor offered a long-remembered feeling in an anonymous junior officer's feet. Windsor went on to develop a new argument, that the ship's non-existent slowdown may have been caused by the fact that Prime Minister John Gorton would have only been available on the day after Anzac Day to take the salute at 7RAR's welcome-home parade.

This cognitive somersault demonstrates the admirable adaptability of folklore, which can be used to bolster either one historically insupportable idea (that the troops were so reviled that they were not wanted on Anzac Day) or its opposite (that the troops were so revered that they could only be welcomed by the prime minister), without its champions ever noting the fact that no battalion before or since 7RAR's first tour was ever greeted by a prime minister upon its return from Vietnam.

'There's a lot more to be probed even on this one,' wrote Windsor.[10]

No, there is not.

It is nonsense.

But, in the perhaps forlorn hope of closing off this argument in which only one side has ever presented a single documented fact, I should point out that all of the previously confidential reports of HMAS *Sydney* are now available at the Australian War Memorial (and online). The captain's report from April 1968 confirms every point in Michael O'Brien's study and includes appendices detailing the total steaming hours, distances and fuel consumed during each day of the cruise between Vung Tau and Sydney, and the exact times spent at anchor and steaming between every port, and there is nothing anomalous about any of the figures. This confidential report was sent by Second World War veteran Captain DAH Clarke, DSO of the *Sydney* (whose honour is impugned every time this matter is disputed) to the Flag Officer Commanding

HM Australian Fleet, who forwarded it to the Secretary at the Department of Navy.[11]

There is no mystery of any kind, and there never was.

As the Vietnam War ground on, the RSL's enthusiasm for the veterans was unflagging. At a function in the Casino RSL Hall in January 1970, forty 'special certificates' were awarded to local men who had served overseas since the Second World War, and the president of the New South Wales RSL 'complimented Casino on their fine action in expressing thanks to those boys who had served in Vietnam'. He added, 'On behalf of the R.S.L. I say we are tremendously proud of you and invite you to join our organisation.'[12]

The biggest cheer of the 1970 Anzac Day parade in Sydney was reserved for the first Vietnam veterans in the march, reported the *Sun-Herald*. In an equal but opposite reaction to Nadine Jensen's 1966 action, a 'woman slipped under the barricades to throw confetti over the young, fresh-faced Vietnam troops, most of whom wore only two medals, indicating they had served twelve months in Vietnam. As police gently escorted her back, the woman said with tear-filled eyes: "Oh, they are so young, as young as my son. It takes me back to when I was a girl and my husband first marched."'[13]

It is puzzling that so many veterans remember Nadine Jensen, the woman with the red paint, but none recall the unnamed mother with the confetti.

In August 1971, Colin Hines formally took office as president of the New South Wales RSL and told the press that one of his three priorities was to 'fight for the welfare of the young, particularly National Servicemen returning from Vietnam'. He declared that 'our war compensation rates are nothing more than an insult' and accused the federal government of 'betraying' the nashos.[14]

The Myths of Vietnam Veterans, Anzac Day and the RSL

In January 1972, Frank Buxton, formerly Field Representative of the Australian Forces Overseas Fund in Vietnam (which provided Christmas hampers and entertainment for the troops) wrote that 'the young veteran [sic] of Vietnam, now ex-servicemen, must be convinced by all means possible to join the League. They must be made aware that the League's future is theirs and that they now have obligations to care for the heritage handed down by past generations of ex-servicemen.'[15]

In March of that year, the last Australian combat troops were withdrawn from Vietnam. In April, Hines's Anzac Day *Reveille* editorial appealed to all sub-branches to 'make special mention of the Vietnam veterans in their Anzac Day services' and allow 'Vietnam veterans to lead their march and take pride of place at any ceremony', as they must 'become the backbone of the R.S.L. of tomorrow'.[16]

The *Sydney Morning Herald* headlined its front-page Anzac Day coverage, 'A new generation leads Anzac march', over a photograph of Vietnam veterans leading the parade. The newspaper reported, 'The proud figures of 600 Vietnam war veterans at the head of yesterday's Anzac March through the city instilled a new enthusiasm into the crowds lining the streets. From the moment they swung past the Cenotaph in Martin Plaza, heads turned in salute to fallen comrades, the crowd was with them ... Australia's newest veterans received generous applause amidst cries of "welcome back, boys" and "good on you, fellers."'

In Brisbane that Anzac Day, 435 Vietnam veterans marched for the first time as a unit, and 200 veterans marched in Perth.[17]

In 1981, Vietnam veteran Peter Young became national secretary of the RSL. By 1983, there were some 12,000 Vietnam veterans among the RSL's approximately 300,000 members.[18] In 1988, Vietnam veteran Alf Garland was elected national president of the RSL. It would be difficult to construct an evidence-based argument (rather than a feeling in somebody else's feet) for Ham's claim that 'most' RSL branches at any time refused or discouraged admission and membership to Vietnam veterans.

So where lie the roots of the myth?

There are, perhaps, some minor technical explanations. For example, in November 1965, the secretary of Mosman RSL Club wrote to New South Wales licensing authorities to complain that a nineteen-year-old who had fought in Vietnam was not legally permitted to drink in his club, as clubs – unlike hotels – were only licensed to serve people aged twenty-one and over. At this stage, it seems, it was not legally possible for younger veterans to join RSL clubs in New South Wales.[19] Anecdotes published several decades later suggest this same law might have been at the root of some RSL-rejection stories. The excitable Tony Bower-Miles, who enlisted in the army at seventeen (although his birthdate on the nominal roll differs from that given in his memoir) and went to Vietnam aged nineteen, relates a story in which he was refused membership of his local RSL because he was one month from his twenty-first birthday. Although the secretary-manager is not going to kick him out, Bower-Miles tells him, 'Stick it in your arse. You got all them pogo c___ here on a Friday night selling raffle tickets.'[20]

Bower-Miles seems to be talking about his local RSL club, not the sub-branch. Clubs and sub-branches were separate organisations. Although the relationships between the two differed in different states and changed over time, it is generally true to say that membership of a sub-branch did not include membership of an RSL club. An RSL member or a veteran could be refused entry to an RSL club if he were not also a member of that club, simply because he had not paid his dues.

The Myths of Vietnam Veterans, Anzac Day and the RSL

Another possible interpretation of the RSL rejection stories is that some commentators cannot help but view the past through the prism of the present. Windsor has described the national servicemen who went to Vietnam as 'veterans of a lost war [whom] many RSL clubs didn't want to know'.[21] But returned national servicemen from Vietnam were not, initially, veterans of a lost war, and were not seen as such until several years after the national service scheme was suspended. Each national service intake discharged between 1967 and 1973 had at worst survived an inconclusive conflict, and none had seen a single unequivocal Viet Cong/North Vietnamese Army victory in his area of operation. When Australian troops finally withdrew, first to Nui Dat and then Vung Tau, they were not pursued by NVA tanks. The war was not over, the North had not yet won, and Australians were told peace with honour had been achieved. It was only with the fall of Saigon in April 1975 that any Australian became, retroactively, the veteran of a lost war.

Our historical memory of the Vietnam War is peculiar in many ways, among them the fact that there is no other war in which the attitude of ex-servicemen's organisations towards the veterans is thought to be important. We know little about the way returned men from the Second World War were treated in RSL clubs by veterans of the First World War, and almost nothing about the experiences of veterans of Korea – much less Indonesia and Malaya – in RSL clubs. Complaints of veterans' mistreatment by the RSL do not seem to have arisen until the dispute between the Vietnam Veterans' Association of Australia and the RSL over the Agent Orange issue. The VVAA was founded in 1979 to pursue claims by some veterans that they had been affected by toxic chemicals during their war service.[22] Although the RSL provided assistance to the VVAA, some veterans felt the league did not advocate their case with sufficient vigour, and certain RSL members and officials were openly sceptical of arguments that Vietnam veterans had suffered any unique hardship.

The VVAA borrowed tactics from the left. In 1980, a hundred Vietnam veterans demonstrated on the Sydney Anzac Day march by wearing orange paper attached to their uniforms and medals, to symbolise the defoliant. 'This is not a political protest,' said the organiser, Rod Smith (although it obviously was). 'We are the conservative element in Australia. We are members of RSL clubs.'[23]

The VVAA spent several years publicly airing various complaints against the RSL, and the RSL fought back with the intemperate rhetoric for which generations of the organisation's leadership have become known, but until the mid-1980s the VVAA's accusations were based on the RSL's alleged neglect of veterans' postwar health issues, rather than the rejection of membership applications. To date, I have not been able to find a published rejection story before 1983, when the Evatt Royal Commission reported that veterans' various medical problems were probably not caused by Agent Orange.

On the other hand, when the RSL genuinely rejected veterans for what might charitably be described as political reasons, its actions were widely reported. For example, it was headline news in Australia in 1964 when a large number of ex-servicemen were officially excluded from an RSL club – and dozens of RSL members stayed away from that club in protest. It happened on May 25 and was reported in the Sydney *Sun-Herald*, although the event took place about 2,750 kilometres from Sydney, in Port Moresby in New Guinea, where members of the local Native Ex-Servicemen's Association were told 'point blank' that they could not enter the Port Moresby RSL Club after their Anzac Day march.

According to the president of the Native Ex-Servicemen's Association, they were informed they were not welcome because they were not returned men. 'But thousands of us died during the war carrying wounded Australian soldiers, guiding them and fighting in the front line,' he said. He denounced the ban as a colour bar and many white Australian ex-servicemen apparently boycotted the RSL to join local veterans in the Pacific Islands Regiment mess.[24]

It was considered scandalous even in the days of White Australia that, even in the furthermost reaches of Australian territory, men who had fought for Australia could be turned away from an RSL, and it was reported because it was remarkable. And it seems ridiculous to have to say it, but the exclusion of Vietnam veterans in time of war would have been considerably more newsworthy – in any society except the fictional, parallel-universe Australia of the 1960s as reimagined in the late 1980s.

The year after the Port Moresby travesty, on 15 February 1965, a busload of Freedom Riders rode into the town of Walgett in northern New South Wales, where almost one-third of the population was First Nations but where First Nations veterans were barred from the RSL club – except on Anzac Day. Freedom Riders picketed the club with signs that read 'Good Enough for Tobruk – why not Walgett?' and 'Bullets do not discriminate'. The incident was extensively reported, documented and photographed. Both sides had their say. 'A club may reserve its prerogative to refuse anyone membership,' said club secretary Tom Hogan, and he warned a journalist not to forget that the club had 'buried two Aboriginal ex-servicemen who died last year at a cost of £75 each'.[25] The actions of Walgett RSL brought about a short-lived, statewide scandal, at a time when First Nations people arguably enjoyed less popularity than the troops in Vietnam.

In May 1967, Second World War veteran Les Waddington, a member of the Cronulla sub-branch of the RSL, was expelled from the league for 'conduct subversive to the objects and policy of the league'. Waddington had begun to feel uncomfortable about the Australian commitment in Vietnam. 'Open discussion at RSL clubs and sub-branches never had a chance,' he wrote. 'Official policy had been stated; it would be impudent to challenge a meeting with a contrary attitude; there was a close-the-ranks philosophy that was oppressive, especially to a small, tentative voice. Macho behaviour was essential, dissenting points of view unwanted; they would not only be weak, they would be treasonable. One's life stuff would be wasted trying to change RSL policy on Vietnam.'[26]

Waddington's offence was to help found the Ex-Services Human Rights Association of Australia, members of which had demonstrated against the Vietnam War and the visit of US President Lyndon Johnson in 1966. Waddington was eventually reinstated to the RSL with support from other league members, but he was the only non-Indigenous ex-serviceman reported as being shunned by an RSL during the Vietnam War.

Ahistorical ideas about the veterans' experience gained strength with extraordinary speed. On 26 April 1987, fifteen years after Vietnam veterans led the Sydney Anzac Day march for the first time, the Sydney *Sun-Herald* reported, 'Australia's Vietnam veterans came home yesterday, at long last. Steady applause, broken by spontaneous outbursts of cheering and whistling, accompanied the record number of about 2,000 veterans as they led the Army in the Anzac Day march for the first time.'[27]

While it is axiomatically difficult to prove that something never happened – and in 2003 Victorian RSL state president Bruce Ruxton conceded that 'some secretaries of individual RSLs may have banned Vietnam vets' – it seems unlikely that many men were ever explicitly refused membership of an RSL branch or sub-branch on the basis of their service during the war.[28] Even Peter Yule's comparatively

The Myths of Vietnam Veterans, Anzac Day and the RSL

vastly resourced, semi-official history of Vietnam veterans was able to unearth written evidence of only one specific example.[29] That said, many veterans clearly felt alienated by the attitude of the RSL to their concerns. A feeling of quiet rejection – a cold shoulder, a limp handshake or a sarcastic sneer – is difficult to invest with narrative drama. It is clearer and simpler to say that Vietnam veterans were turned away at the RSL's doors, and thereby denied entrance to both the clubs and the Anzac pantheon, and banned from marching on Anzac Day. It may not be the truth of what happened, but it is the truth of how some veterans felt.

And the story works for almost everyone. Few on the right question some veterans' version of history in which they are spurned at every turn; the right derives too much enjoyment from the idea that the left in the 1960s was a spitting, blood-hurling, violent, unthinking rabble. Few on the left have much sympathy for the RSL, and an acceptance that even the league was somehow against the Vietnam War lends credence to the contemporary fantasy that the anti-war movement won cultural hegemony in Australia and helped pressure the government to withdraw the troops.

On 9 August 2023, I was invited onto a panel on Philip Clark's *Nightlife* show on ABC Radio National, to discuss the fiftieth anniversary of the end of Australia's commitment in Vietnam. Just as we were finishing up, General Sir Peter Cosgrove asked me if I had looked into the stories that Vietnam veterans had been refused admission to the RSL. I told him I had, and that those stories did not exist before the Agent Orange controversy. He claimed that they did, and when we spoke about it afterwards, the gracious and generous Cosgrove insisted he had heard them before 1985, although he could not specify from whom or exactly when.

Nine days after the broadcast, New South Wales RSL president Ray James issued an official apology to the state's Vietnam veterans. 'Some were spurned by veterans of previous conflicts,' he said, 'turned away and refused membership by some RSL sub-branches in NSW ... When veterans needed the League the most, the RSL community in NSW let them down.'[30]

But James was not a perpetrator admitting and regretting his guilt in the normal way of an apology. He was a Vietnam veteran apologising to other Vietnam veterans for the behaviour of Second World War veterans: a member of a victim group making an accusation on behalf of other victims, against dead men who could no longer defend themselves. He was burying history in myth.

There is a darker side to this historical mischief. In May 1968 in Vietnam, national serviceman Dal Abbott of 1RAR was killed in action at the Battle of Coral. His family, who opposed the Vietnam War, instructed the army to bury his body overseas, and his remains were interred in Terendak Military Cemetery in Malaysia. Dal's father, Trevor Abbott, an army sergeant in the Second World War, called his son's death 'legalised murder'.[31] When the Vietnam War was over, the family asked for Dal's name not to appear on the Roll of Honour at the Australian War Memorial, and a blank space was left where it might have been. Trevor Abbott had passed away by 2014, when the AWM overrode the wishes of the surviving family and added Dal's name to the roll – in the tawdry tradition of denying the wishes of bereaved parents that dated back to the 66-character inscriptions on First World War tombstones. The AWM had been lobbied by Vietnam veterans, most notably former 1RAR platoon commander Garry Prendergast, who argued that the AWM had 'capitulated incorrectly to unfair political anti-war influence reflecting the then morally wrong and negative attitude of the general public at the time towards the Vietnam veterans'.

The Myths of Vietnam Veterans, Anzac Day and the RSL

When Dal's name ultimately appeared on the roll, and Prendergast was asked how he felt about the family, he said, 'I don't give a shit about them. It's nothing to do with them. It's about his sacrifice.'[32]

Prendergast was not the first veteran to take the Abbott family's stand personally. In 1997, Adelaide 9RAR veteran Geoff Williams, who returned from Vietnam in December 1969, 'remembered' wearing his uniform in the city when 'people started waving red flags in my face, shouting abuse, spitting on my country's uniform. A bloke turned around and hit me with a pole. He had ribbons on from World War II but his son had been killed in 'Nam. He was having a go at me personally.'[33]

The attacker in Williams' story can only have been intended to represent Trevor Abbott, even though the Abbott family lived in New South Wales. It is close to impossible that the grieving Trevor might have physically attacked a veteran in an unreported assault at an unreported demonstration in a different state, but Williams might have felt that Trevor's stance was an act of violence against his service and values. Nobody listens to a man with hurt feelings, so he gave himself a hurt head. Once again, myth was employed to put flesh on a feeling – the sentiment that Vietnam diggers were belittled and betrayed by 'the greatest generation'.

The ultimate manifestation of this is the RSL myth, the acceptance of which seems complete. For now. With Vietnam veterans apologising to themselves for the behaviour of Second World War veterans – and enjoying intellectual support from the AWM – it's possible that the denigration of the dead will continue until Second World War historians notice its implications. If the aftermath of a war belongs in the narrative of that war, then the final shameful chapter in accounts of the Rats of Tobruk, the men of Kokoda, and the POWs of the Burma Railway is their wholesale abuse of younger returned soldiers, many of whom were conscripts.

Lest

We should learn of their perfidy in their biographies and unit histories. My guess is that we will not, but the mythology of Vietnam is evolving with such dizzying speed that this revision is no longer unthinkable.

The Myths of Movements

That the Vietnam War was an unpopular war. That soldiers do not like fighting wars. That the anti-war movement helped to stop the Vietnam War. That there was no pro-war movement.

We tend to remember the Vietnam years as the time of huge moratorium demonstrations and one young woman running towards a welcome home parade cloaked in pantomime plasma, staining the honour of soldiers with her silent accusation. This kind of event was so dramatic and new that it's easy to forget that the majority of staid, conservative, Coalition-voting Australians stood firmly behind their government's commitment to Vietnam. At first, the war attracted even less domestic opposition than Australia's earlier deployment to the so-called Malayan Emergency, which drew virtually no protest and not much public interest.[1] And in February 1968, three weeks after the beginning of the Tet Offensive and the broadcast of film of NLF guerrillas in the grounds of the US embassy in Saigon – an event often held to have brought about a collapse in the morale of supporters of South Vietnam – only 24 per cent of Australians believed Australian troops should return home soon.

While the doubtable Alan Tudge was one of the reasons that I wrote this book, another was an elderly man – who, in fairness, will remain anonymous – who complained to the ABC about a radio show in which I had pointed out that there had been a pro-Vietnam War movement as well as an anti-war movement. My attempts to explore and explain the pro-war position provoked an extended, rambling objection from an irate listener (is there any other kind?) who felt that my show breached the ABC's Code of Practice. I had, he wrote, shown a 'lack of impartiality, accuracy and balance', and 'no transparency over presenters' militaristic bias'. The fact that I had described conservative opinions led him to the belief that I must hold them myself – and be devoted to the cause of propagating them with taxpayers' money.

When we neglect conservative voices, history becomes incoherent. The policies of a democratically elected government tend to broadly reflect the opinions of the people who voted for them. Coalition governments started Australia's Vietnam War and were re-elected twice during that war. By the time Gough Whitlam's Labor Party came to power in 1972, the last Australian combat troops had already withdrawn from Vietnam, and in sending combat troops then pursuing and ending Australia's war, Coalition administrations had public opinion on their side. Governments differed from the majority of voters only in their advocacy of the provocative and self-defeating principle that national servicemen should be compelled to fight in Vietnam.

Since ongoing support for the war among Australia's politically inactive conservative majority has been forgotten, it is unsurprising that pro-war organisations have also faded from memory. But the pro-war groups had no less influence on the course of the war than the anti-war groups – that is, neither group achieved anything much at all.

By far the biggest and best-remembered accomplishment of the Australian anti-war movement was the organisation of the moratorium demonstrations of 1970 and 1971. The locally unprecedented scale and prominence of these protests has led to the idea that they somehow helped end Australia's involvement in the Vietnam War. This is simply not the case. US President Richard Nixon announced the withdrawal of 150,000 US troops from Vietnam in April 1969, then a further 25,000 in September, and 150,000 more in April 1970. The first big moratorium in Australia was not held until May 1970, by which time the pivotal decisions about the future of the war had long since been made in the US. The second moratorium took place in September 1970, and Australian forces began to leave Vietnam in November, but it would be disingenuous to link this with the protests rather than the ongoing US drawdown.

Nor were the US decisions made primarily in response to the demands of protesters in the US. The first huge US demonstration took place in November 1969, months after the announcement of the withdrawal of the first 175,000 troops. Even the original US Moratorium was irrelevant.

But to make myself clear: when I write that there seems to be no point in demonstrating against a war, it is not because I am against anti-war protests; when I say that a lot of people support wars and enjoy fighting them, it is not because I think this is a good thing; when I write that there have always been LGBTQ+ individuals and groups in the defence forces, it is not because I think it is important that they (or anyone else) should or should not be recruited to the army. I just want to establish the facts.

So shoot me.

Or, rather, don't.

Another reason to write this specific chapter was a letter I received from a reader of a magazine story I wrote about the Republican and Unionist murals in Belfast. My (inevitably) irate correspondent took me to task for saying that the men of the British

Parachute Regiment were feared in Northern Ireland. She asked who had feared them, and whether I thought that the Paras themselves wanted to be in Northern Ireland.

I grew up in Aldershot which, at the time, was the largest garrison town in the UK, the self-proclaimed 'home of the British army' and the base of the Parachute Regiment. I can say with confidence that everyone was scared of the Paras, including the rest of the British army, and that most Paras wanted to fight anywhere – be it Goose Green, Belfast or Aldershot. By and large, people join combat arms of the military not because they want to go abseiling or skiing or jumping out of planes (well, maybe jumping out of planes) but because they hope to fight a war.

I left Aldershot when I was eighteen years old, but I could not leave military bases behind. More than thirty years later, I enrolled in a doctorate at ADFA (I may have mentioned this before) and it was like coming home. It was at ADFA that I first became absorbed by mythology in military history. My interest grew out of my study of the national service scheme, and the realisation that it was impossible to understand the nashos without taking into account the level of popular support for the Vietnam War. Divorced from this backdrop, the men who willingly served in the army seem like ideological outliers or extreme right-wingers, rather than the doggedly conventional citizens that most of them were. My supervisor was the incomparable Professor Jeffrey Grey, author of the authoritative Cambridge *Military History of Australia*, and the son of Major General Ronald Grey, the commander of 7RAR in Vietnam. It was Jeff who introduced me to former intelligence officer and historian Michael O'Brien, author of the rigorous *Conscripts and Regulars: With the Seventh Battalion in Vietnam*. In this book, O'Brien had used data from questionnaires returned by 230 veterans of the battalion's two tours, but he had not completed a statistical examination

The Myths of Movements

of the results. He generously handed over to me half a room's worth of paperwork for analysis. My aim was to look at differences in the attitudes and experiences of regular soldiers and national servicemen – that is, soldiers by choice and soldiers by chance.

Respondents to the 7RAR survey were asked what they found to be the most exciting/enjoyable moments of their tour. For regulars on the first tour (April 1967–April 1968), the most common response was 'operations', which included 'patrols' and 'contacts', as well as specific operations such as Saigon Guard during the Tet Offensive. One man wrote, 'I enjoyed the excitement of the action. I should have been disappointed to have missed a contact from being back at base.' Some men were keen to separate what they found exciting from what they found enjoyable. One wrote, 'Surviving most enjoyable. The buzz of battle most exciting. Heaven was a bottle of Worcestershire sauce, an onion and a dry cigarette.' Another regular soldier replied, 'Most exciting would have to be all the contacts. Most enjoyable R&C, R&R and the return to Australia.' The thing that regular soldiers enjoyed most about army life was fighting the enemy, which is the purpose of the army. For national servicemen on the first tour, the single most common response to the question was 'R&R'. Among second-tour (February 1970–February 1971) regulars, 'R&C' was rated as the single most exciting/enjoyable experience. 'Operations' came third. By 'operations', men meant 'Finding something out bush e.g. camp bunkers system. Being involved in a contact'; 'The feeling after successful contact'; 'The aftermath of contact. Enemy KIA'. Another regular soldier made the customary distinction: 'Exciting – contacts with enemy. Enjoyable – between the legs of a Vietnamese woman.' But only one second-tour national serviceman gave a response that could be classified as 'operations', and even that was a strictly contingent: 'The occasional contact in which we suffered no casualties.'

For some regular soldiers, Vietnam was a highlight of their life. One said, 'I did it all and had a ball. A great, great learning experience.'

The biggest single distinction between first-tour national servicemen and regular soldiers was that regulars enjoyed their work (that is, fighting) more than their leave, whereas nashos had the opposite experience. And during the second tour, regulars enjoyed their work far more than nashos did. The responses of junior officers in the survey were much more weighted towards operations, as might be expected of men who had chosen the military as a career.

Frankly (and I like to be frank), in an imperfect world it is essential that an army has professional soldiers who want to fight, rather than conscripts who would prefer to be drinking. So yes, I do think the British Paras wanted to be posted to Northern Ireland and regular Australian soldiers wanted to be sent to Vietnam.

When I first enrolled at ADFA, Jeffrey Grey briefly introduced me to my co-supervisor, Dr Robert Hall, but joked that I would not need to have anything much to do with Bob unless he (Jeff) died.

Then Jeff did die.

I was several years into the PhD when Hall took over as supervisor. Hall was a former officer in 8RAR, deployed to Vietnam in 1969–1970, and he gave me the collected wartime Gallup polls and an analysis of the peaks and troughs of public opinion. In 1996, the leader of the Opposition, Arthur Calwell, had said, 'The Vietnam war is unpopular in Australia because practically nobody wants to participate in it.'

But that was not true: Bob Hall did.

'I was a professional soldier,' Hall told me. 'I wanted to participate in the war. I was in Duntroon in 1966 and looking forward – along with my classmates – to going off to war.'

Did he feel out of touch with the rest of society?

'There was a schism in society, clearly,' he said. 'My sister was strongly anti-war. We had our own discussions around the dinner table at home. But a lot of people, I think, wanted to be involved.'

Before Australia entered the Vietnam War, there was little appetite among the public for a war. But as soon as the first Australian training troops were deployed in 1962, support skyrocketed to about 60 per cent and remained around that figure until late 1969, when, as I noted earlier, the US had already commenced its pull-out.

'At that point, most Australians wanted to also withdraw Australians,' said Hall. 'For obvious reasons.'

Contrary to the wild historical distortions of the post-Vietnam War years, Australians supported their troops – more so than they favoured the war.

Although overall backing for the war fell as the years went on, levels of support rose again precisely when they might have been expected to decline. During the My Lai trials and the moratorium marches, Australian enthusiasm for the war actually increased.

I asked Hall why he thought that popular support for the Vietnam War had been forgotten.

'It's been submerged a little under the conscription debate,' he said. 'There was no point in which [support for] conscription generally fell below 50 per cent. But there were two things about the conscription debate which upset people: one was the deployment of conscripts to Vietnam, and the other was the conscription by ballot. Many of the Gallup poll analyses included unsolicited remarks from people along the lines that they supported conscription but didn't want conscripts to be sent to Vietnam; or they supported conscription, but they wanted every twenty-year-old to be conscripted.'

The national service issue is one of the reasons so little is heard about the pro-war movement – which could more accurately be described as the 'anti-anti-war movement'.

The most effective, consistent, vocal and ideologically coherent opposition to the anti-war movement was led by the National Civic Council, whose social and cultural program was a furious rear-guard action against secular modernity. The NCC was the creation of Catholic political activist and polemicist Bartholomew Augustine Santamaria and it maintained an ambiguous relationship with the Democratic Labor Party (DLP), which also owed a large intellectual and organisational debt to Santamaria.

Vietnam was very much Santamaria's war. The dictatorial government of Catholic president of South Vietnam, Ngo Dinh Diem, who resettled hundreds of thousands of Catholics who fled the North, was much more popular among the war's supporters in Australia than in the US. When Diem was assassinated in a CIA-backed military coup in 1963, Santamaria declared, 'The principle of legitimacy is now destroyed,' but he continued to encourage every effort to defeat the Viet Cong until the end of the war.[2]

In contrast, the Second World War had not been to Santamaria's taste. Although he had just turned twenty-four when the fighting broke out in 1939, he sought and won exemption from war service to work for Catholic Action, a lay movement formed to implement Church policies and principles and save the world from anti-clericalism. Like other political figures who vigorously supported national service and the dispatch of conscripts to fight in Vietnam, Santamaria had never served in the regular army. He nonetheless had a wide-ranging influence on the debate over Vietnam in Australia, and his standing among Catholics was so high that even objectors might ask for his advice.

The Myths of Movements

But Santamaria's NCC would have made for an obnoxious dinner guest. It had three overlapping interests: politics, religion and sex. Its newspaper, *News-Weekly*, might begin by calmly discussing current affairs, then suddenly escalate into a foaming, engorged rage about extramarital sex. For example, when university students burned a cross and then laid four toilet seats in front of a war memorial in Kings Park, Perth on 1 April 1966, Santamaria accused the 'young larrikins' responsible of 'endeavouring to handicap the conduct of military operations in Vietnam'. But a story deeper in the body of *News-Weekly* examined in greater detail the 'depraved creatures responsible', and reads more like the confused fantasies of a priapic psychopath: 'This disgusting episode ... speaks eloquently of the depraved level which university "porno-politics" has reached ... It shows that Australian undergraduates are being swept up in the movement originating in Berkeley University, California – where the "Vietnam Day" campaign was conceived – which has passed through the phase of a "Free Speech Movement" to a "Filthy Speech Movement" ... to drug-taking on a massive scale, and the introduction of nude parties, where every kind of sexual perversion is practised in common.'[3]

Huh?

Much has been instances of violence and vandalism by anti-war protesters, but it has been forgotten that Labor Party meetings and anti-war protests were often disrupted by pro-conscriptionist, pro-government demonstrators in the early years of the war.

Most of the anti-anti-war actions seem to have been prosecuted by the DLP. On 17 April 1966 in Adelaide, 'Hundreds of jeering hecklers, shouting, chanting and stamping their feet, gave Mr Calwell a rough passage during his 50-minute speech,' reported the *Sydney Morning Herald*. 'A dozen uniformed police and additional plain-clothes men helped to keep order among the people inside the hall and another 1,000 listened to a relay of the meeting outside. Thirty minutes before the meeting began the hall was about one-third full. Then a side-door was rushed by the anti-Calwell brigade, there was a scuffle, and they burst into the hall.'

On 21 April 1966, when most of 5RAR marched through Sydney in a battalion farewell parade (and don't get me started about those ...), the crowds were leafleted by the NCC, which had produced 30,000 flyers supporting Australia's involvement in Vietnam. On May 24, 5RAR's Errol Noack from Adelaide became the first national serviceman killed in Vietnam. In response, *News-Weekly* attacked Arthur Calwell, in an open letter to him that thundered: 'Australian servicemen, you said, would be kept in safe areas until the elections so that there would be no casualties. Two days later, the first Australian national serviceman was killed, proving that the soldiers were not in safe areas, but already in action, even at the moment in which you were speaking. You did not apologise for your unworthy innuendo; in fact, you set sail on the opposite tack. You rushed in to make political capital out of his death, while his own uncle, who felt a grief which you a stranger to the boy could not possibly feel, said that he had died for Australia and begged people like you not to play politics with his death. The performance was horrifying.'[4]

In fact, it was later revealed – as it had been rumoured at the time – that Noack had been mistaken for the enemy by another Australian patrol and cut down by friendly fire. He had been a reluctant conscript, and while his uncle Herb had asked others not to attack government policy, he attacked government policy himself: 'I'm very much against the idea of a lottery being used to pick those who have to defend us,' he said.[5]

Two events occurred in Sydney in June 1966 which are remembered in inverse proportion to their newsworthiness at the time and their importance in the political history of a nation. On June 8, Nadine Jensen made her blood-bride charge at the homecoming parade for 1RAR. On June 21, Peter Kocan, a nineteen-year-old factory hand, fired a sawn-off .22 rifle at point-blank range at Arthur Calwell, who was sitting in a parked car outside an anti-conscription rally at Mosman Town Hall. Calwell was saved by the safety glass in his car window and suffered only minor injuries from the fragments of flying glass embedded in his face. *News-Weekly* blamed the left for creating the political climate which led to the attempt on Calwell's life. It persistently drew parallels with the attempted murder of Calwell and a demonstration at Kew Town Hall some months earlier, where Prime Minister Harold Holt's car had been rocked: According to *News-Weekly*, two types of activity were creating 'basic conditions of anarchy in Australian life': 'beatnik demonstrations and beatnik morals, often proposed by the same persons'.[6] It was as though Calwell had been shot by an anti-war demonstrator.

News-Weekly blamed foulness and filth, and 'a small group of alienated people, constantly at war with their environment ... their actions derived, at least in part, from a constant diet of sadistic and pornographic reading'. Meanwhile, Holt was the forgotten victim: 'the PM himself, who likes to mix freely wherever he goes, has had to submit to new restrictions on his movements since the Kew Town Hall incident, and the Government's security advisers have tightened their cover of meetings addressed by him.'[7]

In fact, *News-Weekly* felt that it was Holt who had survived an assassination attempt. 'Prime Minister Holt,' it insisted, 'was the first politician whose life was actually endangered by the deliberate injection of violence into politics.'[8] And so it was that as time passed Peter Kocan's deed vanished from memory, and a youth firing a gun at a member of parliament became symbolic of nothing, compared with a young woman smearing paint on a soldier.

Kocan was sentenced to life imprisonment, sent briefly to Long Bay Prison, then transferred to a psychiatric hospital, where he received a letter of forgiveness from Calwell. He was released in 1977, after serving nine-and-a-half years of his sentence. He became a successful writer of poetry and prose – and, of course, a victim. Because it turned out that the assassination attempt had been directed at Kocan himself anyway: 'I think I was trying to achieve a big suicidal crescendo to end my miserable life,' he said. 'I had a vague notion I'd been shot in a hail of bullets by bodyguards.'[9]

The ferociously anti-communist Santamaria flattered his opponents with imitation. He was particularly fond of setting up Leninist-style, single-issue 'front groups'. Among the many NCC stooge organisations listed by his biographer Gerard Henderson – ranging from the Wheat for India Campaign to the Australian Council for Educational Standards – is the anti-anti-war Peace With Freedom (PWF).

The founding president of Peace With Freedom was James McAuley, a robust defender of selective conscription. The arguments used to justify the national service ballot seem hard to credit today, but the principles behind them were as sincerely held as (and virtually identical to) those of the patriotic women of the First World War. McAuley, best known as one half of the hoax surrealist poet Ern Malley, looked back to an earlier time in his defence of national service for Vietnam in 1966: a supporter of conscription '*for others*' (his italics) might easily be made to look like 'a dispenser of white feathers', he said. It would have been particularly easy to characterise McAuley as such, since he had spent the Second World War as a militia lieutenant in a secret unit in Melbourne and Canberra, writing faux modernist poetry and perpetrating the Ern Malley hoax.

The Myths of Movements

Nonetheless, McAuley wrote that military service was a duty, like 'paying taxes or serving on a jury which a good citizen loyally accepts when it is put upon him, though he may dislike it, and avoid it if he can take advantage of any legal exemptions'. While conscription was moral, he argued, it was immoral to give conscripts the choice of agreeing to fight, as the volunteer 'might not necessarily "want" to go' but simply be persuaded by other unknowable factors. McAuley did not believe that the fairest result was necessarily 'produced by leaving it to these private calculations'. Since universal service was not required, he wrote, 'There is a case for not dropping the weight of an unwelcome decision on every individual, taking advantage, as it were, of those who would then feel that they "had better" volunteer.'[10]

These were the strongest arguments that pro-selective conscriptionists could muster, and they do not stand up to what people who do not regularly go to pubs have taken to calling 'the pub test'. They did not even convince McAuley's intellectual comrades. The second most prominent PWF member, the customarily unconstrained former Marxist Frank Knopfelmacher – who, unlike McAuley, had actually seen active service during the Second World War – later admitted he had felt 'inhibited' by 'the "conscription" angle of the debate, which entailed persuading what could have been my sons into the muck of a military machine'.[11]

McAuley's often unsympathetic biographer Cassandra Pybus wrote, 'Peace With Freedom was very loose: no office-bearers other than McAuley himself, no formal membership, no membership fee, no minuted meetings [and] no publications held in the National Library.' Except for Gerard Henderson, who was a student representative at Peace With Freedom, 'no-one who was associated with Peace With Freedom can remember anything much about the organisation or what it did'.[12] However, as Robert Manne has

239

written, the purpose of PWF was indisputably 'to defend Australian involvement in the Vietnam War and to contest the anti-war movement on university campuses'.[13]

Knopfelmacher believed that Peace With Freedom was 'probably the best political training school this country has ever seen'. He was never much for self-deprecation and maintained, 'It would be false modesty not to point to the high average IQ of our gatherings or to deny that our seminars were better than anything I have witnessed at any university anywhere.'[14]

Knopfelmacher held that the war's supporters in Australia performed better than their contemporaries in the US, as they never caved in: 'We fought the local fifth column step by step, in all significant tertiary institutions, in the media, and at public forums,' and 'had it not been for the American surrender in the field initiated by Johnson's "abdication" speech we would have carried intellectual opinion with us (the masses being on side all the time did not have to be turned)'.

He was broadly correct about 'the masses' being largely onside, but Johnson had made the unexpected announcement that he would not again run for president in March 1968, long before the peak of the US anti-war movement.

Since the anti-war movement did nothing much to stop the war, it is difficult to see what the anti-anti-war forces might possibly have accomplished – but it is easier to understand what nobbled them. They were backed into a position of minimising or denying atrocities that everybody today believes to have taken place. In 1968, in 'The Great Napalm Lie Exposed', *News-Weekly* stated that there had been 'no children burned by napalm' in a region where such injuries had been alleged.[15] In a letter to *The Age* Santamaria quoted a doctor with an Australian surgical team who suggested that rather than being napalmed 'many children were burned by overturned oil lamps or by the explosion of kerosene lamps into which their parents had poured high-octane petrol taken from fuel dumps'.[16]

One reason the Vietnam War became so desperately and utterly lost among the intellectuals whom PWF hoped to persuade is the moral defeat occasioned by the broadening understanding of what happened at My Lai. It slowly became apparent that 16 March 1968 had seen the mass murder of villagers in the South, by US troops who were ostensibly fighting to protect them, and an orgy of gang rapes, mutilations and sexual torture of women and children that defied even the most jaded caricature of military purpose.

Santamaria at first described the My Lai massacre as 'a battle' and the dead women and children as 'surrendered combatants', although *News-Weekly* later called for the atrocity's leader, Lt William Calley, to stand trial.

Another grouping in Santamaria's orbit, Friends of Vietnam, produced the magazine *Vietnam Digest*, but its pro-war propagandising was consistently hampered by moral honesty. In the first edition, the historian Geoffrey Fairbairn wrote, 'The Viet Cong do display very great heroism and very great ingenuity ... They die very well indeed ... but they die bravely as part of a Collective which they believe will alter the very nature of man; and they live quite without individuality ... the call that sustains them in their hour of need is the call of the corroboree.' His bigger point was that the Viet Cong were dangerously mistaken, but he had difficulty turning this into a convincing argument as to why Australians should cross the seas and risk their own lives to annihilate them.[17]

Friends of Vietnam was appalled by many of the people who seemed to share its cause. In a later piece in the *Digest*, journalist Peter Samuel bemoaned the tragedy of My Lai but saved his deepest despair for President Nixon and the bellicose, conservative majority of the US people. If people came to think that in wars such as Vietnam 'senseless atrocities and careless killings' were commonplace, then there 'simply would not be the domestic political support to sustain them, and who would argue that that would be wrong?', wrote Samuel. But the support for the killings was there, much to Samuel's discomfort: the Americans who said Calley had been sent to kill and was simply doing his job were 'appallingly numerous'.[18]

Civil organisations outside of Santamaria's ideological empire were more effective than Friends of Vietnam in providing both moral and physical support for the war effort. O'Brien writes of the consistent aid offered to the troops by the Surfers Paradise Rotary Patriotic Fund and its Wounded Servicemen's Convalescent Scheme (WSCS). Under the WSCS, any Australian and, later, New Zealand, serviceman wounded in Vietnam and evacuated to Australia was given a first-class return airfare with Ansett Airlines from any capital city to Coolangatta airport, and provided with a two-week, all-expenses-paid stay in a first-class Gold Coast hotel or similar accommodation, with tours and entertainment included. If the wounded man was married, his wife was sponsored too. Surfers Paradise RSL helped out with meals. Honorary Rotary Club member and ex-serviceman Ken Bromley wrote a weekly column for the Gold Boast *Bulletin* following the recovery of every single wounded soldier (and the newspaper itself, notes O'Brien, always referred to Brisbane-based 7RAR as 'Lt Colonel Ron Grey's superb 7th Battalion RAR'). By the end of the WSCS in 1973, the scheme had cared for 1496 wounded men, 623 wives and an uncounted number of children. Its spirit survives in the Ken Bromley Association which, through the Gold Coast Rotary Club, continues to provide two-week, five-star holidays to any psychologically or physically wounded serviceperson or ex-serviceperson in need of a break.

The pro-Vietnam War movement was forgotten even by John Howard, who played a part in it himself, as the speaker at a meeting in favour of both the war and conscription at Bankstown in April 1970, two years after the massacre at My Lai. On 17 August 2006, on the eve of the fortieth anniversary of the Battle of Long Tan, Howard issued in parliament a formal apology to Vietnam veterans. He prefaced his remarks with the qualifier that it was not his intention 'in any way' to revisit Australia's internal debates about the war (although he rarely missed a chance to do that very thing). He was not even offering his opinion but simply stating a fact, since 'an objective assessment would reveal our nation's collective failure at the time to adequately honour the service of those who went to Vietnam'.

'Those who served in Vietnam were not welcomed back as they should have been,' he insisted. 'Whatever our views may have been – and I include those who supported the war as well as those who opposed it – the nation collectively failed those men.'[19]

He did not explain how veterans had been failed by the actions of the DLP, the NCC, PWF, the Surfers Paradise Rotary Patriotic Fund, or the huge crowds that had welcomed back infantry battalions in the sixteen welcome-home parades that preceded the 1987 reunion. He simply implied that none of this had happened. Nor do the more militant Vietnam veterans seem especially keen to remember pro-war feeling or the pro-war movement, since their argument rests on the proposition that nobody supported them. The left has no interest in maintaining a memory of its enemies, and even sympathetic conservatives do not particularly want to go down in history as priapically obsessed with the sexual proclivities of young demonstrators – or, indeed, as white feather men. And so it is that the pro-Vietnam War movement fell victim to the amnesia that so often claims even the most vigorously prosecuted of lost causes.

The Shape of Myths to Come

On a mild autumn morning in August 2023, I walked into the Australian War Memorial in Canberra, where the delicious smell of fresh carpentry spiced the air in corridors that echoed with the hum of unseen drills – the sound of myths in the making.

The Memorial was in the early stages of a $500 million redesign and refurbishment, conceived under the Scott Morrison government, which in two years had granted more funding to the Memorial than to every other Australian national cultural institution put together.[1] On the upside, this oddest of governments in the strangest of times had not bankrolled any actual wars.

A couple of months before my visit to the Memorial, a judge had dismissed a defamation case brought by Australia's most decorated living soldier, former SAS patrol commander Corporal Benjamin Roberts-Smith VC, MG, against newspapers and journalists who had reported accusations of war crimes against him, many of which originated from inside his own regiment. The judge ruled that Roberts-Smith had broken the rules of engagement and committed four murders in Afghanistan.[2] Roberts-Smith's court actions were effectively underwritten by the billionaire Kerry Stokes, who sat on the board of the Memorial.

Roberts-Smith's Disruptive Pattern Desert Uniform remained on display in a cabinet near the entrance of the Memorial's 'Conflicts 1945 to Today' gallery. Headless and handless, yet apparently self-supporting, it could have been a hollow man.

The Roberts-Smith exhibit was captioned with a statement from Memorial chair Kim Beazley on behalf of the Australian War Memorial Council, acknowledging 'the gravity of the decision' in the defamation case and 'its broader impact on all involved in the Australian community' (by which Beazley presumably meant everyone in Australia, or perhaps every Australian in the world). The judgement was described as 'one step in a longer legal process'. While items relating to Roberts-Smith were still on display, the board was ostensibly 'considering carefully the additional content and context to be included in these displays'. The clatter of building work drowned out the purr of the board cogitating prudently.

The fate of Roberts-Smith and the Memorial were intertwined, both parties locked in a stilted dance of truth evasion that, if I were a better writer, I might be able to work into a metaphor for Australia's deployments in the Middle East.

The offensives that became widely known in the English-speaking world as the War on Terror began in retaliation to al Qaeda's attacks on the US on 11 September 2001. It soon became apparent that the US would invade the Islamic Emirate of Afghanistan to rout the terrorist leadership from its supposed hiding place, and that Australia would send troops to support the operation. Street demonstrations against the bombing of Afghanistan were held in several Australian cities, and about 3000 people marched through Sydney.

As was to become his custom, Prime Minister John Howard took the opportunity to refight the Vietnam War. Addressing the Australian Defence Association, he said, 'I can rule out the introduction of conscription ... in the present strategic circumstances, national service is neither necessary nor appropriate.' He stressed that there could be 'no valid comparison' between Afghanistan and Vietnam, where 'large, conscripted forces [had been] necessary for major land battles and frequent armed confrontations'.[3]

Firstly, there is no sensible measure by which the Australian force in Vietnam could have been considered 'large' (in 1968, at the height of the Australian and US deployments, there were only 8000 Australians in Vietnam and 549,500 US servicepeople), or pivotal in any 'major land battle'. Secondly, the underlying idea that national service had been re-introduced for the Vietnam War is simply untrue.

But why was Howard even talking about this? No serious commentator had suggested that the war in Afghanistan might require a conscript army in Australia. There was no mass movement against the invasion. The prime minister was arguing with ghosts.

The Australian military mission in Afghanistan, said Howard, was 'likely to be pursued through precision, ground operations conducted by small teams of Special Forces', and 'the decision to include Australian SAS soldiers was recognition both of the highly targeted nature of the coming campaign and the important role our soldiers could play within it'.[4] I imagine the message Howard hoped to get across was that there would be few Australian troops on the ground, and therefore few casualties to worry about, and even the small number of soldiers in harm's way would be highly trained superheroes and, effectively, bulletproof.

If I had been a bit younger, a lot braver and considerably more capable, I would have considered joining the military myself. As it was, I stayed in Australia and edited the 'lads' magazine' *Ralph*.

While the job of lads' magazine editor is vital in time of war, I have to face facts: I probably would not have passed SAS selection, but I might have made it into the Australian Army Public Relations

Service. And if the first draft of history is journalism, then the first draft of myth is PR.

The most distinctive feature of the popular image of the war in Afghanistan is that there was not one. For most of the war, for most of the time, most people at home had no idea what was going on. While Australian troops were stationed at Tarinkot in the southern province of Uruzgan, a reporter for *The Age* wrote that 'Australians know little about what their troops are doing in Afghanistan, and they seem not to care. This lack of curiosity about what is being done by Australian soldiers in the name of all Australians is not confined to the public: many journalists and editors seem to share the community's indifference.'[5]

There were plenty of reasons not to care about Afghanistan: it is a long way from Australia; very few younger Australians had ever been there; it was an Islamist theocracy; it had no colonial ties to Western states; and for years on end, the Department of Defence had managed media affairs with such opacity that it was barely possible to get any idea of what was going on anyway. Most Australian troops appeared to be plumbers or boilermakers of some kind, largely employed in building wells and water tanks.

If Australians had any picture of Afghanis at all, it was as the undeserving refugees onboard the MV *Tampa*, which the SAS (*the SAS!*) had been required to board and turn back. They were most likely the kind of monsters who would toss their own children into the ocean for the chance to claim Centrelink benefits in southwest Sydney.

Widespread public apathy made it easier for Defence to self-defeatingly and reflexively hide what was going on – until seemingly out of nowhere emerged evidence of shocking war crimes around the welding, soldering and rigging of a great desert pipefitting project. I spoke with former army PR officer Tony Park, who saw the beginning of Defence's determination to keep the public uninformed about Afghanistan in the context of the military's opening up to the media during the Australian deployment to the UN peace-keeping mission in Somalia in the early 1990s.

Until Somalia, the army smarted from what many in Defence felt to be the part that the media (rather than the Viet Cong and the North Vietnam Army) had played in defeating the US and its allies in Vietnam. In the gap between deployments, the press had become the enemy. But for Somalia, the Department of Defence raised the Media Support Unit to provide journalists in the field with access, accommodation, and the facilities needed to file stories.

'We were developing doctrine that would "group up" the media,' Park told me. 'We were going to make them our friends. We started rolling out an awful lot of media training. And all of this culminated very, very nicely with East Timor [where the intervention of Australian troops as peacekeepers began in 1999]. Commanders were getting used to this idea that in a battle space today, the media will be there, we have to look after them and "control" the media space.

'And it all went swimmingly. Then the war in Afghanistan came.

'But what happened in the intervening period was Children Overboard,' said Park. 'And Children Overboard turned our organisation around 180 degrees in the wrong direction.'

The 'Children Overboard Incident' was an event on 6 October 2001, when asylum seekers crammed onto a ship designated SIEV 4 (Suspected Irregular Entry Vessel) were intercepted by HMAS *Adelaide*, which towed their vessel and caused it to sink.

John Howard claimed the asylum seekers had threatened to throw their children into the ocean then 'irresponsibly sank the damn boat, which put their children in the water'.[6]

He wouldn't have a bar of it.

It was not true. The asylum seekers had done no such thing, but Chief of the Defence Force, Admiral Chris Barrie, gave a disastrous press conference in which he was unable to clarify what he knew about the deception and when. 'Barrie got caned, absolutely slaughtered,' said Park. 'He was not media-aware. If he'd had media training, he showed no evidence of it.'

The Department of Defence concluded that the problem lay not in the government's handling of the affair, but in citizens who asked questions in press conferences – that is, the media.

'I used to see it in the private sector, when I was working as a PR consultant,' said Park. 'There's a big corporation and their PR is going swimmingly, and all the factory managers are encouraged to engage with the local media, and they put out proactive stuff – and then there's a disaster or someone dies, and the whole organisation turns on itself: Who's responsible? How could this happen? Let's centralise control. Let's centralise control of PR so that no-one can ever say something wrong, and no-one can ever release the wrong picture.

'And that happened with Defence in Children Overboard. So all media inquiries, all imagery, all pictures now had to go through Canberra. We had gone from being at the top of our game to being this media-terrified organisation, controlled with an iron fist by the minister's office. You literally had a backlog of press releases about recruitment activities and open days that were waiting on the minister's press secretary to approve them. It was ridiculous. And this was all happening before Afghanistan started.'

I asked Park about the PR strategy in Afghanistan, where most of the early action for Australia involved a Special Forces Task Group.

'There was no strategy,' he said. 'It was like the entire war. Never overestimate how much planning goes into this. Everything was on the fly. At first, the strategy was that the government and Defence would say nothing about what was going on, and certainly nothing about any action our people were getting into. However, when he was defence minister, Robert Hill took a couple of journos on a trip to Afghanistan. The idea was Special Forces Task Group was under the radar, but now the defence minister shows up with a couple of journos and these couple of journos naturally start asking questions. And Lt Col Rowan Tink [of the SAS] starts answering questions.'

Tink gave the media details about the coordinating role played by Australian Special Forces during Operation Anaconda and a battle that led to the deaths of about 500 enemy fighters in March 2002.

'Because you had a policy where the Special Forces Task Group is under the radar, *unless the Defence Minister wants to come to town with some journos*,' said Park.

Defence sent an army camera team to Afghanistan – a PR officer, a video operator, a stills photographer and a journalist from the army newspaper, *Army News*. 'Their job was to generate some product, to get videos of the guys – not in action, but pretending – driving around Afghan villages, not shooting (because we don't want to show that),' said Park. 'We got some really superb imagery. You still see it today. For a few years, that was all that was in the public domain: stuff from that weeklong visit. And I had to choreograph that with the SAS guys, and get them used to the fact that someone was going to be pointing a camera at them so to cover up their faces. And no sensitive gear was on show. The SAS guys on the ground really got into it – they're smart operators and they could see that the public needed to see something, and that they could have some control on what got out there.'

Park and Colonel Tink discussed the message they needed to send home to Australia, and agreed that it was to remind people that there was a war going on, that Australian soldiers were fighting and that Afghanistan was a dangerous country. With that in mind, 'The next time someone gets killed, the Australian media can't say, "Oh my God, bring the soldiers home,"' said Parks. 'They need to know this is a dangerous business.'

Park believed that his strategy would have seen the war covered more normally, even normalised. The public would have been presented with triumphs and tragedies, victories and setbacks, perhaps even characters and journeys – maybe a Simpson with a camel – and Australians would have been able to follow the fighting as if it were an ongoing occurrence rather than a state secret. Instead, they were confronted with long periods of nothing unevenly punctuated by inexplicable surprises.

Tony Park said, 'Strategically, what the government *should* have been doing during my time in late 2002, when the coalition had the upper hand militarily, was using the media to push the case that Afghanistan needed an avalanche of humanitarian and reconstruction aid money, and consolidation and training of its armed forces. When all that came, years later, it was too little, too late.

'As it happened, at the end of 2002 [much of] the US military pulled out and went to Iraq. And it all turned to shit. The world forgot about Afghanistan and the Taliban started coming back.'

In February 2003, I and about 200,000 other people marched in Sydney against the looming Iraq War (so it's a good thing I had not joined the army, really). The way I saw it, a conspiracy of Saudi Arabians, Emiratis and Egyptians had attacked the US under the direction of their Saudi Arabian leader, who was hiding out in Afghanistan – so Australia planned to help invade Iraq to stop it from happening again.

The Shape of Myths to Come

John Howard's justification for going to war for the second time in his third term in government was to deprive Iraq of its weapons of mass destruction, although he also professed concern about 'the use of a human shredding machine as a vehicle for putting to death critics of Saddam Hussein'. I did not believe that Iraq possessed unused weapons of mass destruction, but I had no particular position on the people-eating appliance.

As far as I remember, I marched because I either hoped or believed that if enough people showed their opposition to the war, Australia would not take part. In retrospect, I am not sure how or why I imagined that marching might prevent a war. It's possible I had absorbed prevailing ideas that the moratorium demonstrations had contributed to Australia's withdrawal from Vietnam, but I cannot say for sure.

I was not alone: for once, I was not even in the minority. About half a million people joined anti-war marches throughout Australia. John Howard responded, 'I don't know that you can measure public opinion just by the number of people that turn up at demonstrations.'[7] However, of a dozen pre-Iraq War polls, not one showed majority support for the coming invasion: an average of only 36 per cent of respondents were in favour.[8] Over that same weekend in February, 10–15 million people across the globe demonstrated against the war, in what *Time* magazine called 'by some accounts the largest single coordinated protest in history'.[9]

Of course, the invasion went ahead, because walking from one place to another does not make any difference to anything. I believe there were subsequent smaller demonstrations against the war but I did not take part, since if public opinion could not prevent the military from going to Iraq, it was hardly likely to bring them back.

In March, when Howard announced that Australia would commit forces to 'action to disarm Iraq', he added, 'To those in the community who may not agree with me, please vent your anger against me and towards the government.'[10] By this, he was not calling for a resumption of the huge anti-war demonstrations, he was attacking the Vietnam-era protesters whose memory he could never leave alone.

The idea that would-be demonstrators heeded their prime minister and shelved plans to douse themselves in red paint and charge at the SAS is perpetuated at the War Memorial. The 'Conflicts 1945 to Today' gallery, which was only partially open during my visit, makes the claim that during the Vietnam War, 'some protesters' (Nadine Jensen?) 'directed their anger against those in uniform and their families' which, along with 'union strikes which delayed the arrival of mail and beer', in turn angered the troops in Vietnam. But the good news, according to the AWM, was that 'belated recognition by the Australian public that protests against Vietnam veterans were misdirected has helped servicemen and women serving overseas to avoid similar treatment'.

This is unproven and unprovable. It has never been suggested that there was ever the slightest danger of non-Islamist Australians harassing serving soldiers during the War on Terror. And it is unlikely that Islamist terrorists might have been deterred by a realisation that armies are simply a tool of governments, or that they might hurt the feelings of their victims' families. One of the reasons that opposition to the wars in Afghanistan and Iraq was so muted is that almost nobody in Australia had any political sympathy for the Taliban, al Qaeda or Saddam Hussain's Ba'athists. It is possible that events on the home front might have played out differently if sections of the left had already been coopted into unconditional support of an Islamist ideology. Little has been said about the way Australian Middle East veterans feel about watching tens of thousands of Australians demonstrating for Palestinian freedom. Just as the post-Vietnam War anti-rape protests became wartime anti-war marches in veterans' memories, perhaps Palestinian keffiyehs will turn into Afghan shemaghs, and anti-Israel protests will become pro-Taliban rallies for another generation of returned men and women.

Maybe that will happen in the real world, too.

In Afghanistan, meanwhile, the war rekindled and then set ablaze. Australian troops were redeployed against the backdrop of a renewed Taliban insurgency in late 2005. A Reconstruction Task Force of engineers, protected by infantry, artillery and cavalry, went to Uruzgan province in September 2006. A new Special Operations Task Force, including commandos and SAS, later went out to support them. In 2009, Operational Mentoring and Liaison Teams were embedded in the Afghan National Army. Australian combat troops left Iraq in 2009, but Australians continued to play a role in Afghanistan until the last remaining forces were withdrawn in 2021, two months before the capital Kabul fell to the Taliban once again. However, the conflict rarely attracted much media coverage except when a soldier was awarded a Victoria Cross, or a man was killed.

The four Australian VCs were Mark Donaldson, Ben Roberts-Smith, Dan Keighran, and Cameron Stewart Baird (posthumous). Donaldson was awarded the VC for an action in January 2009, when his SAS patrol was ambushed by a larger Taliban force. Under a sustained bombardment of machineguns and rocket-propelled grenades, Donaldson first exposed himself to fire to draw the attackers' attention away from wounded Australian troops, then dashed out to pick up the patrol's wounded Afghan interpreter and carry him to cover, saving his life.

'Mark Donaldson was paraded in front of the media,' said Park. 'I was in a stand-by pool of officers, and they brought me back to do Mark Donaldson's media training, I was having to continually lift up my lower jaw to close my mouth, because I didn't know there was so much shooting going on! And I had been working at HQ Special Operations. Mark said to me, "Every day, we'd go out of the base, and we knew we'd get shot at." Now, that didn't happen in my time. If someone fired a gun, it was almost going to be big news.'

Roberts-Smith received the VC for almost single-handedly attacking and destroying two Taliban machinegun positions in June 2010. The third VC, infantryman Dan Keighran, whose autobiography was later co-authored by Tony Park, fearlessly broke cover under ambush several times to draw enemy fire, allowing Australians and their Afghan allies to pinpoint Taliban positions and evacuate Australian wounded in August 2010. Baird died leading a commando raid on a Taliban compound in June 2013.

Park told me, 'When Donaldson's story came out and Ben Roberts-Smith's and, to a lesser extent (because he was deceased), Cameron Baird's, we had the protected-identity rules, where we went to great lengths to make sure no photo ever showed anybody's face, and that no names or personal details were given. We used to burn all our mail in Afghanistan (not the letters, but the packaging and parcels that they came in) because the Yanks were saying that the Taliban had guys in Bagram going through rubbish dumps looking for people's names and addresses, so that they could target their families back home. So, we were super-paranoid about all that – *unless you kill a load of guys!*

'The main media events during the war were the funerals. Because once a prime minister has attended one funeral, they can't not attend the next one. I'm the first to say that we have to honour the sacrifices of people, but it was seen by many in Defence to be turned into events – and the politicians could do that. They felt they couldn't talk about action and what was happening in the war, but they could do this other stuff. And I think it created a feeling that we weren't doing that well, that it wasn't worth it.

'Then there was nothing for months or years until we got funerals, then Dan Keighran won a VC. Strike up the band! Roll him out! What's going on? He was in one of the biggest firefights of all time, and his mate got killed. So we had nothing, but then the tap got opened up a little bit when there was a medal winner. That comes back to the failure of PR: in everybody's mind, Afghanistan was about Aussies getting killed, or it was about superhuman Aussies doing superhuman things.'

Ultimately, with Special Forces, at least, 'The pendulum swung the other way,' said Park, 'from not wanting to be seen and wanting to hide away, they were briefing advertising companies for recruitment ads, based on some of the images that we'd shot in Afghanistan. They wanted to use the media – and even advertising – to ensure they had a flow of people.'

Eventually, media were permitted to become 'embedded' with Australian troops and some solid reporting came out of Afghanistan but, said Park, 'The fault in our failure to really use the media and PR during the war was down to governments and this micromanagement. We go out of our way to protect people's identities – except the ones that kill the most people. We put Ben Roberts-Smith on the *Sunday Night* program, wading through the pool with weights over his head.'

Roberts-Smith was by far the most visible of the VC recipients. Malcom Knox, who ghostwrote Mark Donaldson's autobiography, *The Crossroads*, told me, 'When I was writing it in around 2010, and even at around the time it was published, people would ask, "What're you doing?" and I would say, "I'm ghostwriting a book for the first Australian VC winner since Vietnam." People automatically would say, "Oh, that really big guy!" I had to explain, "No, no, there was a guy – *the little guy* – who won one before him."

'Even then,' said Knox, 'the notoriety of Roberts-Smith was way in excess of whatever surrounded Mark – partly, I think, because Mark is such a reserved person, but also partly because of the nature of the action in which they each won their VC. You contrast Roberts-Smith as a guy who stormed a machinegun nest with his automatic weapon and killed a bunch of bad guys, with Mark who was somebody who ran into a field where there were bullets raining down on him to rescue and save the life of a wounded Afghan interpreter. It was such a different way of displaying courage – which is also typical of Mark as a person, as opposed to Roberts-Smith, but it lent itself less to the PR myth-making of that time. What was being mythologised about the VC was the aggressive aspect of soldiering.'

While Roberts-Smith had killed the most enemy fighters in Afghanistan, he later turned out to have also killed a number of people who were not fighting and perhaps not even the enemy.[11] He was not alone. By the time Roberts-Smith's defamation action had failed, The Inspector-General of the Australian Defence Force Afghanistan Inquiry report (more widely known as the Brereton Report) had uncovered evidence of twenty-three incidents 'in which one or more non-combatants were unlawfully killed by or at the direction of Australian Special Forces'. A total of thirty-nine civilians were allegedly murdered, and weapons were sometimes placed with their bodies in order to make them look like enemy combatants.[12]

In an extraordinary statement to a parliamentary committee, retired Special Forces major Heston Russell said, 'I have watched as the reputation of our veterans and all that we achieved in Afghanistan has been raped by elements of the media, while the Department of Defence and the government at large have left veterans and our families to defend ourselves, becoming potential targets for the real threats in this world … The simple fact that the Australian public and media were left to ask if our time in Afghanistan "was worth it" is the most monumental failing of successive Australian governments, who otherwise excel at all forms of marketing spin and rhetoric – failing to educate and engage the Australian public throughout our longest conflict...'

Russell said, 'There were over 11,000 insurgents and terrorists killed, yet our legacy has come down to accusations of illegally killing 39 civilians. That is less than 0.04 per cent of those killed during the conduct of our operations in Afghanistan, yet we hear nothing of the 99.96 per cent of those operations that saw our Australian special forces demonstrate everything it means to embody the Australian spirit and values we readily lack here [in Parliament] today.'[13]

If the Special Operations Task Group really did kill 11,000 people in Afghanistan – and that number seems to have become widely accepted – it is not at all clear who these people might have been. The highest credible estimates count the peak wartime operational strength of the Taliban at only 60,000 core fighters, supported by about 90,000 militia and perhaps another 50,000 facilitators and support elements.[14] If every one of the 11,000 killed by Australian Special Forces alone had been core fighters, they would have accounted for more than 18 per cent of the entire Taliban. Moreover, Australian forces were largely based in Uruzgan province, which is home to only about 2 per cent of the Afghan population.

There seems to have been a high degree of aggregation of the enemy in Afghanistan, which may have been one of the sins of Ben Roberts-Smith.

Part of the problem with the memory of Roberts-Smith lies with the pride in the hero before his fall. He is 2 metres tall, born to be the stuff of statues. He already looks like a statue of himself.

A judge found Roberts-Smith to be a war criminal.[15] In one incident, Roberts-Smith had machine-gunned a man with a prosthetic leg, which he souvenired as a trophy and later encouraged other soldiers to drink from. In another, he kicked a kneeling and handcuffed Afghan prisoner off a cliff and into a dry creek bed. The prisoner fell so hard that his teeth were knocked out of his mouth. He was then shot dead.

I would guess that this is the image that will survive the war – the helpless, handcuffed prisoner tumbling down the cliff. This is what people will remember. But I do not think most people will care.

It is a little early for the war to be reborn in popular drama, although no doubt there will soon be Australian movies about conflicted commandoes, morally compromised SAS troopers, and engineers and infantrymen just doing their job. In the third chapter of this book, I wrote about the Australian War Memorial's travelling exhibition *ACTION! Film & War* – in which the war in Afghanistan was partly represented by props from a movie made by my former neighbour, Benjamin Gilmour. In a glass cabinet, near spangly dresses worn in the 2012 Vietnam War movie *Sapphires*, was the traditional Afghan *perahan tunban* adopted by Gilmour when he filmed his 2018 ultra-low-budget drama *Jirga* in Afghanistan.

Jirga tells the fictional story of a former Australian soldier who returns to Kandahar province after the war to ask forgiveness from the family of an unarmed civilian he had killed during a raid on a village. Gilmour told me that he hoped the movie would 'propose an idea to the audience about what was possible around post-conflict restorative justice – this possibility of healing a relationship between the occupiers and the enemy'. Therefore, he said, he was 'really surprised' to be approached for an Australian War Memorial exhibition. 'I saw the film as an *anti*-war film that explored the negative impact of war on both civilians and combatants,' he said. 'You have a traumatised veteran returning to find some peace for himself, and traumatised Afghans sharing their story and their perspective with him.'

Among other unexpected responses to the movie was the expressed desire among some genuine veterans to follow in the footsteps of Gilmour's central character. 'In 2019 and 2020, I received messages from two former ADF members who had seen *Jirga* and were moved by it,' Gilmour told me. 'One asked me if I thought forgiveness would be the outcome if he conducted a similar journey to my protagonist's and I said, "Yes, possible, but not guaranteed." The other, I put on to a British travel guide doing trips over there, as he wanted to go, but I think COVID stopped him. In 2021, I got a message from a US army soldier with a similar question. I considered at that time actually starting a travel company to facilitate exactly these kinds of healing missions.'

If real-life veterans were to imitate the pilgrimage in *Jirga*, it would be a phenomenon as remarkable as the way in which the First World War white feather women followed the example of Harry Faversham's fiancée in *The Four Feathers*. Fiction would provide the raw material for fact, rather than the other way around. And *Jirga*'s quest for redemption would perhaps come to be remembered among returned servicepeople as a real story that had happened to one of their own. Benjamin Gilmour would have authored a myth, complete with its contestable object lessons about the reception a remorseful killer might receive in Afghanistan.

Before the war-crimes investigation and the Roberts-Smith trial, the war in Afghanistan was an almost blank slate. Tony Park predicted that any future TV story about Afghanistan, would likely 'relay the same footage that my camera team shot in 2002 of guys riding through villages on motorbikes, because there isn't much else'. But there is always the unofficial record. Ordinary soldiers have been making home movies at least since Vietnam, but

Australian veterans of the war in Afghanistan often keep helmet-cam footage of house-to-house operations, which make war look like a frenzied, frenetic videogame. I was first shown footage like this on desktop computers in veterans' homes, and it can be dizzyingly confronting. 'There is an immediacy,' the Australian War Memorial's Daniel Eisenberg told me. 'The camera is at eye level. Both hands are free, which means things like a weapon can come into shot.'

And the pursuit looks unstoppable and terrifying from the point of view of the pursued.

In about 2012, Park was tasked with what he called a 'sneaky job' for the army: 'I was asked to do a review of imagery that was coming out of the war and was going online,' he said. 'By that stage, the helmet-cam stuff was starting to leak out, and by far the most popular videos – if you looked at what were getting the most hits on YouTube – were action-type videos from the field. The official army PR videos were a bit of the mentoring stuff, more often than not ministerial visits or prime-ministerial visits, which no-one watched. And they couldn't work out why it wasn't cutting through.'

The war in Afghanistan remains wide open to reinvention. 'There isn't even the record of it to help shape whatever perception there is of it,' said Park, 'because, by and large, for fourteen years most people didn't know or didn't care about or didn't understand what was going on. I didn't know how much combat was going on – and I was in the bloody army!'

Popular perspectives will change over time – although perhaps not with the dizzying speed and frequency with which they have altered about Vietnam. But it is always dangerous to make a claim for historical singularity, and I am confident in predicting that in the coming years some veterans may feel shamed by association with the crimes of Roberts-Smith and others, and protest that

The Shape of Myths to Come

they themselves did nothing wrong, but there will be a deliberately audible undertone that they had heard whispers about what the SAS bad boys had been up to – because it will seem such an integral part of the story that if you didn't know about it, you were not really there.

There will be a period of hesitation, and something approaching silence from formerly pro-war voices, who will claim to have always harboured private doubts. For a while, it will appear as if nobody had been in favour of the war, even the politicians who prosecuted it. Stronger arguments will be made that the invasion – while unwise – was necessary to maintain our military ties with the US.

Journalists – or, at least, columnists – will turn on better journalists and claim it was the reporting that was at fault; and people who have never been to war themselves will insist that other people who have never been to war could not possibly understand the pressures that might drive a hero to kick a handcuffed shepherd off a cliff.[16] It will be forgotten, or passed over, that it was the hero's mates who gave him up, and the worst elements of the squadron will be elevated over the best, and cowardly murderers will be given more credibility than brave and honourable men.

When the dust settles, we will be told that all veterans are heroes, and it is time we moved on from an isolated incident – or however many isolated incidents there turn out to be – and support our military just as our military support our democracy with their lives.

The official histories will be published, giving jobbing journalists a sturdy factual framework on which to hang sometimes dubious oral histories. On manufactured anniversaries, popular books recounting the 'lost secrets' of 'forgotten battles' will enjoy flurries of credulous publicity. Cryptic old men will claim to know truths they can never tell.

Our Afghanistan commitment will go from an honourable mission to a doomed failure to a waste of lives to a misjudged-but-well-meant intervention to a proud-but-distant memory of a bloody foreign war where Australian troops were let down by treacherous local allies.

John Howard foresaw most of this, in the same speech where he assured a nation unworried that there might be conscription for Afghanistan that there would be no conscription for Afghanistan. He said, 'I've seen many an apparently unassailable argument and proposition for Australians to do one thing or the other in the past, to be lost in the heat and burden and turmoil of international debate and, with the passage of time, the belief on the part of many in the community that the events should be forgotten and left to history. That should not occur in relation to this involvement because what we are fighting against is something that does in a very direct fashion threaten our security ...'

As usual when Howard talked about the Middle East, he was talking about Vietnam. Major Russell had been talking about Vietnam, too, when he accused the government of 'failing to set the conditions to better support veterans once we returned from this conflict, and failing to learn from the exact same mistakes that occurred during and after our commitment of Australian forces to the Vietnam War'.[17] He later said that his Vietnam-veteran grandfather had told him, 'Don't let them do to your soldiers what they did to mine when we came back from Vietnam.'[18]

And here I am talking about Vietnam as well. The myth that Vietnam veterans' PTSD was caused by the anti-war movement should last precisely as long as it takes for the rates of PTSD among Afghanistan veterans to become clear. If anyone truly believes that PTSD will turn out to be less prevalent among these men and women, who returned from a war that was widely supported, against an enemy that was (and remains) broadly despised, then I look forward to their arguments and to the response from the veterans of the War on Terror.

When I began writing this book, I believed myths to be an inherently bad thing. It bothered me that the idea that myths were sometimes necessary for morale or social cohesion was propagated by people who did not believe those myths themselves. Their thinking seemed to me to be based on the concept that there are two levels of truth, one for educated people and the other for idiots.

It struck me as a bit Alan Tudge.

I wouldn't have a bar of it.

Mate.

But now I am not so sure. And I cannot say precisely why. Maybe it is a combination of my age and this age that makes me feel as if things are falling apart (well, I am, anyway), and that we might be justified in doing anything we can to put them back together. Perhaps it is partly that, in an era of deepfakes and alternative facts and AI, worrying about historical falsehoods based on wartime propaganda and misread documents seems as quaintly old-fashioned as the word 'falsehood' itself.

But it is probably just that existential ennui that comes when a writer finishes a book. Every day of my last fortnight working on the first draft of *Lest*, I swore I would never write a volume of non-fiction again. It is too much work. It takes too long. The research is agonising. Who even cares what other people think about the First World War. And why would I know any better? Then, on the eve of the day the manuscript was due, *The Australian* published a confused and confusing story about the upcoming Sydney Biennale. It reported that curators had briefly promoted a previous exhibition, with a 'vision statement' claiming that the work critiqued 'the formation of an Australian national identity as a consequence to the loss at Gallipoli in the First World War, orchestrated from London as an anti-jihad preventive campaign'. The statement had been withdrawn, but for some unfathomable reason, Libertarian Party NSW MP John Ruddick chose to comment, claiming that it was 'factually inaccurate' and that 'by 1914 the Turkish Ottomans were secular, and certainly not jihadis'.[19]

In a single stroke, the climate-change-denying, Covid-denying Ruddick also became the world's first Ottoman Empire denier.

I almost wrote to him to explain that the Ottoman Empire was an Islamic caliphate until 1924; and that the Ottoman sultan was the caliph, the custodian of Mecca and Medina; and that, since only a caliph can call a jihad, Sultan Mehmed V Reşâd's formal declaration of jihad against the Entente on 14 November 1914 was the last genuine proclamation of jihad in history.

Then I thought, Why bother?

I'll just save it for the next book.

Notes

The Myths of Anzac Day

1. See Ministers' Media Centre archive for a transcript of Avani Dias' interview with Alan Tudge, ABC, Triple J Hack, 7 September 2021, <https://ministers.dese.gov.au/tudge/triple-j-hack-interview-avani-dias>.
2. See Ministers' Media Centre archive for a transcript of Chris Kenny's interview with Alan Tudge, Sky News, 9 September 2021, <https://ministers.dese.gov.au/tudge/interview-chris-smith-chris-kenny-show-sky-news>.
3. See <https://www.awm.gov.au/commemoration/speeches/keating-remembrance-day-1993>.
4. Don Watson, 'Digging', *The Monthly*, May 2008.
5. James Brown, *Anzac's Long Shadow: The Cost of our National Obsession*, Redback, 2014, pp. 143–45.
6. Tanya Evans, 'Secrets and Lies: The Radical Potential of Family History', *History Workshop Journal*, No. 71 (Spring 2011), pp. 49–73.
7. In an interview with a prominent Vietnam veteran, I mentioned that I had read about disciplinary issues in his service record. He was surprised and discomfited. About a month later, the service records of Vietnam veterans were no longer automatically accessible on application.
8. See <https://www.awm.gov.au/collection/understanding-the-memorials-collection/researching-a-person>.
9. Harry Murray, as cited in 'Harry Murray VC, CMG, DSO and Bar', 29 August 2019, EHS-ADMIN, <https://evandalehistory.org/?p=261>.
10. James Brown, *Anzac's Long Shadow*, p. 141.
11. Ibid., p. 149.
12. Tom Frame, *Anzac Day Then & Now*, NewSouth, 2016, p. 22.
13. *Byron Bay Record*, 3 May 1919.
14. *Euroa Advertiser*, 2 May 1919.
15. *Lawloit Times*, 4 May 1920; *Murray Pioneer and Australian River Record*, 30 April 1920.

16 *Daily Observer*, 27 April 1920.
17 *Tweed Daily*, 28 April 1920.
18 *Register*, 27 August 1915.
19 *Register*, 14 October 1915.
20 *Register*, 1 October 1915.
21 National Film and Sound Archive of Australia, 'Anzac Day–History, Marches and Traditions | National Film and Sound Archive of Australia', <https://www.nfsa.gov.au/collection/curated/anzac-day-history-marches-and-traditions>.
22 *Advertiser*, 14 October 1915; *Advertiser*, 15 October 1915.
23 *Kapunda Herald*, 15 October 1915.
24 *Mt Barker Courier and Onkaparinga and Gumeracha Advertiser*, 22 October 1915.
25 *Murray Pioneer and Australian River Record*, 21 October 1915.
26 John Monash, *War Letters of General Monash*, edited by F.M. Cutlack, Angus & Robertson, 1935, letter dated 25 April 1916.
27 *West Coast Recorder*, 2 May 1929.
28 *Australia and the Vietnam War*, Department of Veterans' Affairs, 2007. This pamphlet has recently (2023) been revised to reflect a more accurate representation of the homefront.

The Myths of White Feather Women

1 See <http://www.womenworkingtogether.com.au/4.%20anti-suffragists.1900-10.html>.
2 Malek Abduljaber and İlker Kalın, 'An Empirical Analysis of the Women and Peace Hypothesis', *All Azimuth: A Journal of Foreign Policy and Peace*, September 2019.
3 Quoted in Marilyn Lake, 'Women's International leadership', in *Diversity in Leadership: Australian women, past and present*, ed. Joy Damousi, Kim Rubenstein and Mary Tomsic, ANU Press, 2014, p. 77.
4 Malek Abduljaber and İlker Kalın, 'An Empirical Analysis of the Women and Peace Hypothesis'.
5 Ibid.
6 Joan Beaumont, 'Australian Citizenship and the Two World Wars', *Australian Journal of Politics and History*, Vol. 53, No. 2, p. 7.
7 Joan Beaumont, *Broken Nation: Australians and the Great War*, Allen & Unwin, 2013, pp. 99–100.

Notes

8   *The Capricornian*, 7 November 1914.
9   *Brisbane Courier*, 17 November 1914.
10 *The Farmer and Settler*, 30 November 1914.
11 *Brisbane Truth*, 6 December 1914.
12 The votes-for-dudes (as they were then known) fear was perhaps more of an issue than is widely remembered, and much excited the members of the Senate in the first parliament of Australia in 1902, after women had been granted the franchise in South Australia and (to a more limited degree) in Western Australia, but before they received the vote in federal elections later that same year. Senator Thomas Glassey said that he had heard arguments that women would be influenced in their vote by 'the clergy, by good-looking candidates, and by young men'. While Glassey admitted, 'I am not young, and I do not think I was ever very good looking,' he nonetheless supported women's suffrage. Senator Sir John Downer opined that 'the women always like ugly men'. Glassey replied, 'I do not think they do, any more than I think that my honourable and learned friend likes the ugly women.' Senator James Stewart weighed in with empirical evidence. 'We are told that not only are women stupid, but that if they have the vote they will only vote for the young and handsome men,' he said. 'I quite admit that if that were likely to happen, my chance of being returned to the Senate would be a very remote one! [But] the honourable senators returned from South Australia do not number a single dude amongst them. They are all fine big, rough, upstanding men, not particularly handsome.' See <https://historichansard.net/senate/1902/19020409_senate_1_9/>.
13 *The Truth*, 29 November 1914.
14 *The Argus*, 24 October 1916.
15 See <https://historichansard.net/hofreps/1916/19160914_reps_6_79/>.
16 Joan Beaumont, *Broken Nation*, p. 226.
17 *The Age*, 26 July 1915.
18 *The Bulletin*, 18 November 1915
19 *Cumberland Argus and Fruitgrowers Advocate*, 8 December 1915.
20 *Punch*, 6 April 1916, p. 5.
21 *Port Pirie Recorder and North Western Mail*, 18 September 1916.
22 See, for instance, *Mercury*, 20 February 1915; *Geelong Advertiser*, 20 February 1915.
23 *Corowa Free Press*, 12 January 1915.
24 Reported in *Queanbeyan Age and Queanbeyan Observer*, 7 April 1916.

25 *Register* (Ade), 17 May 1915.
26 *Labor Call*, 8 March 1915.
27 *Register* (Ade), 3 July 1915.
28 *Murray Pioneer and Australian River Record*, 27 January 1916.
29 B. M., 'The White Feather', *The Lone Hand*, 1 December 1915, p. 36.
30 Ray Phillips (Mrs M.M. Phillips), *The White Feather*, Melville and Mullen, 1917.
31 *The Argus*, 29 May 1918.
32 E. Sylvia Pankhurst, *The Suffragette Movement: An Intimate Account of Persons and Ideals*, Krause reprint, 1971, pp. 593–594.
33 See <https://sa.org.au/interventions/rebelwomen/brazen.htm>.
34 *Daily Telegraph*, 23 May 1916.
35 Craig Blanch, 'Australian Home Front Badges of the First World War', 12 August 2015. See <https://www.awm.gov.au/articles/blog/australian-home-front-badges-first-world-war>.
36 See <https://vwma.org.au/explore/memorials/3766>.
37 See, for example, <https://www.slq.qld.gov.au/blog/rejected-volunteers>.
38 *Woman's Realm*, 28 December 1917.
39 *Geelong Advertiser*, 23 August 1918.

The Myths of the Gallipoli Landing
1 Speech by Bob Hawke at an official dinner given by Prime Minister Akbulut, Ankara, 23 April 1990, University of South Australia Library, p. 4.
2 Speech by Bob Hawke at the Dawn Service, Gallipoli on 25 April 1990, University of South Australia Library.
3 *Sydney Morning Herald*, 22 September 1983.
4 *The Age*, 18 February 2005.
5 *The Age*, 20 February 2005.
6 *The Age*, 27 April 2005.
7 *Sydney Morning Herald*, 27 April 2005.
8 Quoted in Bart Ziino, 'Who Owns Gallipoli? Australia's Gallipoli Anxieties 1915–2005', *Journal of Australian Studies* 88, 2006.
9 Jenny Macleod, *Gallipoli: Great Battles*, Oxford University Press, 2015, p. 135.
10 Ian Hamilton, *Gallipoli Diary*, Vol. 1, George H. Doran Company, 1920, p. 20.

Notes

11 Thomas James Richards, 'War Diary' entry 24 April 1915, AWM 2DRL/0786, i 226.
12 Hans Kannengiesser, Maj. C.J.P. Ball (trans.), *The Campaign in Gallipoli*, London, 1928, p. 66.
13 Ian Hamilton, 'Anzac and the Iliad', speech reported in *Reveille*, Vol. 8, No. 11, 1 July 1935, p. 2.
14 That said, according to the Australian soldier-artist Ellis Silas, the Turks at Gallipoli would shoot at anything that moved, even the wounded on stretchers, as 'they had been told by the Germans that the Australians were cannibals'. Ellis Silas, *Crusading At Anzac*, The British Australasian, 1916, unnumbered.
15 Quoted in Ulrich Trumpener, *Germany and the Ottoman Empire*, Princeton University Press, 1968, p. 117.
16 Ian Hamilton, *Gallipoli Diary*, Vol. 1, Chapters 1, 2.
17 Robin Prior, *Gallipoli: The End of the Myth*, p. 124.
18 Quoted in Gammage, 'ANZAC: Nationhood, Brotherhood and Sacrifice' in *The Story of Gallipoli*, David Williamson (screenplay), Penguin Books, 1981, p. 53.
19 Quoted in Kevin Fewster, Vecihi Basarin and Hatice Hurmuz Basarin, *Gallipoli: The Turkish Story*, Allen & Unwin, 2003, p. 67.
20 Patrick Balfour Kinross, *Ataturk: The Rebirth of a Nation*, Weidenfeld and Nicolson, 1964, p. 76.
21 Quoted in Kinross, *Ataturk*, p. 81.
22 Charles Bean, *Gallipoli Correspondent: The Frontline Diary of C.E.W. Bean*, 26 September 1915, Allen & Unwin, 1983, p. 158.
23 Ross Coulthart, *Charles Bean*, HarperCollins, 2014, p. xiii.
24 Charles Bean, *Gallipoli Correspondent*, pp. 73–77.
25 Department of Defence, 'A Hero of the Dardanelles', recruitment film script, 1915, NAA: B539, AIF144/1/274A.
26 'The World War I Diary of Percy Smythe', see <https://www.smythe.id.au/diary/>.
27 A.B. Facey, *A Fortunate Life*, Penguin Books, 1981 edition, p. 254.
28 C.E.W. Bean, The Story of Anzac from 4 May, 1915, to the Evacuation of the Gallipoli Peninsula, *The Official History of Australia in the War of 1914–1918*, vol. II, University of Queensland Press, 1981 (first published 1941), p. 910.

Notes

The Myths of the Dardanelles Campaign
1. Kevin Fewster, Vecihi Basarin and Hatice Hurmuz Basarin, *Gallipoli: The Turkish Story*, Allen & Unwin, 2003, p. 140.
2. Ibid., pp. 97–98.
3. See <https://www.everythingturkish.net/eat/gallipoli-and-the-ottoman-jews>.
4. Jeffrey Grey, *A Military History of Australia*, Cambridge University Press, 1990, p. 94.
5. Ibid., p. 91.
6. John Connor, 'The Frontier War That Never Was', in Craig Stockings (ed.), *Zombie Myths of Australian Military History*, University of NSW Press, Sydney, 2010.
7. E.C. Buley, *Glorious Deeds of Australasians in the Great War in 1915*, Andrew Melrose, 1915, fifth edition, 1916, pp. 261–263.
8. *Simpson and his Donkey 'Murphy'*, Hill & Plummer, 1917.
9. *New Zealand Herald*, 19 April 2008.
10. *Berringa Herald*, 18 September 1915.
11. Graham Wilson, *Dust, Donkeys and Delusions*, Big Sky Publishing, 2012, p. 109.
12. Ibid., pp. 108–128.
13. Peter Cochrane, 'WWI legend of Simpson and his donkey a case of selective truths', *The Australian*, 25 January 2014.
14. Peter Cochrane, *Simpson and the Donkey Anniversary Edition: The Making of a Legend*, Melbourne University Publishing, 2014, pp. 18–19.
15. Quoted in *New Zealand Herald*, 19 April 2008.
16. Ian Hamilton, 'Anzac and the Iliad', speech reported in *Reveille*, Vol. 8, No. 11, 1 July 1935, p. 2.
17. Ian Hamilton, *Gallipoli Diaries*, Vol. 1, 30 May 1915, p. 258.
18. Peter Weir, 'Peter Weir on "Gallipoli": "I felt Somehow I was Really Touching History"', *Literature/Film Quarterly*, 1981, Vol. 9, No. 4, pp. 213–17.
19. Bert Facey, *A Fortunate Life*, Penguin Books, 1981, p. 274.
20. Ian Hamilton, 'Anzac and the Iliad', speech.
21. Charles Bean, *Gallipoli Correspondent*, p. 176.
22. Quoted in Peter Pederson, *Monash as Military Commander*, Big Sky Publishing, 2018, p. 137.
23. Bill Gammage, 1981, op cit, p 50.
24. Ian Hamilton, 'Anzac and the Iliad', speech.

25 *Sunday Times*, 27 November 1932.
26 Cengiz Ozakinci, 'The Words "There is no difference between the Mehmets and the Johnnies" engraved on the 1915 Gallipoli monuments do not belong to Ataturk. Part I', *Butun Dunya*, March 2015.
27 Ulug Igdeminr, *Ataturk and the Anzacs*, *Turk Tarih Kurumu Basimevi*, 1978, p. 55.
28 *Mail* (Ade), 26 April 1930.
29 *Observer* (Ade), 1 May 1930.
30 Alan J. Whiticker, *Speeches that Reshaped the World*, New Holland, 2008, p. 294.
31 *Sydney Morning Herald*, 25 April 2012.
32 Jenny Macleod and Gizem Tongo, 'Between Memory and History: Remembering Johnnies, Mehmets and Armenians' in Raelene Frances and Bruce Scates (eds.), *Beyond Gallipoli: New perspectives on ANZAC*, Monash University Publishing, 2016.
33 *Sydney Morning Herald*, 19 April 2005.
34 *The Australian*, 20 April 2019.
35 Ian Hamilton, 'Anzac and the Iliad', speech.
36 Robin Prior, 'The Myths of Gallipoli', in Raelene Frances and Bruce Scates (eds.), *Beyond Gallipoli: New perspectives on ANZAC*, Monash University Publishing, 2016, p. 19.
37 *Sydney Morning Herald*, 31 October 2008.

The Myths of Monash and the Western Front
1 See <https://honesthistory.net.au/wp/centenary-watch-october-november-2017/>.
2 See Mark Dapin, *Jewish Anzacs*, UNSW Press, 2017; Derek J. Penslar, *Jews and the Military: A History*, Princetown University Press, 2014.
3 Cecil Edwards, *John Monash*, State Electricity Commission of Victoria, 1970, p. 1.
4 Don Watson, 'Digging', *The Monthly*, May 2008.
5 Quoted in Mark Dapin, *Jewish Anzacs*, p. 31.
6 Geoffrey Serle, 'Monash, Sir John (1865–1931)', *Australian Dictionary of Biography*, National Centre of Biography, Australian National University, <https://adb.anu.edu.au/biography/monash-sir-john-7618/text13313>, published first in hardcopy 1986.
7 John S. Levi, *Rabbi Jacob Danglow*, MUP, 1995, pp. 81–82.

Notes

8   John Monash, *The War Letters of John Monash*, edited by F.M. Cutlack, Angus & Robertson, 1935, letter dated 16 August 1915.
9   *London Gazette*, 15 October 1915.
10 Monash, *Letters*, France, 4 October 1917.
11 Monash, *Letters*, France, 18 October 1917.
12 John Hetherington, *John Monash*, Oxford University Press, 1962, p. 14.
13 Ross Coulthart, *Charles Bean*, HarperCollins, 2014, p. 287.
14 Ibid., p. 311.
15 Quoted in Peter Pedersen, *Monash as Military Commander*.
16 John Monash, *The Australian Victories in France in 1918*, Hutchinson, 1920, p. 96.
17 Ibid., pp. 56-57.
18 John Monash, *Letters*, France, 1 October 1917.
19 Peter Burness (ed.), *The Western Front Diaries of Charles Bean*, NewSouth, 2018, p. 614.
20 Cecil Edwards, *John Monash*.
21 *Monash*, W.C. Penfold & Co Pty Ltd, 1969, unnumbered.
22 Tim Fischer, *Maestro John Monash: Australia's Greatest Citizen General*, Monash University Publishing, 2004. pp. 59, 210.

The Myths of the Emu War
1   Murray Johnson, '"Feathered foes": Soldier Settlers and Western Australia's "Emu War" of 1932', *Journal of Australian Studies*, 2006, Vol. 30, Issue 88.
2   Leigh Straw, *After the War: Returned soldiers and the Mental and Physical Scars of World War I*, UWA, 2017.
3   Joceyln Maddock, *Westonia: Wheels of change*, Westonia Shire Council, c1998, p. 487.
4   Ibid.
5   *The Wheatgrower*, 3 November 1932.
6   Agricultural Bank, Perth, Western Australia, 'Register of Settlers in Receipt of Advances Under the Discharged Soldiers' Settlement Act, 1918'.
7   Murray Johnson, '"Feathered foes"', p. 150.
8   'Use of Machine Guns for Eradication of Emus in WA and Wild Horses in North Queensland', NAA: MP742/1, 17/5/219.
9   John Connor, *Anzac and Empire: George Foster Pearce and the Foundations of Australian Defence*, The Australian Army History Series, 2011.

Notes

10 *West Australian*, 3 November 1932.
11 *Daily News*, 12 October 1932.
12 Joceyln Maddock, *Westonia*, pp. 481–82.
13 *West Australian*, 18 October 1932.
14 'Use of Machine Guns for Eradication of Emus in WA and Wild Horses in North Queensland', NAA: MP742/1, 17/5/219.
15 Richard J. Cook, Srđan M. Jovanović, 'The Emu Strikes Back: An Inquiry into Australia's Peculiar Military Action of 1932', *Romanian Journal of Historical Studies*, Vol. 2, Issue 1, 2019.
16 Thos J. McMahon, 'On Outpost Duty', *The Queenslander*, 18 November 1916, p. 8.
17 'Guarding Our Northern Outpost', *The Queenslander*, 18 November 1916, p. 23.
18 George McIver, 'The Unhappy Emu', *Sydney Morning Herald*, 19 November 1932.
19 'War on Emus, The First Skirmish', *West Australian*, 3 November 1932.
20 *Merredin Mercury*, 3 November 1932.
21 'Use of Machine Guns for Eradication of Emus in WA and Wild Horses in North Queensland', NAA: MP742/1, 17/5/219.
22 *Daily News*, 3 November 1932.
23 *West Australian*, 4 November 1932.
24 'Lewis Guns Open Fire on Emu Hordes', *Mirror*, 5 November 1932.
25 'Use of Machine Guns for Eradication of Emus in WA and Wild Horses in North Queensland', NAA: MP742/1, 17/5/219.
26 'A Thousand Birds in Luck: Machine Gun Jams', *West Australian*, 5 November 1932.
27 'Use of Machine Guns for Eradication of Emus in WA and Wild Horses in North Queensland', NAA: MP742/1, 17/5/219.
28 *Daily Telegraph*, 9 November 1932.
29 *West Australian*, 9 November 1932.
30 *Western Mail*, 10 November 1932.
31 *Daily News*, 9 November 1932.
32 *Daily News*, 10 November 1932.
33 *Daily News*, 10 November 1932.
34 State Records Office Western Australia Series 36, Cons 1496, Item 1932_0821.
35 *West Australian*, 26 November 1932.

36 *Daily News*, 9 November 1932.
37 'Use of Machine Guns for Eradication of Emus in WA and Wild Horses in North Queensland', NAA: MP742/1, 17/5/219
38 Pattrice Jones, 'Provocations from the Field – Derangement and Resistance: Reflections from Under the Glare of an Angry Emu', *Animal Studies Journal*, Vol. 8, No. 1, p. 5.
39 'R.A.A. DANCE Jolly Affair at the Barracks, Fremantle', *Daily News* (Per), 3 July 1933.
40 'Enjoyable Motor Outing', *Daily News* (Per), 3 February 1936.
41 Pattrice Jones, 'Provocations from the Field – Derangement and Resistance', p. 12.
42 'The Emu War. Paying the Cost. Demand on a Farmer', *West Australian*, 27 November 1933.
43 Commonwealth of Australia, Parliamentary Debates: Senate Official Hansard, 5 December 1933.
44 Gwynydd Purves Wynne Audrey Meredith, Army service record, NAA: B883, QX41376.
45 Pattrice Jones, 'Provocations from the Field – Derangement and Resistance', p. 7.
46 J.A. Bryden and Chris Park, *Letters from the Emu War*, Shawline Publishing Group, 2021.
47 Agricultural Bank, Perth, Western Australia, 'Register of settlers in receipt of advances under the Discharged Soldiers' Settlement Act, 1918'.

The Myths of the POWs
1 Kenneth Harrison, *The Brave Japanese*, Horwitz, 1966, p. 133.
2 Lt.-Col. Galleghan, 'Interim Report', AWM54 554/11/4/ Part 1.
3 David Griffin, 'Galleghan, Sir Frederick Gallagher (1897–1971)', *Australian Dictionary of Biography*, National Centre of Biography, Australian National University, <https://adb.anu.edu.au/biography/galleghan-sir-frederick-gallagher-10270/text18165>, published first in hardcopy 1996.
4 Kevin Blackburn, *The Sportsmen of Changi*, New South, 2012, p. 167.
5 Kenneth Harrison, *The Brave Japanese*, Horwitz, 1966, p. 133.
6 Ibid., p. 135.
7 Ken Blackburn, *The Sportsmen of Changi*, p. 1.
8 *The Age*, 26 January 2005.
9 See <https://pmtranscripts.pmc.gov.au/release/transcript-22680>.

10 Quoted in Hank Nelson, *P.O.W. Prisoners of War: Australians under Nippon*, ABC Enterprises for the Australian Broadcasting Corporation, 1985, p. 34.
11 *Sydney Morning Herald*, 22 December 2022.
12 Alexander Hatton Drummond, *The Naked Truth*, manuscript, AWM371 94/0367.
13 *Smith's Weekly*, 9 February 1946.
14 Australian War Memorial, AWM54 573/6.
15 *The Age*, 10 December 1977.
16 M.D. Cobcroft, 'The Burma Thailand Railway: Myth, Legend and Reality', in Lt Col (Ret'd) Peter Winstanley (ed), *Articles about Prisoners of War of the Japanese, Including the Burma Thailand Railway 1941–1945*, undated c2003, unnumbered.

The Myth of No Poofters
1 *Canberra Times*, 23 April 1982.
2 *The Age*, 26 April 1982.
3 *Canberra Times*, 23 April 1982.
4 *The Age*, 26 April 1984.
5 *Sydney Morning Herald*, 22 November 1985.
6 Quoted in *Sydney Morning Herald*, 23 September 1989.
7 Quoted in Yorick Smaal, *Sex, Soldiers and the South Pacific, 1939–45: Queer Identities in Australia*, Palgrave Macmillan, 2017.
8 Peter Stanley, *Bad Characters: Sex, Crime, Mutiny, Murder and the Australian Imperial Force*, Pier 9, 2010, p. 143.
9 Unknown Author, 'On with the Motley: The Changi Concert Party', The Changi Book, ed. Lachlan Grant, New South, 2015, p. 134.
10 Quoted in Hank Nelson, *P.O.W. Prisoners of War: Australians under Nippon*, ABC Enterprises for the Australian Broadcasting Corporation, 1985, p. 28.
11 Nigel Starck, *Proud Australian Boy: A Biography of Russell Braddon*, Australian Scholarly Publishing, 2011, p. 42.
12 Kenneth Harrison, *The Brave Japanese*, p. 136.
13 Quoted in Hank Nelson, *Prisoners of War*.
14 Alexander Hatton Drummond, *The Naked Truth*, manuscript, AWM371 94/0367.
15 Yorick Smaal, *Sex, Soldiers and the South Pacific, 1939–45*.

Notes

16 *Canberra Times*, 23 April 1982.
17 David Bradford, *Tell Me I'm Okay: A Doctor's Story*, Monash University Publishing, 2018, p. 41.
18 Noah Riseman, *Serving in Silence?: Australian LGBT Servicemen and Women*, NewSouth, 2018, p. 33.
19 'How Not to Join the Army', Draft Resisters Union, 1968.
20 David Collyer, *From Fishnets to Foxholes and Back Again*, self-published, 2001, p. 7.
21 Ibid., pp. 9–10.

The Myths of Victimised Veterans

1 Noel Giblett (ed.), *Homecomings: Stories from Australian Vietnam Veterans and Their Wives*, AGPS, Canberra, 1990, p. 23.
2 For my investigation of Mike's story, and further information on the various otherwise uncredited assertions I make in the coming pages, refer to Mark Dapin, *Australia's Vietnam: Myth Vs History*, NewSouth, 2019.
3 ABC News, 'Did Kerry Discard Vietnam Medals?', 24 April 2004. See <https://abcnews.go.com/Politics/story?id=123495&page=1>.
4 Jerry Lembcke, *The Cult of the Victim-Veteran: MAGA Fantasies in Lost-war America*, Routledge, 2024, p. 36.
5 Gary McKay, *Vietnam Fragments: An Oral History of Australians at War*, Allen & Unwin, 1992, p. 260.
6 Tony Bower-Miles & Mark Whittaker, *Bomber: From Vietnam to Hell and Back*, Pan Macmillan, 2009, p. 90.
7 Ibid., p. 50.
8 Ibid., p. 25.
9 *Mufti*, v10, n1, 7 January 1967.
10 Ibid., pp. 25–26.
11 Tony Bower-Miles and Mark Whittaker, *Bomber*, p. 144.
12 Ibid., p. 143.
13 Carolyn Holbrook, *Anzac: The Unauthorised Biography*, NewSouth, 2014, p. 120.
14 'Rape victims remembered', *Sydney Morning Herald*, 26 April 1982.
15 M. Odlum, '168 arrested as women defy "no march" order', *Sydney Morning Herald*, 26 April 1983.
16 K. Kizilos, 'Vietnam veteran makes his Anzac protest', *The Age*, 26 April 1985, p. 1.

17 C. Botten, 'Police arrest two members of anti-war group', *The Age*, 26 April 1986.
18 *The Age*, 27 April 1987.
19 'Faces of our diggers', *Geelong Advertiser*, 24 April 2010.
20 Peter Yule, *The Long Shadow*, NewSouth and the AWM, 2020, p. 43.
21 Quoted in Ibid., p. 454.
22 Ibid., p. 372.
23 Quoted in Ibid., p. 271.
24 Ibid., p. 145.
25 *Sydney Morning Herald*, 6 August 2023.
26 Quoted in Carolyn Holbrook, *Anzac*, p. 175.

The Myths of Vietnam Veterans, Anzac Day and the RSL
1 Paul Ham, *Vietnam: The Australian War*, HarperCollins, 2007, p. 565.
2 *Canberra Times*, 26 October 1963, p 2.
3 *Mufti*, v9 n3, 5 March 1966.
4 *The Age*, 26 April 1966, p. 1; *Australian*, 26 April 1966, p. 1; *Canberra Times*, 23 April 1966, pp. 1, 3; *Sydney Morning Herald*, 26 April 1966, p. 1; *Australian*, 26 April 1966, p. 1.
5 *Canberra Times*, 28 April 1966, p. 8.
6 *Reveille*, vol. 41, no. 6, 1968, p. 5.
7 Gerard Windsor, *All Day Long the Noise of Battle: An Australian Attack in Vietnam*, Murdoch Books, Sydney, 2011, p. 221.
8 See Rodney Nott and Noel Payne, *The Vung Tau Ferry: HMAS Sydney and Escort Ships Vietnam 1965–1972*, Rosenberg Publishing, Kenthurst, NSW, 2008, pp. 170–73.
9 'Sydney march', *Sydney Morning Herald*, 26 April 1968.
10 *The Australian*, 28 April 2019.
11 See <https://s3-ap-southeast-2.amazonaws.com/awm-media/collection/RCDIG1072694/bundled/RCDIG1072694.pdf>.
12 *Reveille*, vol. 43, no. 6, 1970, p. 23.
13 *Sun-Herald*, 26 April 1970, p. 2.
14 *Sydney Morning Herald*, 11 August 1971.
15 *Reveille*, vol. 46, no. 5, 1972, p. 6.
16 *Reveille*, vol. 46, no. 8, 1972, p. 4.
17 *Sydney Morning Herald*, 26 April 1972, pp. 1, 15.

Notes

18 *Reveille*, vol. 58, no. 1, 1983, p. 11. It is also worth remembering that more than half of the returned men from the First World War never joined the RSL (Inglis, *Sacred Places*, pp. 243–44).
19 *Canberra Times*, 29 November 1965.
20 Tony Bower-Miles and Mark Whittaker, *Bomber*, p. 143.
21 *Sydney Morning Herald*, 31 January 2015.
22 Jacqueline Bird, 'In the matter of Agent Orange: Vietnam veterans versus the Australian War Memorial', *Honest History*, 15 March 2016. See <http:// honesthistory.net.au/wp/in-the-matter-of-agent-orange-vietnam-veterans-versus-the-australian-war-memorial>.
23 *Sydney Morning Herald*, 26 April 1980.
24 *Sun Herald*, 25 May 1964.
25 *Sydney Morning Herald*, 16 February 1965.
26 Les Waddington, untitled, unpublished, undated, p. 54.
27 *Sun-Herald*, 26 April 1987, p. 5.
28 Anne Blair, *Ruxton: A Biography*, Allen & Unwin, Sydney, 2004, p. 152.
29 Peter Yule, *The Long Shadow*, p. 145. Yule writes that there is 'documentary evidence for the rejection of Vietnam veterans by RSL clubs'. This is sort of true, in that he found one instance of one veteran being denied membership of one institution, but there is no evidence that this man was rejected because of his service in Vietnam. In any case, Yule's example is a confusion of two different incidents. Searching through the same files as Yule, I found evidence that another Vietnam veteran had had a membership application turned down. It seems to me more likely that the applicant in this second case was rejected because his only overseas service had been in Vietnam, so I believe this probably did happen – but not at all regularly.
30 See <https://rslnsw.org.au/news/rsl-nsw-apologises-to-vietnam-war-veterans/>.
31 *Tribune*, June 1968.
32 *Sydney Morning Herald*, 14 April 2014.
33 *Advertiser* (Ade), 10 May 1997.

The Myths of Movements

1 In 1955, the year the first Australian battalion arrived in Penang to help stamp out the embers of the communist insurgency in Malaya, Gallup polls showed that 29 per cent of Australians believed that Australian

troops should come home straight away. By contrast, the number who favoured bringing the troops back from Vietnam immediately didn't reach 29 per cent until September 1967, three years into the Australian commitment.
2 Quoted in Gerard Henderson, *Santamaria: A Most Unusual Man*, MUP p. 421.
3 *News-Weekly*, 20 April 1966.
4 *News-Weekly*, 1 June 1966.
5 *The Age*, 28 May 1966.
6 *News-Weekly*, 29 June 1966.
7 *News-Weekly*, 29 June 1966.
8 *News-Weekly*, 29 June 1966.
9 *The Age*, 16 March 1983.
10 James McAuley, 'For Volunteers Only?', *The Bulletin*, 9 April 1966.
11 Frank Knopfelmacher, 'Peace with freedom', *Quadrant*, July 1985, p. 56.
12 Cassandra Pybus, *The Devil and James McAuley*, University of Queensland Press, 1999, pp. 253–54.
13 Robert Manne, 'Knopfelmacher, Frank (1923–1995)', Australian Dictionary of Biography, National Centre of Biography, Australian National University, <https://adb.anu.edu.au/biography/knopfelmacher-frank-29637/text36602>, published online, 2020.
14 Frank Knopfelmacher, letter to the editor, *Sydney Morning Herald*, 2 May 1972.
15 *News-Weekly*, 27 March 1968.
16 Letter to the editor, *The Age*, 25 June 1967.
17 *Vietnam Digest*, No. 1, December 1968.
18 *Vietnam Digest*, No. 6, July 1971.
19 Commonwealth of Australia, Parliamentary Debates: Senate Official Hansard, 17 August 2006.

The Shape of Myths to Come
1 See <https://www.theguardian.com/culture/2023/mar/30/australian-war-memorial-funding-dwarfed-that-of-other-cultural-institutions-in-coalitions-final-years>.
2 At the time of publication, this case was under appeal in the Federal Court. By the time you are reading this, the decision – and the findings

Notes

against Roberts-Smith – may well have been overturned. If that occurs, then there would be no basis for concluding that Roberts-Smith engaged in any unbecoming or illegal conduct, and all imputations against him are unreservedly withdrawn.

3 See <https://pmtranscripts.pmc.gov.au/release/transcript-12374>.
4 Ibid.
5 Tom Hyland, 'Curiously incurious: The Australian media, the Australian military and Afghanistan', in Amin Saikal (ed), *The Afghanistan Conflict and Australia's Role*, Melbourne University Press, 2011, p. 168.
6 *The Australian*, 27 February 2006.
7 See <https://pmtranscripts.pmc.gov.au/release/transcript-20692>.
8 See <https://australianhumanitiesreview.org/2003/05/01/public-opinion-and-the-democratic-deficit-australia-and-the-war-against-iraq/>.
9 See <https://world.time.com/2013/02/15/viewpoint-why-was-the-biggest-protest-in-world-history-ignored/>.
10 See <https://pmtranscripts.pmc.gov.au/release/transcript-20534>.
11 Refer note 2 for this chapter.
12 See <https://www.aph.gov.au/About_Parliament/Parliamentary_Departments/Parliamentary_Library/pubs/BriefingBook47p/BreretonReport>.
13 See <https://www.aph.gov.au/Parliamentary_Business/Hansard/Hansard_Display?bid=committees/commsen/25288/&sid=0002>.
14 See <https://ctc.usma.edu/afghanistans-security-forces-versus-the-taliban-a-net-assessment/>.
15 Refer note 2 for this chapter.
16 Refer note 2 for this chapter.
17 See <https://www.aph.gov.au/Parliamentary_Business/Hansard/Hansard_Display?bid=committees/commsen/25288/&sid=0002>.
18 See <https://www.abc.net.au/news/2023-10-16/nsw-heston-russell-damages-defamation-case-abc/102980564>.
19 *The Australian*, 31 January 2024.

Mark Dapin is an acclaimed journalist, author, screenwriter and historian. He is the author of the novels *King of the Cross*, *Spirit House* and *R&R*. *King of the Cross* won the Ned Kelly Award for Best First Fiction; *Spirit House* was longlisted for the Miles Franklin Literary Award, and shortlisted for the *Age* Book of the Year and the Royal Society for Literature's Ondaatje Prize. *R&R* was shortlisted for a Ned Kelly Award. Mark holds a doctorate in military history. His book *The Nashos' War* was shortlisted for the NSW Premier's Literary Award for Non-Fiction, and won the NIB People's Choice Award and an Alex Buzo Shortlist Award. He has also written three books of true crime: *Public Enemies* (shortlisted for a Ned Kelly Award), *Prison Break* and *Carnage*. He worked as consultant producer on the Network Seven TV show *Armed and Dangerous*, and as screenwriter on Stan's *Wolf Creek 2*. His website is at markdapin.com